P9-CLR-553

IT'S NOT OKAY

IT'S NOT OKAY

ANDI DORFMAN

G

GALLERY BOOKS

New York London Toronto Sydney New Delhi

Gallery Books
An Imprint of Simon & Schuster, Inc.
1230 Avenue of the Americas
New York, NY 10020

First Gallery Books hardcover edition May 2016

GALLERY BOOKS and colophon are registered trademarks of Simon & Schuster, Inc.

For information about special discounts for bulk purchases, please contact Simon & Schuster Special Sales at 1-866-506-1949 or business@simonandschuster.com.

The Simon & Schuster Speakers Bureau can bring authors to your live event. For more information or to book an event, contact the Simon & Schuster Speakers Bureau at 1-866-248-3049 or visit our website at www.simonspeakers.com.

Manufactured in the United States of America

10 9 8 7 6 5 4 3

Library of Congress Cataloging-in-Publication Data
Name: Dorfman, Andi author.
Title: It's not okay / Andi Dorfman.
Description: First Gallery Books hardcover edition. | New York : Gallery Books, 2016.
Subjects: LCSH: Dorfman, Andi. | Television personalities—United States—Biography. | BISAC: BIOGRAPHY & AUTOBIOGRAPHY / Personal Memoirs.
Classification: LCC PN1992.4.D57 A3 2016 (print) | LCC PN1992.4.D57 (ebook) | DDC 791.4502/8092—dc23
LC record available at http://lccn.loc.gov/2015048948

ISBN 978-1-5011-3246-9
ISBN 978-1-5011-3247-6 (ebook)

To all the brokenhearteds of the world . . .

One day all the pain will make sense.

CONTENTS

IT'S NOT OKAY

DAY 1. 12:45 P.M.

My Life Is Officially Over

My life is officially over! Seriously, I'm not exaggerating. It really is O-V-E-R. I feel absolutely mortified, infuriatingly pissed, and pathetically distraught. To sum it up, I am nothing less than the superstar of my own major shitshow. And to make matters even worse, this entire debacle is all over—drumroll, please—a boy. Yup, a freaking boy, who just twelve hours ago was the "man" I was engaged to marry. All because I had let him sweep me off my feet as I fell madly in love with him in the short time frame of only eight weeks. And now he's just another freaking boy, one who has left me utterly heartbroken.

It wasn't supposed to be like this. *I'm* not supposed to be like this. Not after a breakup! It isn't as if this is my first failed relationship. Hell, I've had twenty-five in the past year alone, and that's not even including this one. Damn, saying that number aloud makes me cringe inside. Twenty-five, hold up, now *twenty-six* breakups in a year has got to be some sort of a record, right? If only we got consolation prizes for our breakups, perhaps a new pair of fabulous shoes. Then at least we could drown away our sorrows on the floor of a shoe closet worthy of Carrie Bradshaw, all the while knowing that each breakup came with three to five inches of pep-in-our-step leg-skinnifying stiletto pleasure. But no, life isn't that fair. At least not in my world. All I'm left with is a slew of practice breakups, which should have prepared me for this epic one. However, as I sit here crying and drowning my sorrows with a bottle of rosé (I'll switch to red once the sun goes down), a pen, and this diary, even through a haze of Grenache it is crystal clear that nothing could have ever prepared me for this. Yeah, this one's gonna hurt.

Fuck! How did I even end up here?

Obviously I know the technical answer to that—it doesn't take a genius to understand that in order to get to number twenty-six, you've got to start with number one (not to be confused with "the One"). And of all the ways I could have met a man, somehow *my* way was on a reality television show. I wish I could say I'm joking, but I'm embarrassingly serious.

Where do I even begin? I guess to make a long story short, this new chapter of dating on television began for me late one chilly September night in the great state of California after I'd been flown cross-country from Atlanta to Los Angeles, where I was promptly put up in an undisclosed hotel and stripped of my phone and any other form of communication with the outside world. Seventy-two painfully boring hours later, it was finally time to meet Number One, whom I knew little about except that he had won the romantic lottery by being chosen to date thirty "lucky" women, all handpicked just for him. A single father with Latin heritage, he was a former athlete and looking for love. And so was I.

The night had finally come. Doused with half a bottle of hair spray, my wavy locks had the texture of straw as I slipped into the slinky floor-length Halston Heritage gown I had purchased only days ago from the clearance rack at Loehmann's. I had been impatiently waiting for hours, passing the time with several reapplications of mascara and blush, when finally a producer came to my door and ushered me down in the elevator, through the hotel lobby, and into a waiting stretch limousine. Already inside were four other women, also dressed in floor-length gowns and also ready to meet Number One. I took a seat against the window and observed each woman. One had a pillow shoved in the midsection of her dress resembling a baby bump, which I found quite ballsy and slightly uncomfortable given that Number One was a single father. Another woman wore a sequined gown with a plunging neckline, while another wouldn't stop bragging in a high-pitched screech that she was wearing cowboy boots underneath her black gown, which had a conveniently placed cutout revealing her lower-back tattoo. The fourth woman—the only normal one, in my opinion—wore her hair in a sophisticated chignon that complemented her soft skin, which resembled that of a porcelain doll. A producer hopped into the limo along with a cameraman, and just like that, we were off and on our way to the circus!

A short drive later, the limo was parked in the cobblestone driveway of an enormous Spanish-style mansion, with Number One standing amid bright lights in front of a large fountain adorned with colorful flowers. With a dozen cameras positioned at various heights and angles, he waited as one by one, each of the four other women exited the vehicle and greeted him. Each engaged in a short conversation before sashaying around the fountain and entering the arched wooden front doors of the mansion. When it was my turn, I stepped out of the limo and began what felt like the longest ten-foot walk of my life. The moment I laid eyes on Number One, I was infatuated. His satisfactorily tall athletic build, blond hair, and expensive suit that fit snugly in all the right areas (if you know what I mean) had me both nervous and intrigued. A quick introduction later, with a grin, I too sashayed around the fountain and entered the mansion.

The setup was simple: If I survived the first night, I along with the other survivors would move into this mansion and begin "dating" Number One, who got to go on three dates a week with the women of his choosing; two of those would be private solo dates, while the third would be a "group date." Each week, Number One got to eliminate a select number of women until it was finally down to one who, if all went according to plan, he loved enough to propose to, and the two of them would ride off into the sunset together and live happily ever after. Oh, and all of this while cameras rolled, capturing our every move.

After surviving the first night—which really ended at sunrise the next day—I began what would be a seven-week romance with Number One. Each week brought a new round of dates and with it a new destination, and of course, new drama. Week after week, I found myself on these dreaded "group dates," where I'd sit back and watch the majority of the women flaunt their assets, play damsel in distress, and take every opportunity to one-up each other. Luckily, each woman also got a little private time on these dates. At first I longed for these moments where I'd get to flirt and make out without the prying eyes of the other women, but week after week, as I continued to be bypassed for a solo date, I found the conversation becoming more and more dull. Nonetheless, week after week I stayed, partially in anticipation of getting a solo date, which I hoped would ignite a romance between us, partially because I was traveling the world for free—but mainly because I was just so damn attracted to him. Boring conversations aside, let's be honest, nothing makes a woman want a good-looking man more than other women wanting him too; it's the basic law of human attraction. His position of power created an aura around him that made him attractive enough to justify turning a blind eye to the painfully boring conversations I endured for weeks.

Fast-forward seven weeks, twenty-seven eliminated women later, thousands of miles traveled to incredible countries like South Korea, Vietnam, and New Zealand, and a hometown visit in which I had introduced Number One to my family, who were less than impressed, and I was still in the "competition" along with two other women. Our worldwide journey had brought us to our final destination, St. Lucia, and with just two weeks until the end, this week of dating was far different from the others: It was finally time to take part in what the show dubbed the "fantasy suite dates." This was the moment when I'd get to spend the night with Number One without the prying eyes of cameras or producers. This was the moment where sparks would finally be ignited.

Ha! Yeah, right. Unless if by sparks you mean he blasted Ray Jay and R. Kelly all night long and showed me dozens of videos of his old soccer highlights on YouTube. There was no getting to know me, no romance, and there was most definitely no fantasy involved in the evening. All there was was the realization that I was nothing more than a pretty object he had no intentions of liking, let alone loving, and thus no amount of free travel was enticing enough to stay any longer. In fact, I couldn't wait for morning to come so I could hightail it out of the room, say goodbye to this journey, and go back home to Atlanta.

The following morning, when I tried to explain the disappointment of the night, his disinterest in anything but himself became even more apparent. Delusional, like most men, he insisted everything was just peachy fucking keen, and all he would say, no matter how hard I tried to explain my point of view, was, "It's okay."

Throughout the show he'd used this phrase so many times and in so many serious moments with each and every woman that it had gone from a running joke to a disrespectful annoyance. It was as if those two little words were Number One's way of saying, "I just don't care." And now, here he was doing the same thing to me, yet again. Everything I said was met with the same gag-worthy response. I told him I didn't think we were compatible . . . "it's okay." That he didn't seem interested in knowing me on a deeper level . . . "it's okay." That it was rude to bring up the fact that he had indulged in an overnight date with another woman two days before our own . . . "it's okay." To make matters worse, in the middle of my rant, he actually had the audacity to wipe something off my face! I shit you not! After about six "it's okays," I lost it.

"It's *not* okay!" I screamed. "Everything isn't always okay. Feel something! Respond to something! For the love of God, say anything other than 'It's okay!' "

But all he could say was . . . you guessed it. "It's okay."

Eight weeks of wasted anticipation and painstakingly boring conversations, along with resisting that extra glass of wine so I could fit into skin-tight cocktail dresses and brutalizing my feet in high heels night after night. Eight weeks of missing my family in the hopes of finding love, and it all came to an end in one maddening conversation under the blistering sun of St. Lucia. All I could do was walk away . . . irritated, pissed off, and over it all. Ironically, it was this combination of animosity and the liberation I felt at recognizing and dumping a textbook chauvinist pig that provided a clean break. My heartache was minimal and short-lived, and I left St. Lucia single and ready to put the entire journey behind me.

Little did I know that the ending of this relationship—if you can even call it that—would serve as the catalyst for my next twenty-five relationships and, consequently, breakups. That's because, apparently, dumping the show's lead was groundbreaking in the world of reality television, and honesty was refreshingly inspiring to viewers—so much so that I was asked to return for a second shot at love, only this time *I* would be the lone woman courted and fought over by a sea of hunky men. As irresistible as it sounded, I grappled with the thought of interrupting my life once again to partake in a second shitshow. I had been there, done that, and checked "dating on reality television" off my bucket list, but the hopeless romantic in me was still searching for love.

After debating for weeks, I reluctantly decided to throw my hands in the air, let Jesus take the wheel, and give love another shot. You'd have thought I'd learned my lesson the first go-round, but an unusual optimism told me this second time was going to be different. I don't know what it was, but I just felt it. It was as if all the stars in my world had aligned, and I was about to meet my soul mate and live happily every after.

So three months after saying goodbye to Mr. It's Okay, I was back in Los Angeles, standing in front of that same gaudy mansion, surrounded by cameras ready to capture my every move as I began "dating" twenty-five men. The next eight weeks were going to be the most intense, emotional, and fun of my life, surrounded by hot men and cameras. However, since polygamy is illegal (and gross), I couldn't keep them all, and unfortunately each week I had to break up with one hot stud after another. (So unfair!)

Although each of the breakups came with a different story and different emotions, they seemed so much more amicable than my previous breakup with Number One. The earlier breakups were easier, considering I'd barely known the men long enough to be told their last names. But as the weeks went on, I found that the worst moments throughout the show weren't the hours of exhaustion or the times I felt homesick or overcome with anxiety before a date, but rather when I had to say goodbye to yet another nice guy. The fact that I was standing five feet away from someone I knew I was moments away from dumping was awkward enough, but the guilt I felt afterward was torment. There was a control that came with being the one deciding who went home and when, a power that normally I would have loved to possess, but had quickly turned into a burden I couldn't wait to shed. I found myself wondering, *Why me?* Who had given me the right to dump good, kindhearted men who had put their lives on hold, risked humiliation and heartbreak, and treated me with nothing but respect? Who had made me the judge in this case? Half of the men I dumped were probably too good for me anyway, and yet somehow, by breaking up with them, I felt like I was minimizing them. It got harder as, week after week, deeper relationships formed and I wondered, "Would they be brokenhearted? Was I about to ruin their lives?"

And now here I am, the one not all right. The one brokenhearted. The biggest and hardest breakup of them all is without question Number Twenty-Six. This is going to be one of those breakups that will define me for the rest of my life, haunt me wherever I go, a permanent skeleton in my closet. Not only is the entire world going to know about it, thanks to the making of this entire relationship being broadcast to millions, but this blunder will be the ultimate "I told you so" from every single viewer of the show. I'll have gone from being a successful attorney to a reality television star to the laughingstock of the nation. I'll be seen as just another woman who "couldn't keep a man." And if the devastation and embarrassment of that aren't enough to set this breakup far apart from the first twenty-five, it will also brand me with a label I'll have to wear forever. It won't be a Prada or Dior label; no, this will be more like a cheap knockoff you get on the streets of Chinatown. In all my years and fashion faux pas (of which there are plenty), this is the worst label I have ever worn, and it's called . . . ex-fiancée.

Because that's the label you get when you fall in love, get engaged, and it doesn't work out. You can't cut it out, sell it on eBay or pretend it's not yours. No, this one belongs to you forever. You now get the privilege of telling people—what do they call it these days?—oh yes, that you have been "previously engaged." How delightful!

How did it go so wrong? Did I make a mistake that will shape the rest of my life by picking and getting engaged to Number Twenty-Six?

Of course I did! Was I blind to who he really was? Of course I was! I fell in love with a man who was everything I'd dreamed of—a family man who promised to protect and support me, who looked at me with the adoration in his eyes that every woman dreams of. A man who made me the happiest woman in the world. It was all so perfect . . . until it wasn't. And despite knowing how toxic and unhealthy our relationship became in the end, I don't know how and why it got to be that way. I just know that the odds of my ever getting over this breakup are about as slim as me waking up tomorrow as Beyoncé.

All right, so maybe life isn't really over, but if you're anything like me, your relationship certainly is. Why am I telling you all this? Because we've all been there—maybe not breaking up with someone on national television, but we've all known the kind of heartbreak that knocks you on your ass and leaves you feeling hopeless. Yes, at some point in our lives, we've all found ourselves going from the land of sunshine and roses to being smack dab in the heart of the storm. In fact, odds are if you're reading this, you're either a) going through a breakup, b) getting over a breakup, c) about to break up, or d) just want a good laugh at the disaster you've been lucky enough to avoid. (Note: if you fall into the latter category, I don't blame you. I'd probably enjoy it a little too! But don't laugh too hard, your time might be just around the corner.) Whatever the case, I'm here for you. Here to bare it all, one catastrophic moment at a time. No sugarcoating, no denying the brutal reality of heartbreak. Just my story along with a little advice on how to survive a breakup. It won't be easy—survival never is. In fact, getting through heartbreak can be one of the hardest things you'll ever do in your lifetime. I mean it. It's worse than a death and harder than battling an illness. With a death comes finality, with an illness comes an opponent to beat. But when it comes to heartbreak, it's just you fighting . . . your own pain.

So buckle up, because it's going to be a bumpy ride. Get ready to go from hysterically crying all day, to suddenly becoming a raging lunatic who hates the world, to finding yourself in front of a fireplace literally burning away every memory of your ex. And—believe it or not—all the way to being able to look back, laugh a little, cry a bit, learn a lot and most importantly realize that happily ever after might really be happily *never* after. I'll tell you how I went through it all, and spoiler alert—I *did* come back, and so will you!

But before you do, you'll have to ride out the storm. It will pass, and when it does, you'll emerge better than ever. But you have to survive it first. So head to the wine shop and grab a few bottles (don't forget the corkscrew), stock up on tissues, get a Netflix account, and pretend you've just gotten an invitation to your very own pity party! It's yours and you can cry if you want to. For now, there are no words comforting enough, no amount of positive-thinking bullshit wise enough, and certainly no type of booze strong enough to bring you solace. It's time to lie in bed in your yoga pants, smelly white T-shirt, and cry in between sips of rosé as you think to yourself, *My life is officially over.*

Lesson learned: *Welcome to the Pity Party! Check your pride at the door!*

DAY 2. 1:10 A.M.

It All Started with Free Drinks

I should be sleeping right now, but despite being emotionally and physically exhausted, I'm wired. I am like the depressed eternal flame longing to be put out ever so badly, but no matter how much rain or wind comes my way, I just keep flickering. I can't stop thinking about how I find myself in such a predicament. It's mindblowing that in a matter of just eighteen months I went from a young, promising lawyer to one of thirty crazy chicks dating one guy on TV to the one crazy chick dating twenty-five men on yet another show, to engaged, to where I find myself now . . . a single train wreck living in the guest bedroom at my friend Kelly's house.

How the hell did this happen?

That's a damn good question. I guess the answer can be summed up in two words: free drinks. Well, free drinks and assertive girlfriends.

Flash back to the summer of 2013—I was a twenty-three-year-old single gal living in my hometown of Atlanta, Georgia. I'd finished college, gone on to law school, passed the bar exam, and was working as an assistant district attorney prosecuting gang crimes. I was quite content with my pseudo normal life. When I wasn't working, I was hanging out with my girlfriends or enjoying wine-fueled Sunday dinners at my parents' house. Life was simple but full, minus one obvious thing: a man. With both my parents and sister happily married, I was the token fifth wheel of the family. Though this title afforded me my own room on family vacations, it came at the cost of my pride. Trust me, the only thing worse than a table for one at an all-inclusive Mexican resort is a table for five.

When it came to finding a boyfriend, I was ready, willing, and able, but found myself stuck in that peculiar zone somewhere between disdain and obsession. I guess you could say I was aloof when it came to dating. Sure, I wanted a man, but I wasn't willing to fight tooth and nail to get one. I was young, my eggs were still fertile, thus I figured when the time was right I would find a man in one of the many traditional ways: work, the gym, a bar, or perhaps one of those strippergrams that show up at the door, courtesy of my married girlfriends. But up to this point, I hadn't found the right guy—hell, I hadn't even found one I wanted to go on a date with. No man seemed to make a free meal worth an hour of getting ready followed by hours of awkward, shallow conversation.

And when it came to casual hookups and one-night stands, though I had ample opportunities (which isn't all that hard in Atlanta, especially if you find yourself in certain Buckhead dive bars around last call), the idea never appealed to me. I'm feisty and good at playing hard to get, but my bark has always been bigger than my bite. Truth be told, when it came to hooking up with random men, I didn't have energy to (a) shave my legs, (b) deal with putting out, or (c) engage in the awkward morning after, which consists of either a walk of shame or my telling a guy he didn't have to go home but he had to get the hell out of my place. Though *I* was happy being single, my girlfriends didn't seem to share the same sentiment. They had one concern when it came to me, and it wasn't my job or wardrobe—it was my love life.

Those most concerned with this search were Sarah, Leslie, and Caroline, three of my best friends from law school at Wake Forest. I met Sarah on Facebook, thanks to a mutual friend who knew I was looking for a roommate. We immediately hit it off, and decided to live together. Over the course of three years, she'd become the best roommate I ever had in my life, in part because she was more studious than I was, which kept me focused, but also because we shared the same taste in clothes and wine. Sarah was in a relationship with Phil, a baseball player at Wake Forest. I'd always liked Phil; he was tall, somewhat goofy, adored Sarah, and most important, was always willing to set me up with his hot single teammates. Soon after we graduated law school, Phil realized he had outkicked his coverage and proposed to Sarah. (Note: In girl terms, "outkicking coverage" is like finding a killer pair of Burberry pumps mismarked by a good $300, heading straight to the register, swiping the card, and speeding home, knowing you got away with one hell of a steal.)

Leslie was married to Wade, a classmate of ours. She was a tall, pretty blonde with a dry, sarcastic sense of humor. I envied her for the way curse words rolled so eloquently off her tongue. Nobody could say "fuck" like Leslie—it was an art that I tried to imitate but could never quite replicate.

Then there was Caroline, engaged to Lee, whom she had met in college. Caroline was a quintessential Southern belle from Nashville, Tennessee, and was the fashion captain of our group.

She was smart, but had no qualms expressing her love for a good DVF wrap dress paired with Kate Spade wedges and anything with sequins, which made her the resident comedian as well.

All three would joke about how lucky I was to not have to deal with dirty boxers or joint checking accounts, but ultimately, they were happily in love and wanted me to be too. Cut to me, having been without a boyfriend for the better half of a year, on a random weekday when I found myself in a typical group text with the four of us. Typically, we used these group chats to keep up with one another, talk about the latest Kate Middleton news, make inappropriate jokes, and most important, notify each other of that day's sales on Gilt, Rue La La, and HauteLook. But on one particular day it wasn't about the sales or the gossip; it was about me and my "future husband." Not just "Are you dating?" but loads of questions pertaining to my love life (really, my lack of one). I quickly grew suspicious of a conspiracy, but shrugged off the questions until Sarah "randomly" suggested I go on a reality dating show. Leslie and Caroline wasted no time chiming in with encouragement for this stupid idea, which provoked me to respond with six full lines of "HAHA." I couldn't believe they even watched these crappy TV shows, let alone thought I would ever be the type of cray-cray who would go on such a thing. But they had clearly been researching and planning what I swear must have been called Operation Get Our Only Single Friend Married, led by General Sarah and Sergeants Leslie and Caroline.

SARAH: So, Andi, have you thought about doing a dating show?

ME: So, Sarah, no. What are you talking about a dating show?

SARAH: Like on television . . . one of those reality shows where you find love.

ME: Umm. No, definitely no. Actually, HELL NO!

CAROLINE: Oh, Sarah, what a great idea!!!

LESLIE: Kudos to Sarah! Come ooooonnnnnn, Andi, you totally should!

SARAH: Seriously, you have nothing to lose.

ME: Ummm . . . except my dignity.

CAROLINE: Oh lookie here! There is a casting call 2.3 miles from your office on June 20th.

SARAH: It's meant to be . . .

ME: Umm . . . How do you know this?

CAROLINE: I just happened to be on the Internet and saw it.

ME: Yeah, okay . . . sure.

LESLIE: It's totally meant to be!

CAROLINE: It's like as meant to be as a pair of Tory Burch flats in your size on Gilt!

SARAH: That's so rare.

LESLIE: It's a sign. Wait, Caroline, is Tory Burch on Gilt?

CAROLINE: Not until Thursday.

LESLIE: Fuck that noise.

ME: Girls . . . my love life does not equal Tory Burch sale shoes.

LESLIE: I'm just saying it's a sign.

SARAH: I mean really, what do you have to lose?

ME: Again, my dignity.

SARAH: Yah . . . Ummm dignity is overrated.

LESLIE: Agreed.

CAROLINE: Ditto.

ME: You three are crazy. Headed into court. TTYL!

CAROLINE: Fine, but don't forget casting call June 20th.

SARAH: We can talk outfits when it gets closer!

These conversations went on for weeks until finally, the morning of June 20th came along and I found myself in yet another group text. The pressure was on more than ever, and the girls weren't even attempting to play coy.

SARAH: So, Andi . . . I'm not pressuring you, but I just got a reminder on my calendar that there is a casting call for your future . . . and it's today.

LESLIE: Today is the daaaayyyyyy.

CAROLINE: Wait, what is Tory Burch on Gilt today, again?

LESLIE: No, Caroline . . . it's casting call day.

CAROLINE: Oh riiight! So the location of the event is exactly 2.3 miles from your office and it starts at 6 p.m.

ME: Not going. And P.S. you girls are insane.

LESLIE: and fucking married.

CAROLINE: engaged.

SARAH: engaged!

ME: Haha. Fuck y'all.

SARAH: Don't worry, we still love you.

LESLIE: And by love she means pity . . .

CAROLINE: Okay, focus everyone! So Andi, from your office, you take a right on Peachtree, then left onto Roswell. Take that 1.4 miles and the bar will be on your right.

SARAH: Casting goes from 6 to 9 p.m.

LESLIE: Should she get there early or late? What do we think?

CAROLINE: Well, early reads desperate, fashionably late reads cool.

SARAH: But don't show up at 9 because they might have already found enough good girls.

LESLIE: So how about 7:30?

CAROLINE: Agreed. That will give a 10-minute cushion to get there and plenty of time to do a quick outfit change after work.

ME: WTF? No! *No!* NO!

CAROLINE: Ok, fine, you don't have to change your outfit as long as you're wearing that cute black Theory skirt suit I like . . .

ME: Haha, not no to the outfit change, no to all of it!

LESLIE: Seriously, what the hell do you have to lose?

ME: Again, my dignity.

SARAH: Andi . . . don't get me started. I lived with you for three years, don't make me discuss your dignity . . .

ME: Sarah, low blow!

LESLIE: Think of all you have to gain.

ME: Umm . . . Like what?

CAROLINE: A husband!

LESLIE: New friends? Though they won't be nearly as fucking cool as us.

ME: Ok, real talk here . . . Ya'll seriously expect me to go to a casting call for a reality television show?

CAROLINE: Well, duh! Isn't that what this whole conversation is about?

SARAH: The casting call info sheet does say free drinks . . .

ME: Hmmm . . . free drinks, really?

SARAH: Bible! You know I would never joke about free drinks.

LESLIE: I see it on here too!

ME: What time is the event?

And that's all it took, really . . . Three of my best friends on my ass and the promise of free drinks.

That afternoon I got off work at the abnormally early time of 6:00 p.m. My plans to meet a girlfriend for dinner had changed due to a scheduling conflict that involved dinner with her boyfriend's mother or some other I'm-not-single-and-have-more-important-things-to-do bullshit. Plan B was to grudgingly hit the gym. But, the fact that I hadn't packed gym clothes and would have to drive *past* the gym in order to go home and get dressed *for* the gym was inconvenient enough to nix that idea altogether. I mean, yeah I guess I could have sucked it up and gone the extra mile to my house, at least in the name of single sexiness, but instead, I just began driving north through downtown Atlanta. Ready to fight the grueling rush-hour traffic, I was pleasantly surprised by the steady flow of the cars. With the music cranked up and my foot on the gas more often than the brake, I must have subconsciously taken a right on Peachtree followed by a left on Roswell Road, because next thing I knew I was in the parking lot of none other than the location of *the* casting call. My car had literally steered me to this bar and into this parking space.

I sat staring at myself in the rearview mirror asking my reflection, "What the hell am I doing here?" All the while, scantily clad girls were lining up outside the front doors of the bar. As the line got longer, the heels got higher and the necklines plunged farther down. There was a well-balanced mix of brunettes and blondes, which was surprising considering most Southern girls start bleaching their hair before they hit puberty. Not a surprise: the teased heights of each girl's mane (another thing Southern girls learn to do before hitting puberty). After all, we were below the Mason-Dixon Line, which meant, "The higher the hair, the closer to God!"

"Fucking shit," I muttered as I looked down at my modest ensemble of a black Theory pencil skirt and matching blazer, nude pumps, black blouse, pearl necklace, and tan stockings (which I wore to appease conservative judges). In all of this mess, I'd forgotten that I should have gone home and changed out of my prudish knee-length suit before I went to a casting call for a dating show. Caroline would have been mortified to call me her friend (though I do think she said a Theory skirt would suffice). I began frantically rifling through my center console in search of any and all makeup that could salvage this fatal fashion faux pas. Through headphones, business cards, and pens, I managed to find a pink tube of dried-out Maybelline mascara, ChapStick, and a half-empty bottle of embarrassingly old Clinique Happy perfume. I threw off my blazer, removed my strand of pearls, stripped off my panty hose, and reached down my blouse to perk up my boobs. I was as ready as I was going to get. With a deep breath, I opened the door, and took one step toward insanity.

The line had died down enough by this point that I didn't wait long before being greeted by one of several peppy girls manning the check-in desk.

"Name?" one of them asked.

"Andi Dorfman," I replied as she began to write it onto a dry-erase board only to stop after AN before looking up confused and asking, "Angie or Annie?"

"No, it's Andi, A-N-D-I," I replied.

"Oh, got it, and what was that last name, dear?"

"Dorfman."

Seeing the puzzled look on her face, I decided to spare her any extra brainwork. "D-O-R-F-M-A-N."

"Age?" as she continued to scribe.

"Twenty-six."

"Hometown?"

"Here."

Again, puzzled look. Maybe *I'm* the idiot here?

"Atlanta."

"Do you have a job?"

"Yes, I'm an attorney." What, did she think I normally dressed in a knee length, all-black ensemble? I guess maybe I had pulled off the impossible feat of "making it work." Kudos to me!

"Atny" she abbreviated to complete my nametag.

Though she'd abbreviated my profession incorrectly, I decided to let it slide, since I was, after all, there to make a good impression.

"All right, dear, step over here and we are going to take some pictures. Can you hold the sign under your chin?"

Flash after flash, I stood stoically as I posed for my "mug shot" before finally I was allowed to pass Go, collect $200, and enter the bar. Okay fine, I didn't get $200, but I did get access to the open bar, which became the setting of the most insane scene I'd ever laid eyes on. Hmmm . . . where do I even start? Close your eyes and imagine an entire store filled with Herve Leger knockoffs, each of them accompanied by a pair of matching glittery platform peep toe pumps. Now, breathe in and get you a good whiff of that Elnett hairspray stench. Do you smell that hint of cucumber? Why, yes you do! That would be the Bath & Body Works Cucumber Melon lotion permeating the air (the kind with a hint of shimmer, of course). Look to your right—those girls slamming shots are the "party" girls and are already sloshed. To your left is the group of "pretty prissy girls" conversing with each other (though I doubt any of them are actually listening to one another). And then there's me. The girl in work clothes who's found herself in bandage-dress HELL!

I made my way to the bar to order a glass of Chardonnay, keeping it classy, of course, but before the bartender even poured the wine, I was whisked away by a brunette woman wearing leather leggings and a black V-neck with the sleeves rolled up far enough to see her tattooed wrists. She introduced herself as a casting producer and asked me to follow her into a back room before directing me to take a seat on a stool, where a bright light blinded me and a camera with a blinking red light stared me down, scaring the living shit out of me.

She began by asking me various biographical questions like where I grew up and what I did for a living. The more I responded, the more the bright light made the room sweltering hot and me on the verge of sweating like a skank in church. *Please don't sweat, please don't sweat,* I thought to myself. Finally, I couldn't hold it in any longer. "Shit, is it hot in here or is it just me?" I said as I wiped the moisture off my forehead. As I said "shit," I covered my mouth like a five-year-old and stared into the camera and then back into the eyes of a very unfazed producer.

"Fuck, I just cursed on camera, didn't I?"

I covered my mouth again.

"Shit, I've just said 'shit' and 'fuck,' and we just met. Sorry."

"Oh, please, it's fine . . . not a big fucking deal at all." She chuckled.

I had liked this tatted-up chick from the beginning, and now, hearing the way the word "fucking" rolled off her tongue so effortlessly, I liked her even more. We continued to "shoot the shit" for a few more minutes, and even figured out that we were from the same hometown. There we were; just two gals chitchatting away in the back of a bar, forgetting we were at a casting call, before another producer politely popped in to remind us that there were more girls waiting to be seen. We hugged goodbye before she handed me off to yet another producer who took me into yet another back room.

"Don't show anyone else this envelope," she instructed as she handed me a thick manila envelope.

"Okay . . ."

"We really like you! Now we need you to fill out this packet exactly how it says and make sure to send it back within seventy-two hours!"

"Umm . . . okay, sure," I naïvely responded, unaware of what covert operation they were running here.

"Also, if you don't mind, can you go out the back door so none of the other girls see you have an envelope?"

"No problem," I said.

Feeling like a Bond girl, I pushed the door marked EXIT, slipped the manila envelope in the waistband of my pencil skirt, and stealthily made a beeline to my car. Ironically, the entire ordeal was over before I even had a sip of the advertised free drinks. I drove home, took my high heels off, uncorked a bottle of red (which I prefer anyway), and poured a glass as I sat on the couch, forgetting that the envelope was still sitting on the passenger seat of my car. It wasn't until the next day while driving to work that I saw it and remembered the "seventy-two-hour deadline." I stuck it in my tote bag and walked into work.

By 9:00 a.m., Sarah, Leslie, and Caroline had already asked how the casting went. In an effort both to downplay the entire ordeal and get them to abort their mission altogether, I decided to keep the details to a minimum by simply responding, "Ehhh . . . it was stupid. I don't think they liked me." Little did they know, I had totally Bond girl–ed the shit out of it! They tried to cheer me up by saying things like, "I'm sure you did great," and, "Yeah, right, they probably loved you."

Over my lunch break, I sat at my desk and opened the envelope. Holy shit! An entire tree must have died at the expense of this packet because no lie, there were at least fifty pages of forms to be filled out, asking everything from my bio to my dating history to my tax information, hobbies, citizenship, etc. You name it, it was in this packet. The last page was a "Photo Submission," instructing me to send seven photos of myself, and myself only, with natural makeup and under no circumstances any Photoshopping or filters. As if I wasn't turned off by the intrusion into my past and present, the photo request was just enough for me to chuck the entire packet in the trash. *What a waste*, I thought. Cut to a few days later, the packet still remained in the basket. Was this another sign, like my car steering me to the casting call, or had the cleaning lady just gotten lazy? Reluctantly, I retrieved the packet and placed it in my top desk drawer.

Days went by before I received a phone call from yet another casting producer inquiring into the whereabouts of my packet, which was now overdue by about eight hundred hours. Without wanting to give the impression that I was too cool for school or, in this case, too sane for reality television, I told her I'd been really busy and would try and fill it out over the weekend. I mean, how do you tell someone that you were only there for the free drinks? Feeling guilty, I decided to begin the arduous task of filling out the questionnaires. When I got to the "Photo Submission" page, I realized how screwed I was. Where in the hell was I going to come up with these seven photos? I stalked my own Facebook profile only to find that I didn't have a single decent photo of just myself, and as I scrolled through the photos on my phone, the only solo photos of me were very much unsuited for public viewing (thank goodness iCloud wasn't around then). I knew I was going to have to find a way to secretly get headshots taken.

Enter my sister, known to me as Shishy, who luckily was flying into town for a big family gathering celebrating our grandfather's birthday. Despite being a nerdy-scientist-free-spirit-hippie-dippie who still had a flip phone, when I asked for her help, she happily agreed to take the photos. We snuck off during the party, and after thirty exhausting minutes decided enough was enough and whatever photos were on my phone would have to suffice. I went to the local CVS and printed out the pictures before half-assing the rest of the questionnaire, leaving many of the repetitive pages blank. Exhausted, I mailed the packet back. I figured, if worse came to worst, all I had lost was some time, dignity, and $3.45 in postage. I was finally done . . . or so I thought.

A week later, I was invited to the "final round" of casting in Los Angeles. I decided mum's the word and lied, telling my parents I was going to visit Shishy in San Diego rather than going to a casting call for a reality TV show.

When I arrived in Los Angeles, I was hastily whisked off to an airport hotel just a few minutes away with strict instructions to wait in the car upon my arrival. Another black-clad producer greeted me and led me into my hotel room where another packet sat upon my bed. A few dozen forms and a five-hundred-multiple-choice personality test later, I finally received a knock on my door from yet another producer. How many of them were there? I followed her down the hall into a room set up with a lonely chair, a camera, insanely bright lights, and you guessed it, another producer. She asked me the same background questions along with a few new ones. I can hardly remember what I said except for one horrible answer.

"So who's your favorite person from the current season?" the producer asked.

Fuck! Do I tell them I haven't seen this season—or any season, for that matter—or do I wing it? Luckily while at the airport, I had come across the duty-free shop (where I often read magazines to pass the time and to avoid having to actually purchase them). On the cover of one such mag I remembered seeing a story about the current season. I quickly blurted out the only name I could remember.

"Oh, really? Interesting. Why do you like him?" she asked with a puzzled look, which was enough to assure me that if I had actually read the article, I would have known he was the one who had broken the star's heart.

"I don't know, I just think he's, umm . . . he seems honest," I reluctantly responded.

The interview wrapped, and I was whisked into another room with not one, not two, but about twelve producers. I sat in a chair in front of them with a screen behind me showing a familiar scene.

"Have you been watching my interview in the other room?" I asked.

"Why, yes, we have." They laughed.

Several rapid-fire questions and generic responses later, I was finally done. I returned to my room with the same feeling I had after the very first casting so many weeks ago: Thank God it's over! The next morning I was off to spend time with Shishy in San Diego. (So I guess I had really only told my parents half a lie.) I recounted the previous day's events and told her there was no way they would pick me, and even if they did, it wasn't my thing. A few days in the sun and I was back home to Atlanta and my regular life.

That is, until a few weeks later when one phone call changed everything. I remember it as if it were yesterday . . . I was huffing and puffing on the treadmill when Rihanna's "Rude Boy" was interrupted by my ringtone. It was from a number I didn't recognize, but I knew the 310 area code belonged to Los Angeles. Normally, I never answer a call from a random number, and I don't know why I did this time—probably so I could take a breather. It was the head of casting and she was officially inviting me to be a contestant on the upcoming season. My mind began racing faster than the treadmill beneath me. I told her I wasn't sure if it was my thing, but that I'd mull it over. I hung up the phone and cranked up the speed and put Rihanna back on. When I got home that evening, I poured myself a glass of red wine, sat on my bed and debated. Should I do the show or not? I mentally listed out the pros, which included traveling, making new friends, making out with a hot guy, playing hooky from work, and, of course, the chance to find love. The cons, however, included total humiliation of not just myself but also my family, friends, coworkers, third-grade teacher, and anyone else who was my Facebook friend. Other cons included destroying my career, going broke, and . . . finding love.

It wasn't lost upon me that finding love was both a pro and

con. I had to ask myself, Was I really ready to fall in love? I had been in relationships, but the thought of possibly falling in love and being engaged in such a short amount of time was overwhelming. It's one thing to be ready to fall in love and have months or even years to make sure it's with the right man before taking it to another level, but it's a completely different ball game when there's a time limit on all of that. Oh, not to mention it's all on national television.

I spent days going back and forth from yes to no to maybe and back to no before making a decision that would become the biggest mistake of my life . . .

Lesson learned: *Nothing good comes of free drinks.*

DAY 2. 11:15 P.M.

Off I Go!

Considering you know why I'm in my current state of depression (though keep that a secret because it hasn't "officially" been announced yet. Gag! I could do without the shitshow that'll create). I guess it's no secret that I accepted the gig. It wasn't an easy decision. In fact, I pondered for days. And days. And days. With my pros and cons list changing more often than my underwear, I didn't know what to do. Until one day, out of the blue, I said to myself, *Screw it! What do I have to lose?* I figured I could handle my alcohol just fine and had a pretty good grip on the words that came out of my mouth, so the fate of my reputation and career was in my hands. And if I fell in love, well, then, dammit, I guess it was just meant to be.

But, it wasn't that simple. See, before I could phone the producer back with the "good news," I had to figure out one major obstacle: my job. How do I tell my bosses? It's not like I worked for a glamorous magazine where I was surrounded by chic women who watched reality television and would go absolutely bananas at the idea of their co-worker being one of the contestants. No,

I worked in the courthouse and on the streets of Atlanta—in the gang unit, no less. My supervisor was a man in his forties who undoubtedly had never watched the show, and had no qualms about giving me a hard time for being a cute preppy girl from the rich suburbs who wore stilettos to jailhouse interviews. And now I was going to tell him that I was about to go on a reality television show? I stalled for days before finally mustering up enough courage to walk into his office.

"So, I need to talk to you about something," I said.

"Are you quitting on me already?"

"No, no."

"Oh, thank God. What's up?"

"I might need some time off."

"For what?"

"Oh, how do I say this . . . get ready to laugh. I got invited to do a dating show."

"Like on television?"

"Yeah, on television. Basically, I would be one of several girls vying for one man."

"Well, damn, that sounds awesome. Not for you, but for the guy."

I laughed. "So what do you think, can I get some time off?"

"I'm sure we can figure something out. We'll talk to Boss Ross. But *I* have one condition."

"What is that?"

"If I give you time off, you better win the damn thing."

"Haha, please, I'll probably be gone for less than a week."

I was shocked at how amenable and even excited he was about the idea. Now I just needed Boss Ross to be on board.

"Boss Ross," aka the head bitch in charge of the Homicide/

Gang Unit, had hired me straight out of college after taking me under her wing during my internship the previous summer. The first words she ever spoke to me were, "You ready to see some dead bodies?" A tall, slim brunette, she was smart as a whip and owned any courtroom she walked into with her stilettos and take-no-prisoners attitude. Basically she was a badass, which I aspired to be, and now I had to ask this badass for time off from putting away gangbangers so I could go on a dating show. But, to my surprise she was also oddly thrilled for this opportunity and readily approved.

With my bosses on board, and even more enthusiastic than I was, it was time to tell my parents, who had been left completely in the dark and were about to get the shock of a lifetime. I waited for that Sunday's family dinner, which was the one day a week my mom actually made something other than reservations. On my way I picked up wine for Mom and a bottle of scotch for Dad to ensure they were, at a minimum, tipsy when I broke the news. As the three of us sat around the dinner table, I took a large gulp of red wine before spastically blurting out, "So, I think I'm going on a dating show."

"What?" my mom squealed as she nearly spit out her wine.

I looked at my dad, who wore his familiar stoic I'm-not-going-to-say-anything-until-you-give-me-the-full-story expression he always had whenever my sister or I dropped bombs on him.

"Well, Pookie"—my mom's favorite nickname for me—"I think it's time that you start dating, so I am all for it. But I have to tell you . . . you do know that you have to actually try out and get chosen, right? You can't just *go* on a show."

"Yeah, about that . . ." I could see my dad's smile go from patiently inquisitive to *what the hell did you do?*

"So . . . remember how I visited Shishy in California? Well, I might have . . . ummm . . . also . . . gone to the casting call."

"What?" my mom squealed again, as my dad sat in silence.

"Yeah, so a while back Sarah, Leslie, and Caroline basically made me go to this casting call, and then I got a call back and they flew me to L.A. and long story short, last week they asked me if I wanted to join the next season."

"That's amazing! Does this mean you're not a lesbian?" my mom said.

I scowled. "Really, Mom? No, I'm not a lesbian."

"Oh, I'm just kidding, lighten up! I say go for it! You're single, you're smart, and you have nothing to lose."

"Except my dignity."

"Hah, dignity?" My dad finally spoke. "I think it's fun as long as you don't embarrass yourself, which I know you won't. Go have a good time, just don't fall in love."

"Well, you know that's the whole point, right?"

"Yeah, okay, whatever you say."

"I could go on the show and get engaged!"

"Yeah, let's not start that crap," he said.

With my parents' approval, I called the producer and told her that I was in. Though I'd been sworn to secrecy, I couldn't help but tell my sister and a handful of close friends including Sarah, Leslie, and Caroline. Word got around throughout my office, but I remained coy until my last day before leaving for the show, when I said goodbye to everyone, including Boss Ross. As I walked out the door, she said, "Do me a favor."

"What's that?"

"Drive it like you stole it, honey, and don't stop 'til you see blue lights in the rearview."

"No other way to drive it," I replied with a grin.

And with that, I walked out of the office and toward my next adventure.

I had the weekend to pack before I had to leave for Los Angeles. I probably should have looked at the suggested packing list I was supplied well before forty-eight hours prior to departure because, let me tell you, when I did, I was put into a total tailspin considering all it said was: IN TWO SUITCASES ONLY, contestants should pack the following:

- clothing for both cold and warm weather
- athletic wear
- bathing suits
- heels, tennis shoes, and sandals
- cocktail, long, and casual dresses
- heavy coats

First of all, how broad and thus useless is this kind of list? Why don't they just tell you to pack your entire life? Oh, wait, they would, except you get only TWO suitcases. Somehow by the grace of God I managed to fit a couple of cocktail dresses, some workout clothes, one gown, and absolutely zero bikinis into the TWO suitcases.

Sunday evening arrived, and instead of my parents seeing me for dinner, they were driving me and my two stuffed suitcases to the airport. Though we were excited, we had such low expectations, that what I was about to do didn't really feel like a big deal. After checking my luggage curbside, I gave my mom and dad a hug goodbye and walked toward the double doors that led to the terminal. Turning, I waved and shouted, "See you in a few days!"

"Maybe a week," my mom optimistically replied.

"Or who knows? Next time you see me, I could be engaged!" I said, dangling my left hand in the air at my father.

He laughed. "Get the hell outta here."

And off I went . . .

Oh to think, if I had just had the strength to resist the free drinks (that I ironically never got) I wouldn't be here now. In fact, I would have never laid eyes on Number Twenty-Six, never fallen in love, never found out he was nothing like he seemed, and most of all would have avoided this heartbreak altogether. Where's a time machine when you need it?

But if I'm being honest, I have to say that something far more powerful than alcohol really got me here: it was fate. Though I'm not one to believe that "everything happens for a reason" or "it's all part of a plan," in a time like this, it's comforting to know that eventually those free drinks that led to a broken heart will lead me to yet another destination.

In the meantime, the first stop on the journey is Depression-ville. Welcome! Here you'll find an excuse to drink like no one is watching and eat like your jeans have elastic waistbands. Take advantage of this place! There's a pity party going on here but you won't be allowed to stay forever.

And along with some good food and wine, every party needs some killer music. Thus, I present to you your very own breakup playlist. Don't worry, this list won't send you into a tailspin but rather give your broken heart what it needs to get in the right mood and get over the blues (or at least keep them at bay for a few moments). From country to pop, to hip-hop and rock 'n' roll, I give to you . . .

THE ULTIMATE BREAKUP PLAYLIST:

- "We Are Never Ever Getting Back Together," Taylor Swift
- "Since U Been Gone," Kelly Clarkson
- "Caught Out There," Kelis
- "Break Up with Him," Old Dominion
- "No Scrubs," TLC
- "You're So Vain," Carly Simon
- "On to the Next One," Jay-Z
- "Survivor," Destiny's Child
- "Nookie," Limp Bizkit
- "Cry Me a River," Justin Timberlake
- "So What," Pink
- "Love Yourself," Justin Bieber
- "Tubthumping," Chumbawamba
- "Riding Solo," Jason Derulo
- "Blank Space," Taylor Swift
- "Love Don't Live Here," Lady Antebellum
- "Love Stinks," J. Geils Band
- "Single Ladies," Beyoncé

Time to jam out, sister!

Lesson learned: *Let's get this (pity) party started!*

DAY 4. 5:25 P.M.

The Announcement

Everyone knows now.

This morning, I awoke to a phone call from our publicist telling me that later today she'd be issuing a statement confirming my breakup. I didn't bother to proofread the statement she emailed me, considering just the thought of it makes me want to vomit. It's strange enough to have a publicist, let alone have my breakup be "officially announced." I feel like Khloé Kardashian right now, not in the lavishly rich and enviable way, but in a get-ready-for-everyone-to-judge kind of way.

The truth is, though our split may come as a shock to strangers, it's been a long time coming. For the nine months we were engaged, I'd say four of them were blissfully happy, about three of them were filled with tense ups and downs, and the remaining two? Well, those two months were pure torture. We had gone from completely smitten and in love to hating each other. I guess that's what happens when you're in a roller-coaster relationship filled with the highest of highs and the lowest of lows. My relationship changed so drastically in such a short amount of time, just like my life has.

Once upon a time, I was just a normal girl from Atlanta, Georgia, who'd been plucked from obscurity and put on a dating show. But now I was a "public figure" who has gone from single to engaged and back to single, but it's not just my Facebook status that has changed, it's my identity as well. For one, my social media has taken on a life of its own. I used to hope that the number of likes on my Instagram photos would hit double digits, now I just hope my thousands of followers don't notice that I've used a filter to cover up my latest blemish. Secondly, I now have to be aware of those blemishes whenever I go out in public because I am always at risk of being snapped by a lurking paparazzi. I can't even believe I'm saying the word "paparazzi" in reference to myself, but it's true. Every so often, I'll see a photo in a magazine of me and Number Twenty-Six grocery shopping, exiting a restaurant, or walking the dog. Sometimes I spot the shooter, but usually I didn't even notice they were hiding in the bushes snapping away.

From strangers coming up to me on the street (or at the mall) to free meals and red carpets, all the notoriety made me feel uncomfortable. Though I was flattered that people were so supportive, I didn't feel worthy of the attention. It wasn't as if I was a person with talent to be admired, or performing a service to making the world a better place. Instead, I was just a random girl who had made out with multiple men on national television. That was it. While I struggled with the attention, Number Twenty-Six relished it. He thrived in the spotlight. This didn't bother me at first. In fact, I had wanted it for him. I wanted him to have the spotlight that he had missed out on all of his life since his younger brother had gained notoriety as a college and then professional athlete.

But, with the help of one reality television show and a very public engagement, he was no longer second fiddle, and I couldn't have been happier for him.

We had agreed to balance our newfound fame by laying down some rules when it came to fans and photos. I guess I should say *he* decided to lay down some rules. Rule number one was that I was not to take photos with other men. Though I found this request a bit alarming, the fact that 99.7% of people wanting photos were young girls made it an easy rule to follow, along with the fact that I didn't care about taking photos with men and had just gotten engaged before millions of viewers—the blinding ring on my finger serving as a convenient reminder.

Rule number two was mutually agreed upon: no photos at dinner. We decided that dinner was a time for the two of us to enjoy, and any fan photos could wait until after.

These rules worked for a while, but as our relationship deteriorated, I started to notice their enforcement becoming more lax. Photos of Twenty-Six with a bevy of girls began popping up on social media, and he had gone from a man preaching the value of privacy to a man who not only obliged photo requests during dinner, but went so far as to offer them. The more attention we got, the more I began to question what he loved most: the fame or me. My wish for him to have a spotlight had backfired and I questioned if his new status as a "celebrity" had changed him, or if this was the person behind that megawatt smile all along.

I guess I'll find out now that our breakup news is out. In an attempt to avoid reality, I've decided to stay away from the Internet and all forms of social media, but as the moments pass, I suspect the announcement has officially gone public because my phone has begun blowing up! One after another, the texts and calls pour in. I'm actually worried it might catch on fire. Some of the calls and texts are from friends, others from acquaintances so distant I don't have so much as their names stored in my phone. All of them asking if the rumors are true, how I'm doing, what happened, and who dumped whom. My closest family members and friends already know, but now it feels as though the entire world knows too. I can't find the courage or energy to respond to the texts. What would I even say? I feel so incredibly embarrassed right now that I just want to get back into bed, curl into a ball, and hide under the fluffy down comforter.

As much as I wish this entire breakup could be handled privately, I know it can't. I forfeited that luxury by getting to do all of the amazing things I did. And now I must pay the price, and that means I must get ready for some judgments and criticism. You'd think by now I'd be used to the insults strangers seem to constantly hurl my way, but I'm not. You can't even fathom the things people in this world are willing to say, or should I say type and post on the Internet. I get it, "I signed up for it," but I didn't know that signing up for a reality show would essentially be like getting naked, tying myself to a tree, and being pummeled with cheap shots and jabs while not being able to let out so much as a squeal. They shouldn't bother me, but they do. I can't help it. And now, with this announcement, I feel tied right back up to that tree, too weak to break free.

And despite the publicity of this breakup, the truth is I feel the same things anyone does when it comes to this type of news. With every breakup, notable or not, comes the same common realizations:

It's real now.

There's something about your breakup going public that makes it feel so much more real. Whether it's telling your friends and family, having to change your relationship status to "single" on Facebook, or in my case putting out a press release, the fact that it's over doesn't seem to hit you until someone other than you and your ex know about it. There's no more hiding the fact that you are now—say it with me—"S-I-N-G-L-E." And as much as it sucks that people now know about your new status, try to think of it as both a relief and a way to hold you accountable. It's a relief because now that everyone knows, you don't have to personally break the news to your entire list of contacts. They already know! Plus, it means you've gotten through the second hardest part of a breakup, which is the actual breakup conversation. Your recovery marathon has begun! Sure, you'll endure a few miles of pain and anger followed by a second wind of reflection and revenge, but by the end, you'll cross the finish line a brand-new person. Plus, don't they say half the battle is just showing up?

Secondly, the "publicity" of your breakup will serve as a way to hold you accountable. You've gotten out of a relationship that clearly wasn't right for you, but despite knowing that, it's easy to find yourself (especially in moments of weakness) contemplating going back. But the last thing you want is for others to see that weakness in you. As much as I know how toxic my relationship became, at this moment, I miss it. I miss my ex. I miss the love we once had, the memories we made, and the security I felt. I find myself wanting to go back to those days all the time, forgetting about the bad times. But the fact that people know about the breakup makes me think twice. I can only imagine the field day the tabloids would have if I went from engaged, to single, to re-engaged.

Okay, so maybe not everybody has to worry about the tabloids, but think of it in terms of something we can all relate to: credit card debt. You've got loads of it when all of a sudden you learn that the fabulous pair of shoes you've been eyeing for months are on sale! If nobody knows of your financial crisis, you're obviously getting the shoes. But let's say a friend knows about your debt. You know damn well that the minute she sees you wearing those new shoes, she's going to have something to say about it. So, you think twice, you feel accountable, and thus you avoid making a poor decision. The same goes with your breakup. It's bad enough that people are going to ask you about the breakup, imagine what they'll ask about the makeup.

It's embarrassing.

You feel like an idiot. How could you actually think you had found your soul mate? You feel ridiculous for having been so happy. You were the picture-perfect couple—when others fought, you kissed. While your girlfriends complained about their significant others, you felt grateful. Now that it didn't work out, you feel shitty, stupid, and self-conscious.

Trust me, I feel your pain. There are two things in life I hate most: delivering bad news, and embarrassment. And now, here I am doing both. I've never felt stupid for believing I had fallen in love on a reality show and met my soul mate in just eight weeks. Everyone predicted we would break up, and though we were hell-bent on proving the critics wrong, in the end they were right. I had been sashaying around for nine months with a giant diamond ring and a giant smile to match. I loved being able to show people how in love we were, because we actually were, and because I had never had that chance in my life. And now it's all gone. All that's left is the single girl, with no home, no fiancé, no future, and a dream ring that producers are going to ask me to return any day now. I'm ashamed it didn't work out and now that shame is out there for everyone to know, laugh at, and judge.

But the truth is, the last thing you should feel over a breakup is embarrassed. Feel pain, feel hatred, guilt, remorse, whatever you want, but don't punish yourself with shame. This is *your* breakup, and people will talk shit about you either behind your back, or behind a keyboard, but fuck 'em! They don't live in your world, they don't know what you're feeling or what went on behind closed doors. Have you ever met a hater who was doing better than you? Yeah, me neither.

It's identity theft.

The person I have become, the person people have come to know me as, is gone now. Nobody knew me as an attorney or a good friend or a loving daughter—they knew me as the chick on a reality show who got engaged and became the happiest fiancée in the world. Now, I'm another statistic, just half of another couple that called it quits. I am . . . "formerly engaged."

And it's not just the title that changes, it's our way of life. When we get into relationships, we blend our life with our partner's in so many ways that we don't recognize the person we were before the relationship. Your friends become his friends and vice versa. Your weekend plans are joint plans; your lives intertwine into one. So when that joint life is taken away, you can't help but question who you are now, right? Think of this identity theft as a gain, not a loss. It's a fresh start; a clean slate. A chance for you to reinvent yourself, reevaluate the person who you want to be, the places you want to go, and the people who you want to be in your life. And though the reinvention takes time, take comfort in knowing that it awaits you whenever you're ready.

It's a failure.

You failed at choosing the right man, at making it work, at living happily ever after. I get it. I've never felt like such a failure in my entire life than I have during this breakup. I couldn't make it work, no matter how hard I tried. I couldn't be the person he wanted me to be, no matter how many concessions I made. I couldn't be happy despite the privileged life I was getting to live. I failed at it all.

But why is "failure" such a bad word? Why do we put such negative emphasis on failing? It's as if we are supposed to go through life having succeeded in everything we do. But the truth is, everyone fails! Nobody has the magic touch that turns everything to gold. I mean, think of all the successful people who have failed:

- Oprah: fired from her first television job
- Steven Spielberg: rejected by USC
- Thomas Edison: made 1,000+ light bulbs that *didn't* work until one finally did
- Lady Gaga: dropped from her first record label
- Michael Jordan: cut from his high school basketball team
- Jennifer Lawrence: auditioned for *Twilight* and got rejected
- Bill Gates: dropped out of college

All of these people have one thing in common: they failed before they succeeded. I'm not saying you're going to be the next Jennifer Lawrence or Bill Gates or Oprah, but if they can overcome their failures, so can you.

It's wasteful.

You probably feel as though you've wasted your time, your energy, and your love on your broken relationship. And you have. You're not getting that time back. Sorry. When I think about all of the things I experienced with Number Twenty-Six, I think of all the many "firsts" and "bests" I spent on him. Obviously, it was my first engagement, which I won't ever get back. But it was more than that. It was the first time I'd felt love at first sight, the first time I felt as in love as I did. There were so many best dates, best moments. There were the first kisses, the first time he said, "I love you," the first time I met his family, our first holiday together.

But here's the thing, they are only firsts, not lasts. The lasts are what count! The firsts are starting points, you learn from them, so you can master the lasts. I mean come on, do you care about the first tooth you lost, or the last one that meant you were officially an adult. Do you care sixty years from now about the first kiss you had with your high school boyfriend, or the one you have with the love of your life?

It's normal.

Lastly, and most important, remember that you are not the first person to go through a breakup, nor will you be the last. I promise. Think of the countless celebrity couples who have broken up, even the ones with their own super-couple nicknames: Bennifer, TomKat, Tay-Squared to name a few. Yes, you and I are just like them! Trust me when I say you are not the first person to cry in the shower so nobody hears you, or call in sick for work because of an ailing heart. You are not alone in feeling angry, regretful, or just plain bummed out. It's one of the few times where feeling unoriginal actually brings you solace.

So know that everyone may seem to care now, but let 'em gossip away. You may be the hot topic today, but someone else's fuck up will be the latest juicy news tomorrow. :-)

Lesson learned: *Anyone who says a breakup isn't embarrassing is lying.*

DAY 5. 1:33 P.M.

Self-Help Ain't Helping

I went to sleep last night crying only to awake this morning to tears streaming down my face. How is it possible to literally wake up crying? I haven't been awake long enough for any thoughts to make their way into my pounding head, thanks to my new best friend Mr. Cabernet (which I desperately needed after yesterday's official breakup announcement), and yet I'm already bawling. I just can't seem to control it, not with a box of tissues or with every ounce of my depleting determination. They just keep fucking flowing! How does my body even have this much water in it? It seems both scientifically and physically inconceivable to shed this many tears. I mean, I learned in fifth grade that humans are 80 percent water (though at the moment about 5 percent of that is currently red wine), but still, this seems impossible, not to mention completely unfair.

Through my puffy wet eyes, I glance over at my nightstand to reach for the same thing I reach for first every morning . . . my phone. It's sitting amid an embarrassing amount of used tissues next to a blinking digital clock. Shit! It's 11:47. How did I sleep this late? Next to my phone, I discover a wine bottle. I pick it up and immediately notice it's rather light. As I peer into the bottle, I can see straight down to the bottom, solidifying that I finished it all by my lonesome self last night . . . Double shit. That would explain why the room is spinning.

Where am I in life right now? Am I already the girl who polishes off a bottle of wine and awakens mere moments before noon with tears rolling down her face? Dear Lord, this *really* is going to be rough. I know it's only been a few days since the end of my nine-month engagement, but I'm ready for this pain to go away already. It doesn't help that my days consist of waking up no earlier than 11:00 a.m. (crying), and the first thing I do is reach for my phone and check social media. At which point, I cry some more as I scroll through everyone's posts showing off their "awesome" lives, followed by afternoons filled with pouting around in unwashed pajamas, making some lunch, which will include bread to soak up the wine I drank the previous evening, and watching several episodes of *Judge Judy* On Demand until 5:00 in the afternoon when I will undoubtedly pour a heavy glass of wine.

Some schedule, huh? Thank the good Lord above that I am currently "funemployed," because I don't think I could handle having to go to work and actually come face-to-face with human beings. I have to admire those girls who show up to work days after a breakup and manage not only to be productive but also stay dry-eyed the entire day. They deserve a damn diamond-encrusted medal and a sexy young pool boy as a reward.

Since I have nothing on the agenda today, I decide to wash my leggings and V-neck and change into some fresh clothes, but then I remember I have no fresh clothes. They are back at Number Twenty-Six's place, aka our old home we shared, and there is no way in hell I'm going over there to get them looking like this. Instead, I rummage through Kelly's laundry room, find some Febreze, and douse myself in it. I'm embarrassed that I just admitted that.

Thank God for Kelly. She was the first person I called after we broke up. At that moment, I knew I should leave our home immediately, but given that it was close to midnight, I told Kelly I would just sleep on the couch and head to her place in the morning.

"Umm, are you fucking kidding me? You're not staying there. Come over immediately," Kelly instructed.

"It's fine, it's almost midnight, and I don't want to put you out."

"Stop. There is no way in hell I am letting you stay there!"

"Are you sure?"

"It's not even an option. Do you need me to come pick you up?"

"Okay, thanks! I can drive. Be over soon."

It took me only ten minutes to arrive at her house, but that was long enough for her to open a bottle of wine and have a glass waiting for me when I walked in the door.

Kelly had recently moved into a mansion with her fiancé just down the road and had room to spare for a pathetic and now homeless single friend like myself. She has become one of my closest friends even though I pretty much despised her the very first time I met her, which was on my journey to find love with Number One more than a year ago. I was the last girl to arrive at the mansion, and when I walked into the house to meet twenty-some-odd other women, the first person I saw was Kelly, a tall, thin brunette dressed in a floor-length red Nicole Miller that showed off her ample curves and tiny waist. I recognized her immediately because we had both been featured in a local Atlanta magazine as some of the city's most eligible singles. And though we lived in the same city and ran in the same social scene, we had never officially met. She was intimidating in stature, and with her thicker and daintier Southern accent, ruined any chance I had at playing the Southern belle card. Of course I immediately saw her as a threat but, it took only about two days for me to realize that she had zero chemistry with the lead (and she knew it), was wicked smart, and had a salty sense of humor I found utterly hilarious. This quickly moved her off my "Threat List" and onto my "Friend List."

After the show wrapped, we became even closer, largely due to the fact that we lived within ten minutes of each other. She soon became a friend for life, and I needed her now more than ever. She told me I could stay as long as I want to, but her generosity makes me feel pathetic and weak. My lack of motivation doesn't help my cause, nor does the disconcerting realization that I am drowning my sorrows with wine. I've read enough self-help articles online in the past twenty-four hours to admit that when they say, "Don't drink away your pain," they're probably right. But right now, I really don't give a damn.

While I'm on the topic of self-help articles, am I the only woman who reads them and actually ends up feeling worse? A million articles pop up with every single Internet search I do of "Ways to Get over a Breakup," but each of them spouts the same bullshit garbage. The top five:

1. Grieve
2. Accept
3. Believe

4. Don't drink away your pain
5. Don't stay in bed all day

Just once I'd like to read an article that tells the truth: "You are about to embark on the shittiest time of your life. Be prepared by stocking up on wine, girlfriends, and tissues. Buckle up, it's going to be a bumpy ride, you train wreck, you." Now *that* would make me feel normal.

Or, you know what would be even better? How about a self-help article to read *during* the relationship? Something that tells you, "Hey, there's a major red flag, you might want to read into it a little more before you end up in heartbreak with a bunch of hind-sight information you could have used . . . umm, like yesterday"?

I can't help thinking if only I had read into the red flags a little more, maybe I wouldn't be here now. Despite everything starting off perfectly, Twenty-Six and I had actually had our first fight while on the show, and though it never aired for millions of viewers to see, in hindsight I saw a fight that foreshadowed many of our future difficulties.

It had been five weeks since I'd met him. And in those five weeks I had made out with him an ungodly amount of times, and even enjoyed what can only be described as a magical first solo date with him in France. He'd written me a poem that said the next time he said "I love you" to a woman, she would be the woman he'd marry, and I couldn't help hoping that I'd be that woman. He had shown me that it wasn't just our kisses that made me swoon for him; it was the comfort and ease I felt whenever I was around him.

But then I found myself in Italy on yet another group date, with six men including Number Twenty-Six. The guys met me in the quaint countryside of a town called Monselice, where we walked around enjoying the annual food festival. He noticeably trailed in the back and stayed rather distant throughout the day, but I didn't read much into it because I knew from experience how awkward the transition from a solo date to a group one could be. After the festival ended, I brought the group to a medieval castle and guided them into a dark, cold, stonewalled room adorned with spears, daggers, and other terrifying armory.

"So do you guys want to know what we're doing in this war room?" I asked.

Cue the dramatic music as two Italian men dressed in suits appeared. As if the men in black and the surrounding weaponry weren't intimidating enough, I informed the group that we would all be taking a lie detector test! Yay! The horror on their faces made the feminist inside me squeal with excitement. Now mind you, this is television, so odds are pretty high that our production crew scooped up two random men walking down the cobblestone streets, put them in suits, gave them a laptop and heart monitor, and told them they were "experts" for the day, but we did it anyway!

I decided to go first to prove to the guys that I was a team player and directed them to wait outside. I was nervous as I sat in the chair, but it took only a few questions to realize how janky this test was—not only could I hardly understand the questions through the "experts'" thick Italian accents, but the heart rate monitor had slid from my sternum to my waistline without any indication on the graph. Having feared the men would see this activity as completely psycho-girlfriend-worthy, I was actually relieved at how fake it all felt.

Next, it was each guy's turn. The questions ranged from serious, such as "Are you ready for marriage?" to ridiculous, such as "Do you wash your hands after you pee?" and "Do you prefer blondes over brunettes?"

The guys waited outside before entering the dungeon, looking terrified. One after another, they exited with smiles of relief. After every man had bared his soul—or lied—the results were in, and we were all given the option either to read the results or "trust" each other and throw them away. The men immediately jumped at the chance to read mine. Knowing the sketchiness of the entire thing, I wasn't concerned about what they'd see and didn't feel that by reading my results they didn't trust me. I, however, used this as my chance to "earn the men's trust," and opted to rip up their results and throw them in the trash. Okay, in all honesty, it wasn't just to earn the men's trust; it also made for some riveting television, and I knew would serve as an easy topic to get me through some of the more lackluster conversations. But the main reason I ripped up the results was that, despite my skepticism, I couldn't help fearing that some of the guys had admitted to things I had wished they'd lied about. And when I say "some of the guys," I really mean Number Twenty-Six. What if he answered that he preferred blondes? Okay, that I could totally get over because truth is, even though he has brown hair, I prefer blondes too. But what if he admitted that he wasn't ready to get married, or that he wasn't falling in love with me? I might not be able to handle those two answers. (And, truthfully, I'd have second thoughts about any guy who told the truth about hand washing.) With the results ripped up and in the trashcan, I figured, no harm no foul, right?

Ha! Wrong. That evening we had our usual cocktail party in which I mingled with each guy privately before it was time for me to get Number Twenty-Six alone. As we took our seat on a bench in the courtyard with a moonlit view overlooking the town, I could sense that something was on his mind. A little small talk, and I asked if everything was all right with him. And that's when he unleashed his inner beast and began telling me how much it bothered him that I would make him take a lie detector test right after we had just had a great date where we talked about trust. I was surprised that he had he gone from laughing about it in front of everyone else to feeling upset. After all, it wasn't as if I had planned the date in the first place, and *I* didn't make him take the test, and come on, there was no way he actually thought it was serious! Oh, and let's not forget the most important part of it all . . . I didn't even read the results.

But what shocked me the most was his tone. He was aggressive and combative, playing the victim and practically asking, "How dare you make me prove my honesty?" And though he was obviously careful in his words as the cameras rolled, no amount of restraint could hide the look in his eyes. It was a look of disgust and rage. This was a side of him I had never seen, or even knew existed. There I sat, stunned. It wasn't the merits of the fight that had jolted me but the vision of this person not being the same man I had already begun to fall in love with. The conversation settled down, and without really solving the issue, we somehow moved on and subsequently got back into our normal state of smooching and laughing. But the damage was done. I had seen a vision of my perfect love story becoming the biggest disaster of my life.

Although the conversation ended with kisses and groping, this fight rocked me harder than any past arguments with boyfriends. When I arrived back at my hotel room, I crawled into my bed and cried as the argument played over and over in my mind and I recalled the look in his eyes and the anger in his voice. I felt as if this relationship with him was over before it ever officially started. I had built him up to be this perfect man, and as a result I forgot to look out for any flaws as well. I had let my feelings blind me, prompting infatuation with one man to get in the way of the possibilities with the other men, and all for what? Unfounded accusations about a stupid game? There I was, undoubtedly the luckiest girl in the world as I sat in my sprawling Italian hotel room with a floor full of suitors beneath me, but one man, one fight, had put me in a complete tailspin.

The next morning I woke up still grieving but had to go on a date with a different contestant, this time a one-on-one in Verona. Luckily I was meeting my date there, so I had time to try and regroup during the long drive. I rode in the back of the van, along with three producers, and peered out the window at the beautiful Italian countryside. With headphones on, I listened to the saddest songs I could find on my iPod as I obsessed about last night's fight and sobbed.

I could hardly pull myself together, but my date didn't know it. I felt numb and exhausted from the night before, but most of all I felt guilty. My mind was elsewhere when it should have been on a guy who deserved someone better than me, someone attentive to him—basically he deserved anyone else but a puffy-eyed woman still devastated over a fight with another man.

And though I had seen the way Number Twenty-Six fought, and I didn't like it, like any girl smitten, I turned a blind eye. Plus, it wasn't as if we were operating under the most natural circumstances. Having done the show before, I knew the stress that weeks cooped up in a house, with no access to the outside world, could put on a person. And despite our little fight, I still had strong feelings for this man. Hell, the fact that I was even concerned about it showed me the strength of my feelings. I decided this fight was to be a mulligan for us. The ones that followed, though, not so much.

I guess there's no point beating myself up over missing the significance of that first argument. I am where I am now, and though thinking about the red flags don't change that fact, I'm not going to lie, they do make me feel a little bit better.

As for now, I get it. I *should* put my big-girl thong on, suck it up, and address my feelings in a sober and rational way as I begin to grieve the loss of my relationship. But that's easier said than done. It's day five, I've just gotten out of an engagement, I'm single, homeless, and depressed, and the only thing that makes me feel better is feeling nothing at all—and the only times that happens is when I'm asleep or buzzed. It could be worse: I could be popping Xanax like Tic Tacs, dancing on bar tops, or spreading my legs for anything with a penis, right? Plus, it's not as if I plan on staying in this bed forever; Kelly is bound to get sick of me at some point. For now, my bed is my boyfriend, Mr. Cabernet is my best friend, and no self-help article is going to persuade me otherwise.

No amount of pretending to be strong is going to rid me of these shitty feelings that accompany heartbreak. Sorry, it's true. I'm not about to start sugarcoating it for you now. This is the brutal period, when you realize just how much heartbreak BLOWS. It is likely the most pain you have ever been in and possibly (hopefully) will ever have to be in. Truth is, heartbreak weakens you; it literally hurts you, from the inside out—and right now in these first few days, nothing will change that. People can try and cheer you up, and they will, because they care, but it won't help. You can find some upbeat quote on Pinterest to cheer you up, but no amount of pretty cursive font and gold stripes will be enough for you to actually believe whatever it's saying. All of that will come later, I promise! For now, you are still in survival mode. Do whatever you gotta do to stay afloat. Besides, how many of those "self-help" authors are actually in relationships anyway?

Lesson learned: Stay away from the self-help, but don't stay away from the red wine.

DAY 6. 12:50 P.M.

Tears and Sesame Chicken

I'm still feeling an overwhelming sense of embarrassment and sadness from the public announcement, despite it having happened days ago. I'm trying to stay afloat, I really am, but this shit is hard! I figure, things can't get much worse than this, so I might as well bask in the misery. Thus, I've called the closest Chinese restaurant that delivers and ordered the sesame chicken lunch special, which is one hell of a bargain. Did you know that for $8.95 you can get sesame chicken, fried rice, an egg roll, *and* a fortune cookie? It's perfect for a day like today, which I plan to spend engulfed in a marathon *Scandal* binge. It's long been my favorite television show, and I'd be lying if I said the phrase "It's handled" isn't part of my daily vocabulary. I make it through the first episode when the doorbell rings and my Chinese food arrives. Opening up the fortune cookie first, I add my traditional "in bed" to the end in order to make myself laugh. This one isn't that great: "Small opportunities are often the beginning of great enterprises . . . in bed." *Booooo!*

As I press play on the second scandalous episode, I realize that I am watching it all wrong—the popcorn is missing! How could I forget such a necessity? Somewhere, Olivia Pope is rolling her eyes at me over this mishap. I quickly pop a bag in the microwave while I continue eating my sesame chicken during the minute and forty-five seconds before the popcorn is ready. The fact that I am scarfing down Chinese food as I simultaneously wait for my popcorn to finish popping is not lost upon me, but, screw it, the brokenhearted deserve hall passes too, right? Sorry we can't all have a home-cooked meal with our significant other. I mean, don't get me wrong, once upon a time I totally got to be that hot girlfriend who dressed up in nothing but heels and an apron and had dinner (and my body) ready when my boyfriend got home. But clearly that's not a recipe for happiness. Maybe the single girls have had it right all along. They don't have to have dinner hot and ready for their man the second he walks in the door, they certainly don't have to shave their legs, let alone worry about a man seeing them naked. Basically, being single gets you a free certificate to avoid slaving away over a hot stove and instead indulge in however many carbs you want and nobody can say shit to you about it.

Feeling a flicker of self-righteousness, I pour the popcorn into a bowl and assume my position in front of the television. As I watch Olivia Pope take names and kick ass, I realize that what once was my all-time favorite hour-long pleasure now leaves me on the verge of tears and feeling even more depressed than I was moments ago. My eyes well up as I watch the relationship between the main characters, Olivia and Fitz. It's the most fucked-up relationship in the world. I mean, good Lord, Fitz is the freaking president of the United States who is married to crazy First Lady Mellie (aka "Smellie Mellie"), and Olivia is the badass lawyer/head bitch in charge/wearer of all white hats/power player of Washington, D.C. They can't be together, it's political suicide, and yet they can't be apart. I can't help but look at the two of them and, despite how insanely complicated their relationship is, think, *That is love right there.* God, I wish I had that kind of love. I mean, when Fitz looks at Olivia with those sexy presidential eyes as she tells him, "I am not a prize," and when her voice cracks when she whispers, "I want to make jam, I want Vermont," I lose it. Their love puts the Hope in hopeless and the Rome in romance (despite being nowhere close to Italy). And every tumultuous conversation between them includes Olivia berating the most powerful man in the world, but in a loving way, leaving him speechless before she storms off with her Prada bag and infamous Olivia Pope grin.

While I've never had a Prada bag, I have, once upon a time, had that grin . . .

I had it the first time I ever saw Number Twenty-Six. There I was, on yet another chilly California night, this time in March, standing in front of the same infamous mansion where I had met Number One. But it felt different this time. For starters, I had spent the weeks leading up to this first night in a sprawling mansion of my own, with access to my phone and the Internet instead of sequestered in a secret hotel. This time, instead of haphazardly stuffing clothes into TWO suitcases, I was supplied with a glamorous wardrobe by my very own stylist. And though it was the same mansion as last season, it seemed bigger than I remembered. It felt glitzier and, most of all, this time it felt filled with hope rather than fear. Now I was the woman calling the shots, and twenty-five men were going to compete for *me.*

I was dressed in a hand-beaded floor-length gown that my stylist and I had selected. Custom-tailored to enhance some assets

God forgot to give me, the nude-color dress was worth more than any car I will ever own, or even have a high enough credit score to lease. Rivaling the valuable gown were real diamonds dripping from my ears and wrists. I had never felt more expensive in my life as I stood with lights fixed on me and cameras in place as the handpicked men waited down the driveway in shiny black limos. All of them vetted just for me. All of them—well, most of them—ready, willing, and able to fall in love, just like me. My heart was pounding hard enough to make me worry that the sequins on my chest would give way at any moment, and the sky-high stilettos were already making my calves ache, but all of my feelings were drowned by an overwhelming sense of excitement as I wondered, *Is this really my life? Am I really about to meet my future husband mere moments from now?*

I took a deep breath as the first limo arrived. One by one the men stepped out, walked toward me, and introduced themselves. Each was hotter than the next. Maybe it was the lighting, maybe it was the adrenaline, but I had never seen a group of such hot-ass men in my life. Some of them made cheesy entrances, some brought gifts, others were fairly normal, and all were nervous as hell. I greeted them and made small talk in an attempt to ease their nerves before guiding them inside. Having done this before, I knew there would be anywhere from twenty to thirty men, so I tried to keep a tally in my head to see how many were left. I lost count somewhere between nineteen and twenty-four. And that's when *he* stepped out.

Tall, dark haired, with an athletic build, perfectly structured face, and a megawatt smile, it was as if God had made him with a ruler. He took a step toward me as my heart leapt. The closer he got, the more the chills ran down from my beach-waved, now frizzy hair to my blistered aching toes. Suddenly, the California air wasn't as cold anymore. He greeted me with a hug that felt different from the previous twenty-four; it was warmer, it was tighter, it was . . . euphoric.

He introduced himself and told me he lived in Atlanta. It seemed too good to be true, but I couldn't deny the indescribable magic I was experiencing. I guided him to the mansion just as I had done with the others, and as he walked inside, I checked out his ass (just as I had done twenty-four times before).

That was it, I had met them all. Twenty-five men awaited me inside as I stood alone in the cobblestone driveway soaking it all in. Before I walked into the house, I paused and made a pact with myself: No matter what it was that I'd just felt for *him*, it was under absolutely no circumstances love at first sight—just lust, that's all. This wasn't the time to get ahead of myself. I was supposed to be open and get to know each of the men and take my time, well, what little time there was. I mean, come on, there's no love at first sight on reality television, right? I took a deep breath and walked inside.

Despite there being twenty-five insanely hot, successful guys under one sprawling California roof, I couldn't seem to keep my eyes off Number Twenty-Six as I made my first toast to "finding love." I also couldn't keep my eyes *on* him, because I feared I'd find myself paralyzed and completely blow my cover, which would have been disastrous given that it was the very first night. And though I had known him for only about forty-five seconds, I already felt the desire to impress him, which was the antithesis of how I was supposed to feel as the empowered female.

We'd barely spoken a word to each other after our nervous introduction, but once the party had begun, he pulled me away and walked me outside to a bench where we'd sit and finally have a conversation. He offered me his jacket and I happily accepted. Truth is, it could have been a thousand degrees outside, but I was taking that damn jacket so I could get one layer closer to seeing what kind of bod he was working with.

He began the conversation with a compliment, telling me I was his mother's favorite from last season. Smooth move. Always nice to have Mommy's approval before we play tonsil hockey. The guy was hot, and not just reality television hot but regular life hot! As he talked about God knows what, I prayed for X-ray vision so I could see the pecs and abs that were sure to be hiding beneath his shirt. But no matter how hot he was, I had to make sure he knew that there was only one boss here: me. I overcompensated by playing up the tough-girl act and challenging him with rapid-fire questions and teasing. The game was on, but we both knew I was failing miserably, and regardless of how well I was able to control the words that came out of my mouth, the cheek-hurting grin that made its way across my face was a dead giveaway. The undeniable chemistry and banter back and forth made me feel like a sixteen-year-old schoolgirl crushing hard on the star quarterback. In that moment, it was as if I wasn't in the mansion with twenty-five men but simply sitting on a bench, eyes locked with his, swooning over every word he uttered.

Our chat ended, and I sent him off to join the pool of waiting men in suits, making sure to give him a hug tight enough to cop a feel. Abs . . . check. Pecs . . . check. And, as he walked away, I took the opportunity to check out his backside again. Ass . . . check. Butterflies . . . check. Damn, I was screwed.

Get it together, I told myself. It was only the first night and the options were plentiful inside. For all I knew he could have a girlfriend, be a total douche bag, be the token drunk of the group who gets wasted and jumps in the pool, or even be a serial killer. The possibilities were endless, but one thing was sure, I was into him. So into him, in fact, that I actually contemplated sending him packing that very first night. Call it insecurity or fear, but he seemed too good to be true. Our romance had the makings of a Nicholas Sparks novel. Here I was in California surrounded by cameras and a crop of handsome men from all over the country, and he was a guy from my very own city. Had I really traveled all the way to Los Angeles, moved into a mansion, gotten dolled up, and agreed to be taped by a massive camera crew all to fall in love with a man living in my backyard the whole time?

And then there was that first kiss. Oh that kiss. It was hands-down the best first kiss of my life, though it wasn't the first kiss of the season. No, that one went to Number Twenty-Four. I *wanted* this coveted first kiss to belong to Number Twenty-Six, but he totally bombed the chance when he had it. I had decided that for the first week of dates, Number Twenty-Six would be on a group date, rather than one of the two solo dates. This was largely due to the fact that I was afraid of falling even more in love with him, but also because I wanted to make him sweat it out a little bit. I mean, he was undoubtedly the type of guy that didn't have to do so much as buy a chick more than a drink before they were naked in his bed, but with all the power that came from twenty-five men vying for me (and an open bar), I wasn't going to be conquered that easily.

After the first date (a solo one), which included no chemistry and therefore no kiss, it was time for a group date. Without a clue as to what they'd be doing on the date, a slew of men, including Twenty-Six, met me at a dimly lit nightclub in downtown Los

Angeles. After greeting each of them, I showed them inside and led them toward the stage. The music began blaring through the speakers as the strobe lights lit up the room before the curtains drew back to reveal five male exotic dancers in midroutine. As terrified laughter filled the room, I announced that today's date would involve each man getting dressed in cheesy costumes and performing an exotic dance in front of a live audience, all in the name of charity.

That one magical word, "charity," made the most inappropriate activities seem irresistibly right and thus I was selflessly giving back to the community one firefighter, soldier, and oiled-up cowboy at a time. After a few hours of practice, the men had nailed down their routines and it was time to see what they were made of. Joined by my friends from the previous season, Kelly and Sharleen, we watched from the front row as shirts were ripped off, booties were shaking, and sweat was dripping. As we sat in what could only be described as single-lady heaven, the men's performances left me certain that a) this wasn't their first time stripping, b) it wasn't the first time lathering up in baby oil, and c) it most certainly wasn't going to be their last time doing either of the above.

The date ended, much to my dismay, and it was time for the men to wash off the baby oil and meet me for a cocktail party. With the first group date in full swing, the testosterone and Fireball were flowing, causing one man in particular to become utterly shit faced. While it was amusing at first, after he jumped in the pool and tried to fight some of the others (bless his sweet heart) the vibe of the evening took a turn for the worse. I found myself exhausted and annoyed and certainly in no mood to flirt. I took a break from the chaos and went upstairs to a private terrace to catch some fresh air.

Enter Number Twenty-Six, who had come upstairs and conveniently found me there alone (not planned or anything wink, wink, cough, cough). He asked me how I was doing before moving behind me and placing his hands upon my shoulders as he gently massaged the knots that had made their home there. His massage turned into a full embrace. With the warmth of his arms wrapped around my bare shoulders and the spectacular view of downtown Los Angeles, I thought to myself, "Kiss me dammit, kiss me!" Though my back was turned toward him and I was bitching about how pissed I was, hardly an invitation, I wasn't exactly telling him to get off me either. But he didn't make a move. Silent moments ticked away until his time was up. The night was over and he had bombed, majorly. The next day I would have another solo date with Number Twenty-Four and as a reward for not bombing, he would score the coveted first kiss.

A few nights later, I arrived at the mansion in a sequined black dress with quite the revealing neckline, which I was instructed to not spill on because Selena Gomez would be wearing the dress the following week (no big deal). It was elimination night and thus I had to converse with each of the men to determine who wasn't there for "the right reasons" or who was just not right for me. Conversation after conversation, I found myself becoming more and more anxious to have time with Number Twenty-Six, in anticipation of whether or not he'd kiss me or bomb again. With about eight conversations down, I took a break to freshen up in the upstairs bathroom (aka brush my teeth and pop in a Listerine strip) before making my way to the spiral staircase where Twenty-Six stood at the bottom with two glasses of champagne. He asked if I wanted to go outside "to talk privately" and guided me out to the front of the house. We took a seat on the stoop and began flirting and bantering back and forth, just as we'd been doing for days. And then, he nervously asked me to dance. Totally cheesy, totally predictable, but whatever it took for him to kiss me was fine by me. No less than ten seconds into our musicless dance, it happened. There in front of the mansion where I had met him just days ago, where he didn't know it but he'd made me believe in love at first sight, we had our very first kiss. It was nothing short of magical. A fire had been ignited and nothing or nobody was going to be strong enough to put us out. Ahhh, those were the days . . .

And now, about ten months later, in an ironic twist, the same man I fell in love with at first sight has me drowning in wine-filled tears and scarfing down sesame chicken (and popcorn). Ugh, if only I was Olivia Pope. I can picture her pointing her finger at me and scolding me, "Girl, what were you thinking!" And she'd be right. But I wasn't thinking, I was feeling. Isn't that what we all do as we fall in love? Check our mind at the door and let our heart blindly lead the way? I should have known it was too good to be true. All of it. How quickly we fell in love, how fast our relationship moved, how perfect everything felt.

It's impossible in these early days not to reminisce about the past, especially the good times. Why is it that when we feel pain, our brains automatically forget about the bad times that brought us to this point? Because just like love is blind, so is heartbreak. By blindly reminiscing about the good times in our relationship, we make ourselves feel even worse than we already do. We make ourselves feel guilty as we think of the things we could have done differently and what we should have done but didn't. But you shouldn't ponder on the could haves because the reality is, if they should have, they would have, but they didn't. For now, you have to force yourself to be what you've been taught your whole life not to be . . . a pessimist. The fond memories can be remembered later, when you've gotten past the point of no return and successfully (and healthily) moved on from your relationship. But that's in the distant future (sorry to say). Your present task is to remind yourself why you are where you are. And let me tell you, honey, you ain't moping around eating sesame chicken because the shit was good.

And the shit wasn't good for one of two reasons: either it wasn't *really* love or it was *only* love.

It wasn't *really* love:

Think of this as perceived love. Sure, right now you might think it was real love, we all do. You wouldn't be hurting this bad if it wasn't, right? But what is *real* love, anyway? Think about that for a moment. If you actually paused and decided what qualities define a person whom you really love, would your ex make the cut?

Time to find out. . . . Grab a paper and a pen. Start by writing down anything that comes to mind when you ask yourself: *What do you love in a man?* Don't think about your ex, just think about visions of your future soul mate.

For example:

I love a man who . . .

- Has a good sense of humor, preferably dry and dirty
- Will be a good father
- Trusts me
- Believes in me
- Loves his family, and mine
- Lets me talk for hours about nothing important
- Knows I will overanalyze every situation
- Has guy friends

- Isn't known around town as a douche bag
- Is ambitious
- Is a manly man (can use a hammer and a chainsaw)
- Thinks I'm pretty, even with no makeup on
- Is affectionate
- Is physically attractive
- Accepts my flaws

Now, let's compare your list to your ex. How'd he score? Not well, I'm guessing. Sure, your ex possesses some of those qualities, otherwise what the hell were you doing with him in the first place? But can you honestly say that your ex embodies the majority of the qualities you listed? I'm not suggesting you go around dating with a checklist, but perhaps reminding yourself of what you envision love to be allows you to see, not what you or your relationship was lacking, but what *he* was. And by doing so you come to the ultimate conclusion that it wasn't really love to begin with. In which case, congratulations, you've just cut your recovery time in half.

It was *only* love:

You've made your list and he passes with flying colors—now what? How do you reconcile the pain that comes with a real love that didn't work out? Logic says if you truly love someone and they truly love you back, then everything should work out. But, the truth is, the Beatles had it all wrong when they sang, "All you need is love." (Sorry, Dad, I'm not hating on the Beatles, I swear.) Because, as much as we want to believe in the romantic idea that love is all you need, it's simply not true. Love is not enough to make a lifelong relationship work. You can't expect to love someone and therefore you will spend the rest of your life with them, because life isn't that simple. Instead, love is more like your base. Like the key ingredient to a perfect recipe. You see, you don't just bake a cake with flour and nothing else. It may be the most important ingredient, but you still need a little sugar, some baking powder, and a few eggs among other things. And just like a relationship, where love is the main ingredient, there has to be a little compromise, some support, and a few moments of tolerance as well. It just doesn't work if all you have is love. And your relationship ending is proof of that.

Whether it wasn't really love or it was only love that described your relationship, it doesn't change the outcome that it's over. But it does put things into perspective, at least enough to make you stop reminiscing about the past like it was filled with the best moments of your life. Instead, realize that in hindsight, those moments probably weren't worth all the hype you gave them. Which makes them that much easier to forget about.

Lesson Learned: *When it comes to Love 101,*
if he fails the test, he fails the course!

DAY 8. 2:19 A.M.

The Ring Didn't Mean a Thing

It's almost 2:30 in the morning and I can't sleep. This tossing and turning in my bed has become a nightly ritual, but tonight it's worse than ever. And I'm thinking it has everything to do with the dreadful fact that tonight I finally decided to take off my engagement ring and have no intention of ever putting it back on.

This isn't the first time I've taken my ring off, but I know deep down that this time it's off for good. The first time it happened was months ago, back in late September. We were in New York City attending a charity event when we got in a huge fight. I was talking to a guest at the event, who happened to be a man, when Number Twenty-Six pulled me aside and told me how disrespectful I was being. I explained to him with a laugh that I was actually talking to the guy because he wanted me to set him up with a nice girl, and I had just the right one in mind for him. Despite my laugh, he didn't think it was very funny. And after he told me I was acting like a "whore," I didn't find it funny either. Needless to say, the rest of the night was filled with tension, which turned into a massive fight the moment we returned to our hotel room. Behind closed doors, we shouted in fury at one another until he held out his hand and I placed my engagement ring into his open palm.

We went to bed in silence. As he slept, I wept quietly before finally getting up and going for a walk in the city. Dawn was breaking, and with a few hours to spare before a car was scheduled to pick us up and take us to the airport, I found myself walking aimlessly through Times Square alone, shielding my tears behind dark sunglasses. I didn't know where I wanted to go; I just knew I didn't want to go back to the hotel room.

As I strolled the side streets, I came upon an open church. I walked up the steps and inside to sit in the first pew that didn't have someone sleeping on it, and I looked up in amazement at the architectural ceiling and beautiful stained-glass windows. There I was sitting in a pew, alone in a random church in the middle of New York City as I cradled my head in my hands and began to sob.

And for the first time, I thought, *I don't think we're going to make it.*

With little time to spare, I pulled myself together and dashed back to the hotel. Twenty-Six asked where I'd been, and I told him I had just gone for a walk. We got into the car and rode to the airport in silence.

We stayed silent as we got on the plane. It wasn't until takeoff that he leaned into me and whispered in my ear that he was sorry. I looked at him to find tears rolling down his face. I had never seen him cry. Without hesitation, I wrapped my arms around him and began crying as well. It had been one of the worst fights we'd ever had, but I wasn't ready to lose him and he wasn't ready to lose me either. He reached into the zippered front pouch of his carry-on and pulled out the ring. As he slipped it back on my finger, it was as if we were getting engaged all over again. There was no speech, no bending on one knee, and no cameras. This time, it was just the two of us, sitting on a plane bound for home; we had hit the Reset button on our relationship and this was a new beginning, a beginning that would take the love we had for one another and leave behind the drama of the show and the insecurities that came with it. It was our first real breakup-and-makeup, but as time would tell, it wouldn't be the last.

Now, my left hand feels as empty as my heart and brings with it a bag of mixed emotions. On one hand, the shallow part of me will miss the ring terribly, since I have to return it per the rules of the show. I practically designed the thing by dropping hints to producers daily about what I wanted. I shouldn't even call them hints, considering I was pretty precise in describing my wishes: round, halo, and big. And that's exactly what it was! The moment I first laid eyes on that ring I knew it was meant for me and only me, just like the man who was giving it to me.

But now I see that the ring and the man are a package deal; the only way the ring makes sense is when the man makes sense. You don't want one without the other, regardless of how beautiful (and big) it is. As I look at my left finger, I have to admit that I feel queasy seeing the tan line my ring has made. My bare finger serves as tangible proof of my embarrassment. And I wonder if people notice immediately that the ring is gone. Will they pretend to check out my manicure just to get a glimpse of my naked finger? But most of all, there's a feeling of sorrow that comes with parting ways with this ring, because it's not just parting ways with a piece of jewelry. No, it's more than that. It's parting ways with my relationship.

It's interesting how a keepsake like that can make letting go so much harder. I never really had a problem moving on from relationships in the past; after all, my past led me to being able to fall in love with a complete stranger in just eight weeks. I admit it's completely and utterly batshit crazy not only to fall in love but also to get engaged in such a short amount of time. Trust me, if a friend of mine told me she was engaged to someone she'd met on TV two months ago, I would Google the closest psych ward and enroll her in it immediately. But having done just that, I've changed my tune, partly because I don't want to be committed, but mostly because, despite being the skeptic that I am, I actually did it. Though not alone—no, I did it with the help of a perfect storm that had everything to do with my past meeting the present and producing my future. (Well, short-term future.)

Oh my past . . . Deep breath! Here we go.

Growing up I had been through plenty of boyfriends, as I became somewhat of a serial dater once I reached eighteen. The late age wasn't by choice but rather because nobody seemed to want to date me prior to that. I had grown up with the same group of people since fifth grade when my parents moved us from one suburb outside Atlanta to another just seven miles down the road. While the steadiness of living in the same place for a decade made for everlasting friendships, it wasn't great for my love life. I wasn't necessarily a "guy's girl," but I was flat chested, sporty, abrasive, and living among daintily prim and proper girls who, unlike myself, didn't quit cotillion after two days. I wasn't the steady girlfriend type, apparently, but I wasn't the whore type either, and with all the boys calling me by my last name or "the Dorf," I was living every teenage girl's nightmare . . . in the friend zone.

So when I ventured off to college at Louisiana State University (Geaux Tigahs!), I was bursting at the seams to get a boyfriend. I went to a school far enough away to start fresh, but close enough to be only a road trip away from home. Plus, the fact that I was going to an SEC school appeased my father enough to continue bankrolling this four-year excursion of mine. I had kept all of my friends from home, but I was determined to break free of the "friend" stigma and finally become viable dating material.

After pledging a sorority and taking advantage of my sister's fake ID, I found myself with a starter boyfriend. He just so happened to be the quarterback of the football team, though not the starter. That relationship lasted all of a few months, if that, and to be honest, I use the word "relationship" pretty loosely considering we never had the exclusivity talk. I downplay this relationship because after we broke up, I started dating his friend, who later became his roommate. Oops! It wasn't as weird as it seemed, considering our fling was brief and I ended up dating the second guy for the remaining three years of college.

My college boyfriend was on the football team as well, which made me quickly realize that I had a type, and my type was a man who wore cleats. I couldn't help it; I was just more physically attracted to burly athletes who came home sweaty and smelly. They made the pretty frat boys in their seersucker, bow ties, and side-swooped hair look like pussies. Saturdays in Baton Rouge were game days and nothing else, so forgive me if I would rather date a guy on the field versus a visor-wearing drunken slob in the stands.

The three years we dated were great; he was the epitome of a gentle giant, and I loved him . . . in a college way. But after we graduated, I packed up and headed off to my next venture: law school in North Carolina. We made separate plans for our lives with no real intention of ever merging them together. We said our goodbyes and I made the drive back home. It was the last time I ever saw him.

In law school I had yet another relationship. See, I am the relationship type, after all (take that, high school losers!). I don't even know where to begin with this relationship except to say by the time I was twenty-four years old, I had known him for a decade. Yes, your math is right, I was fourteen when I first met him. I was a freshman in high school and he was a senior who just so happened to be the star football player. Somehow we had met at school and started talking on AIM or some other ancient dial-up that required a modem that would be interrupted the minute someone picked up the landline. There was always a flirtatious tone to our conversations, but given our age difference—I was too young to act on the natural attraction I felt for him, and he was too old—we indulged in nothing more than a flirty friendship. On the rare occasions we found ourselves walking side-by-side during class changes, we would make friendly small talk and laugh at the whispers and giggles it sparked from the catty high school girls. We knew what we were, and it was nothing more than friends.

That all changed a few years later when I was a senior in high school and we started hooking up every time he returned home on college breaks. He was the first guy I ever thought I loved, but I was young, and all the chemistry between us wasn't enough to take the plunge into being exclusive. We stayed in touch throughout my collegiate years all the way up to law school, which was when we decided, in his words, to finally "do the damn thing." We were for the first time in our lives no longer just hookup buddies, no longer just friends, but in a full-blown committed relationship.

Though I was in law school in North Carolina and he was playing professional football in Texas, we managed to see each other quite often. When he had a home game, I would fly to Houston and spend the weekend with him, and we'd have a blast. He wasn't a big-time player, I wasn't a supermodel, and therefore we defied the mold by being two kids who had known each other since high school, utterly in love and living a life far glitzier and exciting than either of us had ever imagined.

We dated for three years, in which time he stopped playing football and moved back to Atlanta. When I graduated law school, I also returned home to take the bar exam and—I hoped—land a job. I moved in with him for the summer while I studied for my exam, and everything was great. We played house, he came on family vacations with me, and we alternated Sunday dinners at our parents' houses. We hardly fought. Everything with him was good and easy, but it wasn't great or exhilarating.

After passing the bar exam and landing my dream job as a prosecutor, I got my own apartment and we started living separate lives. I had changed, and our relationship had steadily plateaued, becoming so comfortable that it was boring. At times, part of me wondered if the only reason we were together was due to our shared history. He was looking to settle down and get married, and although I was looking for the same thing, I just couldn't seem to do it with him.

It wasn't that I was unhappy being with him—he was a great guy—but I couldn't help but feel restless as I wondered if something more was out there for me. At twenty-six years old I found myself at a crossroads. On one hand, I was ready to settle down, but in order to do so, I needed more than just "good." I needed passion, and I needed that spark, that magic intangible that differentiates a good relationship from a great one. Looking back, had I been just five years older and ready to accept that "good" was good enough for me, I would probably have ended up with him. And I would have been happy, and we would have had a good life, but I wasn't ready to accept good, I wanted greatness, I still do. No matter how I feel in this moment, I will never regret having passed up good for the chance of great. In fact, I'd rather be single forever than settle. (Well, at least for now . . . ask me in ten years and I might be singing a different tune.)

Six months after breaking up with him, I was on the way to L.A. about to meet my next "boyfriend," aka Number One. Ugh, I hate that I have to include him on my "list." But I guess that's what I get for dating him publicly. Where do I even start with Number One, except to say the only similarity he has with my exes is that he was an athlete and had a good butt. What can I say, I like good butts (and I cannot lie). In addition to being good looking, Number One had a swagger to him.

Unfortunately, he also had the asshole gene and in my opinion was one of the more narcissistic humans I had ever met. Narcissistic *and* ungrateful. I mean this guy had been lucky enough to date not just one, or a dozen, but thirty women, all of whom had been handpicked based on his desires. You'd think anyone in his shoes would have seen this as a divine gift, but not him. Instead, he made it seem like a burden. Everything he did and said came with a justification. He was honest to the point of offensive, entitled to the point of elitism, and pompous to the point of disgust. But, I have to say, as much as I wish he wasn't on my list, there was a lesson learned with Number One. He taught me that I had been pretty fortunate to have dated good, decent guys who treated me well. I guess you could say Number One made me appreciate all my former "good" boyfriends. I'd seen the good and the bad and now I wanted greatness. I wanted that undeniable chemistry, the spark!

Number Twenty-Six had it, or so I thought. Being my type from the start created a level of comfort between us, which put our relationship on a much faster track than any other relationships I was forming on the show. It was as if we had skipped over the "Do I like you?" phase and instantly jumped into the "Do I love you?" phase.

I immediately felt that he was the piece that had been missing in all my previous relationships. He was, in essence, my type on steroids. He seemed to have everything I had ever wanted, and despite knowing him for only eight weeks, I fell in love. I loved him for so many reasons—for the way he made me feel young and vibrant, his looks, his kisses, the comfort of our conversations, the banter, and the way I could see him being the man I still loved after fifty years. But the man I fell in love with doesn't exist anymore. The protective, loving man I saw as my future isn't the man I know today. To see someone go from the love of your life to your ex-fiancé forces you to question if it was all one big ruse that led to the ultimate failure, yet again.

Perhaps we shouldn't look at our past relationships as failures, but rather as stepping-stones; each guiding us to dry land, or in our case toward the right man. Each teaching us a little lesson about what we like and more importantly, what we *need* in a relationship. Let's think about that for a second . . .

If each former boyfriend is a stepping-stone, then each holds a significant lesson. For example, my starter boyfriend taught me that I *could* in fact land a boyfriend. He ultimately led me to my college boyfriend, who taught me the value of friendship in a relationship. Though we weren't on the same page when it came to the rest of our lives, he led me to someone who was, my law school boyfriend. Law school boyfriend taught me that

I could be content in a relationship, but that contentment wasn't enough for me, which led me to Number One who taught me that I needed someone who actually wanted similar things in life that I did (and that most men are assholes). This epiphany led me to Numbers Two through Twenty-Five, who showed me the difference between good and great, which led me to Number Twenty-Six. Which is where I am now. So the question remains, what has Number Twenty-Six taught me? Where does he lead me?

If you think about your past relationships in the same chronological way, I guarantee you can find at least one valuable lesson that you carried with you to the next relationship, right? Maybe if we stop thinking of our past relationships as failures and start thinking of them as small discoveries that we improve upon, then one day, all of those discoveries will lead us to the ultimate exploration . . . Mr. Forever.

Maybe . . .

Lesson learned: *You gotta kiss the frogs before you find the prince.*

DAY 10. 4:03 P.M.

Alone Forever

It's Day 10 now, and I have yet to leave Kelly's house. It's pretty pathetic. I am a twenty-seven-year-old woman, and here I am a week and three days after my breakup still moping around in unwashed, Febreze-doused T-shirts, devouring empty calories by day, guzzling wine by night, and crying around the clock. While God created the entire world in seven days, it's taken me ten to muster enough strength to make my way to the couch and watch trashy television. And to make matters worse, this morning was the morning from hell, all because of mother-effing tissues!

I awoke to tears running down my face, yet again, along with dark red-stained lips (damn Mr. Cabernet got me again) and immediately had that pit in my stomach that today was just not going to be my day. Without hesitation, I clasp my hands, look up to the ceiling, and say aloud, "Dear God, please don't let me run out of tissues. I will do anything you want if, when I look over to the box of tissues, it is not empty. Please!" I reach over to the cardboard box on my nightstand. Empty. Shit!

My initial thought is, *Why the hell does nobody deliver tissues?* It's 2015 and I've managed to hole up in my room and survive without ever leaving this house, every necessity at my fingertips thanks to the Internet and restaurant delivery—but I can't find a way to get tissues. My second thought is "What the fuck am I going to do?" The first option would be the environmentally friendly decision to reuse the crumpled tissues that are piled past the rim of the trashcan. But as low as I am I just can't bring myself to stoop even lower by recycling my own snot. Thus, I'm left with only one option: make my first public appearance since this breakup. Can't wait to be the chick roaming the aisles of Target with snot permanently baked into her skin and eyes so large and puffy they deserve their own zip code. Lucky me!

As much as I hope this isn't a preview of the rest of my life, I can't be so certain. I'm pretty positive that I will be alone forever. This isn't an exaggeration, at least not in this moment—it's just probability, taking my age and track record into account. I'm not saying my eggs are dried up yet, but being on the verge of twenty-eight means that I might have passed my prime and in doing so wasted four-fifths of my twenties on failed relationships. I have nothing to show for it except a shattered heart and a bunch of baggage that includes an ex-fiancé. Don't get me wrong, I certainly wouldn't mind *physically* being twenty-eight for life, but I could do without having to check the "single" box on my tax forms every year.

It wasn't supposed to be like this. In fact, if someone had asked me a decade ago where I would be at twenty-eight, I would have said, "happily married with a child and another one on the way." Perhaps it's a tribute to my Southern heritage that I expected to marry and procreate by my midtwenties. After all, when you grow up in the Bible Belt, if you aren't married by the time you hit twenty-five, everyone starts to whisper, wondering one of two things: Are you psychotic? or Are you a lesbian? Southern mothers want to be young fabulous grannies while Southern fathers want their expensive daughters off their tab as soon as possible, and Southern men want young and fertile trophy wives. Luckily for me, my mother is a Yankee and doesn't give me the ole Southern mother guilt trip. In fact, she rarely misses an opportunity to tell me she is not ready to be a grandmother, so if I could hold off, that would be delightful. Apparently, babysitting grandchildren would conflict with her biweekly mah-jongg game at the country club, and I *certainly* would not want to put a damper on that.

I've clearly missed the boat on becoming a member of the Young Southern Wives Club or the Belles with Babies Association. And as if a bare ring finger and my monthly period don't make this point firmly enough, the fact that I am almost the only single girl I know puts the nail in the coffin. I can only name two friends who are single like me—one is days away from being engaged and the other is divorced, so she doesn't really count. Therefore, the way I see it, by the time I do reach twenty-eight, I'll be the last single gal standing. Despite the pleasure I get when my friends bitch about their husbands and the hardship of giving birth and "pumping and dumping," I would trade places with them in a heartbeat. The more I think about how many of my high school friends and ex-boyfriends have tied the knot and are starting families, the more I realize I may have won the Zero Obligation battle, but I have certainly lost the Happily Married war. Plus, by now, half the good guys have been snatched up because, like an experienced farmer, they know to pick the crops when they're young and ripe while the other half of the good guys have come out of the closet by now, making both ripeness and women in general irrelevant to them, and leaving me totally screwed. At this rate, my time line has been shot to hell and it's only going to get worse. Best-case scenario, my new life looks like this:

- Age 28: single and still heartbroken
- Age 29: begin dating
- Age 29½: become desperate enough to go on Tinder
- Age 29¾: become embarrassed enough to get off Tinder
- Age 30–31: continue dating
- Age 31: freeze eggs
- Age 32: have a steady boyfriend
- Age 32–33: find a boyfriend willing to propose to me
- Age 33: get engaged
- Age 33 + 1 day: begin planning a wedding
- Age 34: get married
- Age 35: unfreeze eggs and start trying for a baby (if my uterus still works)
- Age 36–40: pop out a bunch of babies
- Age 40: my vagina falls off

So according to this new plan, I have screwed up my time line by, oh, only twelve years. Basically, not only will I be the oldest mother in the neighborhood, but while my friends are hiring babysitters for their young children and having couples' nights out, I'll be at home with a baby latched on to my nipple. In essence, because I have wasted my twenties on countless failed relationships, I will now have to waste my entire thirties on dating and birthing children. FML!

And that's the best-case scenario, because if you really think about it, the odds of falling in love and staying in love forever absolutely *suck*! If you do wind up finding love, becoming one of the lucky ones sporting a nice diamond ring on your left hand as you walk down the aisle, guess what you get? A 50 percent chance of living happily ever after! How shitty is that? Half us are doomed from the start. I am officially destined to be alone forever, aren't I?

Okay, fine, maybe we won't be alone forever. Sure we think we've already had that pure, undeniable, can't-imagine-life-without-him love that's so extraordinary that it only comes once in a lifetime, but we're wrong. Not about the undeniable and pure part, but about the once in a lifetime part. Nothing in life is final, except death, and if you're reading this, you are very much alive. There is no one shot at love, no end all be all, not when it comes to a man. Dammit, you found it once, girl, you can find it again! In the meantime, might as well enjoy our time alone and relish the perks of being single. There are plenty, trust me:

THE PERKS OF BEING SINGLE

- The entire bed . . . it's yours!
- You can take as long as you want to get ready.
- You can follow whoever you want on Twitter.
- Hello closet space, I'm back!
- Christmas just got a lot cheaper.
- You can #MCM any hottie you want.
- Girl trips whenever you want.

- No need to get that painful Brazilian wax every month anymore.
- You don't have to worry about anyone searching your web history.
- The remote control is all yours. Can you say *Real Housewives* marathon?!
- Bye bye uncomfortable sexy lingerie, hello boy shorts.
- That hot guy at the bar? He's fair game, baby!
- Curfew? No such thing!
- You get to do what you want, when you want, *how* you want.
- You are officially allowed to dance to Beyoncé's "Single Ladies."

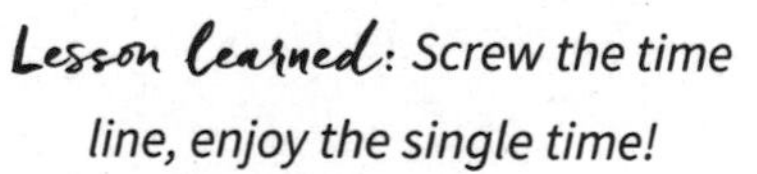

Lesson learned: Screw the time line, enjoy the single time!

****UPDATE****

In case you were wondering, I successfully made the trip to Target to replenish the tissues without any major meltdowns. Round of applause for me! Eighty-seven dollars later, I had not only tissues but the latest Essie nail polish, three packs of Sour Patch kids, two bottles of red wine, Buffalo Wing Pretzel Thins, Twizzlers, and a box of Junior Mints, all of which is sitting in a giant mound next to me on my bed right now. I figured, "Screw it, if I'm going to have a pity party for myself, there at least needs to be junk food involved." I'm not going to lie and say that I haven't spent the day giving myself a pedicure and picking all the red gummies out of the Sour Patch bags, and no I definitely did not break each Twizzler in half in an effort to convince myself that I was practicing moderation, when really I ate twice as many halves as I would have wholes. But dammit, this is *our* pity party and we can cry and eat Twizzlers when and how we want to, right? (And Sour Patch Kids, and Pretzel Thins, and Junior Mints . . .)

DAY 13. 7:22 P.M.

The Fantasy Suite

Is it bad that even in my state of self-pity I'm also horny? The last time I went this long without sex was, Jeez, probably a year ago. I mean, isn't one of the rewards of getting into a relationship sex whenever you want it? My horniness makes me want to call Number Twenty-Six and indulge in a quickie, but I know I can't handle the aftermath.

Speaking of sex, I remember the first time Number Twenty-Six and I did the deed. It was about seven or eight weeks into my "journey," and it was time for the highly anticipated overnight dates. Part of me was excited, considering I'd been surrounded by hot men for so long without anything more than a make-out session, and I was finally going to get time away from all of the cameras and producers, but I was also apprehensive, given how disastrous this date had gone for me in the previous season.

There were three men left; I'd gone on several dates with each of them, met their families, heard them say their "I love you"s and was now less than two weeks away from potentially getting engaged to one of them. There we were, just the four of us (and cameras and producers, of course) in the Dominican Republic, where the rum was flowing and the sexual tensions were blowing the ozone layer off the Caribbean sky. In other words, it was the time where every girl finds herself ready to pull the car over, pop the hood, check out the engine, and examine the dipstick. And I was no different. I had spent days preparing for this moment. I did extra crunches in the gym, I shaved my legs, and I even got the unbearable but necessary Brazilian wax. The physical part of the preparation, albeit painful, was considerably easier than the mental part. The thought of bedding three different men in a period of ten days didn't sit well with me. I was never, nor did I intend to start being, the girl who recklessly threw around her vagina simply for the thrill of it.

Luckily for me, it was really down to only two men at that point, a number that was much easier to justify. The real competition was between Twenty-Five and Twenty-Six, both of whom had long been the front-runners, with Twenty-Six slightly in the lead. I liked them both, but their pronounced differences left me puzzled as to who would be the right man for me.

Number Twenty-Five seemed like the intellectual type; he came off as more polished and profound, there was a depth to his words. He was transparent in his emotions, leaving no doubt as to where I stood, thus making him a safe bet. But there was excitement, too, when it came to him and the big city life he lived. He made me feel desired, he made me feel sexy, and he made me feel like a grown-ass woman. And to top it off, he had a secret weapon hidden behind his kisses that included him tenderly placing one hand on the side of my face while he ever so coyly slid his other hand around my rib cage and firmly pressed in, sending tingles through my entire body. It was as if he had discovered the above-the-belt G-spot, and I was dying to see what else he could discover.

Number Twenty-Six was definitely rougher around the edges yet charming, charismatic, and possessed the unique ability to make an uptight woman like myself feel like a young teenager in love. His kisses were nothing short of steamy, and he didn't have to stroke my rib cage to indulge my body with the same tantalizing tingles. There was a comfort between us that made me feel as though I'd known him all my life, and better yet it was accompanied by the spark I'd been waiting for all my life. But despite the comfort, he was anything but safe. With the thrills came a looming dark cloud that I feared would create a torrential downpour at any moment. I had seen his temper during our fight in Italy and I wondered what he would be like without the cameras—would he bring up the lie detector test again or, even worse, other problems that he had been hiding? Had I let the strength of my feelings build him up into something he wasn't only for it to come crashing down in one night? At times, I found myself putting all my eggs in Number Twenty-Six's basket, with no certainty that the risk would pay off. He was my type, which hadn't worked out so well in the past, and I wondered if he would follow in the footsteps of my past lovers. And though I didn't know, I was damn sure going to find out.

With a million emotions swirling in my head, from fear to anticipation to pure giddiness, it was time for the most important week of dates to begin. First up, Number Twenty-Five. He met me at an airport with a helicopter fueled up and ready to go. Though I hadn't seen him for days, the passionate kiss he immediately placed on my lips brought me right back to him. It was only a matter of time before those kisses would turn into more, and we both knew it, but first we had to get through the actual on-camera portion of the date. After a romantic chopper ride across the island, we landed on our own private island and enjoyed a day filled with sipping champagne and frolicking (and kissing) in the ocean. Rough life, huh? Seeing him shirtless on the white sand with the most unbelievably blue water I had ever laid eyes on should have been picturesque, but the dark mystery of what he would look like naked on top of me blurred my vision. I had one thing on my mind: sex.

When nightfall finally came, we found ourselves alone in a private villa with no cameras, no producers, no microphones, and no rules as we uncorked a bottle of wine and made our way into the candlelit bedroom. **DAD STOP READING NOW!** More passionate kisses (complete with rib cage groping) ensued, and as one thing led to another, I found myself having full-blown sex with him. Thirtysome odd minutes later . . . I had experienced the most cringe-worthy, lady boner–killing, awkward sexual encounter of my life.

Not what you expected to hear? Yeah, me neither. And it was all because of one very distinct, mortifyingly awkward conversation that I wish (and he probably does too) I could erase from my memory forever.

Oh, where do I even begin? Everything was going so well, he was on top of me as he gazed adoringly into my eyes. As he opened his mouth to speak, I was certain he was going to tell me he loved me. But instead, he asked, "Would you rather?" Naked, and caught completely off guard, I thought, *What the fuck?* I got it—this was a game he and I had played a few times, where one person asks "would you rather" *this* awful thing or *that* awful thing and then the two of us would hysterically go back and forth with outrageous answers. But in twenty-seven years on this earth, never have I ever (there's another good game) played it while having sex. Though mortified for him, myself, and this moment, I still decided to throw him a bone and go along with it.

"Umm . . . would I rather what?"

"Would you rather make love . . . or fuck?" he asked without hesitation—or the slightest sense of how bizarre this conversation was.

What the fuckity fuck? We're finally doing the deed, I'm trying to make the scenario less embarrassing by leading him toward romance, and all he can ask is would I rather fuck or make love? What was I suppose to say in response? If I say fuck, then I sound like a slut; if I say make love, then I sound sappy, if I say nothing, he goes limp—or maybe not, actually. I decide to spare myself the slut shaming and in an effort to avoid whatever kinky shit I feared could come next, I reluctantly responded.

"Ummm . . . make love."

Considering we are still having sex at this point, this should have been the time to take the hint and stop talking, right? Yeah, right! Men, taking a hint . . . ha ha ha, now *that's* funny.

"Well, if I had four times, I'd like to fuck the first three times and make love the fourth," he said.

So now, really, *WHAT THE FLYING FUCKITY FUCK FUCK FUCK?* Mind you, we are still having sex at this point—our first time having sex (or should I say the first time we are fucking?), and this is our pillow talk. We'd gone from passionate tingle-producing kisses, to a debilitating arid joke in a matter of one conversation. And while I'm all for overlooking first-time jitters, I'm sorry, but under no circumstances do you play a game like Would You Rather. This is sex, dammit . . . kiss me, love on me, and if you can't talk without making an utter fool of yourself, then stay silent.

Mind you, had the sex been mind-blowing, I could have maybe overlooked this blunder . . . but it wasn't. It wasn't anything he did wrong. The fireworks between us just weren't there. All of the kissing and groping and chemistry we had atop the sheets just wasn't the same underneath them. And as promiscuous as it may sound, I was no longer sexually attracted to him, and began to question if I was emotionally attracted to him anymore either. All I could think was, *I endured a Brazilian wax for this?*

A few days passed before my next date, and as I sat on the beach I couldn't get Twenty-Five's question out of my mind. Despite feeling like a disappointed five-year-old who didn't get the Barbie Jeep she wanted for her birthday, I knew I had to get over it. Not just because I was an adult and temper tantrums were no longer cool, but because I was an adult who had two more dates this week.

Next up was Number Twenty-Four. We'd had pretty decent chemistry initially, but as the weeks passed, that chemistry plummeted and we'd become more friends than lovers. I think deep down, we both knew it wasn't going to work out in the long run, but in an environment filled with pressure and drama, comfort seemed to fill the romantic void. I knew, however, that no amount of security was enough for me to bed him. I couldn't risk impulsively using him for sex, since clearly my urge had not yet been satisfied, and though the feminist in me kind of wanted to "hit it and quit it," I wasn't ballsy or bitchy enough to do it. The thought of sending him home weighed heavily on me, since he had been my source of comfort; while I exhaustively overanalyzed the other two men, I could relax and sip bourbon with him. But I knew he wasn't my future husband, and so he had to go.

Another few days passed, and I sat on the beach again, this

time feeling less mortified and disappointed and more anxious for my final date of the week with Number Twenty-Six. By now, I had gone from seeing him daily to not having seen him in almost two weeks (which felt like a month) and I was in withdrawal mode. I missed him. I wanted him. Hell, at this point, I physically needed him. In a seven-week-long two-man race, he was in the lead going into the homestretch. In order to win, pretty much all he needed to do was get it up and not royally fuck it up.

He met me in the city of Santo Domingo. As soon as he kissed me, I felt relief, knowing that if our time apart had done anything, it made me adore him even more. We spent the day walking through town before joining in on a baseball game with some local kids. As I sat in the dugout talking to the young kids, I watched Twenty-Six coach them on the field. And I saw it . . . I saw the future father of my children. Images of him teaching our kids how to play baseball and sitting next to me in the stands at a varsity game as we cheered on our son or daughter played in my head like a movie, making the day one of the greatest dates of my life, and it wasn't over yet.

After the baseball game was over, we each went our separate ways so we could get ready for the evening portion of the date. I had saved one of my favorite dresses for this special moment, a nude silk gown that conveniently didn't allow for a bra. It was soft and sexy enough to give the illusion of skin, and just revealing enough to leave him tantalizingly curious as to what lay underneath. I slathered my body with baby oil (my secret weapon) and went for an all-natural rolled-around-in-the-bed hairstyle. I was in a car on my way to meet him for dinner when disaster struck. Chewing gum in preparation for a night of making out, I bit down on something hard. As I spit the gum into the palm of my hand to examine what the hell I was chomping on, I saw what looked like a tooth. I felt around my mouth and discovered a massive gap in the back.

"Holy shit!" I screamed as I turned to my producer.

"What, what is it?" he panicked from the backseat.

"Don't freak out, but something bad just happened."

"Oh, my God, did you get your period?"

"No, worse."

"What? What happened?"

"I just lost a tooth!"

"What do you mean? Like you have baby teeth? What?"

"No, I think it was a crown, but yeah, here's my tooth." I opened my palm to reveal my molar.

"No, no, no, this can't be happening."

"Well, it is. Great, I am about to go into the fucking fantasy suite missing a tooth."

"Hey, it could be better for him, if you know what I mean," another producer joked.

The entire car burst into laughter until tears streamed down our faces. I couldn't tell if I was crying from laughing or just utter panic, probably a mixture of both. Here I was moments away from spending my first night alone with Number Twenty-Six, and it was all going to go down with me missing a tooth. Would he notice? Should I tell him?

We sat down for dinner—which I clearly would not be eating now—and it took about five minutes for me to blurt out that my tooth had fallen out. I figured he would laugh, which he did, but he then wasted no time sticking his finger right into my mouth and examining the gaping hole! He joked that maybe *he* would be getting lucky after all, and we both burst into laughter. My uneaten meal still sat on my plate when the time came to finally get the hell out of there and get the real party started. We arrived at a beautiful house lit with tiki torches that led to a backyard pool, slipped into our bathing suits (thank goodness I hadn't eaten), and frolicked in the water. Okay, maybe frolic is putting it lightly; we really indulged in a steamy make-out session. I looked up and noticed the crew packing up, which I should have been ecstatic about, but instead I was terrified. It wasn't the intimacy that scared me—it was the anticipation of what the next few crucial hours would bring. What would he be like now that the camera was off and it was just the two of us alone? Would our conversations be just as good, or would we find ourselves awkwardly making small talk? The disappointing romp with Number Twenty-Five caused trepidation. Would Number Twenty-Six also let me down by surprising me with some freaky fetish game? He was the only one left with whom I could see myself, and thus this night was make it or break it.

With the crew packed up, I figured in a matter of moments we would be in the bedroom, but instead after our lips couldn't take any more, he gently picked me up and placed me on the edge of the pool, leaving my feet to dangle in the water. He hopped up next to me and there the two of us lay on our backs side by side as we looked up to the night sky, lit with sheets of unbelievably bright stars, and just talked. We talked about life, about the past few weeks, about family and friends, about the future. It was so natural that I actually forgot we hadn't had sex yet. It must have been an hour of conversation before I realized how bad my back hurt; all the while I had been glancing between the stars and his face as he spoke. With every word, I kept thinking, "*This is it, he's the one.*" A therapist would call it a breakthrough, Oprah would call it an "aha" moment—whatever it was, I was having it and there was only one way to describe this realization: it was love.

We spent the evening swapping stories, laughing until our stomachs hurt. We talked about our future, our beliefs, and our goals in life. We talked about almost everything except for the other men, and the previous overnight dates I had partaken in. I guess because it was ten days since I had last seen him, there was this unspoken truth that I knew that he knew that I knew that he knew he wasn't the first overnight date, and most likely not the stealer of my V-card. It was the night I had wanted, but never got from Number One or Twenty-Five. We drank wine and gorged on the dessert spread that had been left for us in between trips beneath the sheets (obviously). Let's just say, yes, he got it up, yes it was great, and yes he was undoubtedly in the number-one slot.

We were still in midconversation when the sun came up, beaming through the sheer window panels of our bungalow.

"Did we even sleep?" I asked him with my head pressed against his chest.

"I don't think so," he responded as he kissed my forehead.

As producers came to whisk us away separately, I begged and pleaded for more time. But with our tight schedule—which now included my having to go into town to get my tooth glued back on—our time was up. It was the best night of my life. And unlike the other fantasy evenings, I dreaded getting out of there and having to miss him again. All I wanted was to be back in bed, wrapped tightly in his arms. All I wanted was for the fantasy to last forever.

You know how people ask you what the best night of your life is, and you usually respond with something like your twenty-first birthday, or your first concert, or your senior prom, or even the night you got engaged? Well, mine wasn't any of those. It wasn't when my parents surprised me at college and threw me a helluvah twenty-first birthday party, or that TLC concert I went to in fifth grade where my girlfriends and I all wore matching outfits and blue bandannas tied around our heads (really showing my age and poor style choices there), or even my engagement. No, the best night of my life was that night. The night I lost a tooth, found myself in complete fear of being alone with him, and ultimately, I realized I loved him.

It's difficult reminiscing about what I considered the best night of my life. So instead, I'll just blame it on good ole tunnel vision. I had gone on this journey with one goal: to find love and come hell or high water, that's exactly what I was going to do. I didn't feel external pressure to get engaged, I felt it internally. I think I wanted so badly to be successful and meet my husband on the show, that I put Twenty-Six and our relationship on this extraordinarily high pedestal.

I think every single person involved in a relationship experiences this delusional and debilitating disease. It happens when the fairytale ending is your only focus. And as you intently envision it, you neglect your peripheral view, which contains the unpleasant picture of what your relationship truly looks like.

But, if we look beyond the narrow tunnel that we found ourselves in, would it still be the best relationship we've ever been in? No, it wouldn't. Because if it were, it wouldn't have ended. That's the thing about tunnel vision, you can't live in it forever. Sooner or later, you get out and everything that was outside comes into view. And that's when you realize, the fantasy was just that, *a fantasy.* And we ain't got no time to be living in fantasyland.

So get your head out of the clouds, take your ex off the high horse he rode in on, and take comfort knowing the best hasn't happened yet.

Lesson learned: *It's called a fantasy for a reason.*

DAY 15. 2:30 P.M.

Holy Hairy Legs

Nothing new. Still wearing my usual ensemble of V-necks and leggings because I haven't had the courage to go get my stuff, which remains at Number Twenty-Six's apartment. Word of advice: When you know it's over, make sure you pack a suitcase before you drop the breakup bomb. I'll have you know, however, that I have at least added some pieces to my breakup uniform, thanks to speedy free shipping and tissue tees from Jcrew.com. Still, my clothes are begging me to bite the bullet and go get my belongings, but I can't muster up the courage yet. Instead, I find myself still loafing around Kelly's house, something I've surprisingly become quite familiar and bored with. There are only so many days I can take being pathetic, but I'm not sure what to do instead. What was supposed to be a temporary period of depression has now gone on for over two weeks. I just can't seem to get out of this funk. I'm surviving versus living. I may not be trapped on a deserted island fighting for my life in the wilderness, but I am fighting for my sanity.

Instead of doing anything productive, I wander into the kitchen and do a wine inventory. Bad news—only three bottles left. I open the freezer and take out a box of Thin Mints that Kelly brought home yesterday. As I open the green box and dig into the plastic wrapper, I am saddened to find only one cookie left. Poor thing, all alone in the clear sleeve it once shared with so many of its friends (who are now in my belly). The lonely cookie is just like me. After I devour it, I go to the pantry, where I've hidden a reserve box, only to find that it's empty as well. How the hell have I gone through two boxes of Thin Mints in one day? Not that it's entirely my fault; they shouldn't make them so tasty. As I hold the two empty green boxes in my hand, I can't help wondering if *this* is my rock bottom.

I toss the boxes into the recycling bin and make my way to the living room, where I plop down on the couch, turn on the television, and channel-surf until *Judge Judy* graces the screen. I've taken a keen liking to this show because not only is Judge Judy one badass bitch, but also because seeing that other people are bigger shitshows than I am makes me feel slightly better about my pathetic self—until, that is, I reach down to scratch an itch on my leg and discover just how tragic my life has become. *When was the last time I shaved my legs?* I wonder as I examine the forest that has grown on my shin. The hair is so long I could probably braid it into a fishtail, if I actually knew how to braid or fishtail for that matter. I don't even want to raise my hand for fear the forest is even thicker under my armpit. I realize I have let myself go emotionally over the past few weeks, but while I have good reason to, letting myself go physically is completely unacceptable.

My motto's always been: Look good, feel good. Feel good, play good. It's why I splurge on lululemon and matching Nikes for my gym ensembles and why I never leave the house without concealer and blush. Same goes for a Friday night out. My mood for the entire evening can be dictated solely by my outfit. Bad outfit equals bad mood. Good outfit equals party time! There is a direct correlation between the way I look and my attitude. Simple, yes. Shallow, maybe. True, hell yeah.

Feeling disgusted by my lack of cleanliness, I make a bargain with myself: As soon as this episode of *Judge Judy* is over—it's a classic "my baby mama owes me money because she burned the baby's diapers that I paid for" type of case—I will get my fat ass up and shave my legs.

Thirty minutes later and it's time to make good. It takes five minutes longer than normal, but as I dry off and look in the full-length mirror with one towel wrapped around my body and another twisted around my wet hair, the payoff is unreal. I feel like a new woman! I feel empowered as I strike different poses and purse my lips in front of the fogged-up mirror. If I had known the reward would be this damn sweet, I would have done this days ago. "I'm back, bitches!" I say to my reflection.

And then my towel slips off. Yikes! I look down and examine the spare tire that has manifested itself around my waistline. It's squishier than usual. All those Girl Scout cookies have literally run from the kitchen and straight onto my stomach. *How did this happen?* I ask, but I know. I take one last look in the mirror and promise myself that my indulgence period is over. Time to decrease the wine intake ('cause I sure as hell am not giving it up); say goodbye to Thin Mints (which by the way do *not* make you thin, so it's kind of false advertising); and reintroduce myself to the gym . . . starting tomorrow.

"She really let herself go."

The five words no woman ever wants anyone to say about her. But it happens to the best of us. Our physical appearance is a direct reflection of our emotional happiness, and I'm not talking about having fancy clothes or a pretty face. What I mean is, when you feel pretty and confident on the outside, that tends to be how you feel on the inside as well. It's as if your outside is a lead for your inside to follow. Yes, internally you may be a bit of a disaster, but externally you don't have to be. Plus, you have to face the fact that you are single now, and at some point down the road, you might actually want to be un-single. If there's any hope of that, whatever is happening to your body, whether it's hairy legs, a few extra pounds, a few too many pounds lost or grown out roots, can't happen. A broken heart is not an excuse for a muffin top!

The time has come to start pulling yourself together. Don't worry, nobody expects perfection just yet, and you're still allowed to be a wreck on the inside, for now. But you've got to start replacing bad ideas with productive ideas, starting with a few simple ground rules . . .

THE DO'S & DONT'S' OF POST-BREAKUP RECOVERY

DO:	**DON'T:**
Cry	Pretend to be strong
Reminisce about bad times	Reminisce about good times
Get a haircut	Get a pixie cut
Start journaling your feelings	Start tweeting your feelings
Get a Tinder account	Go on any other social media
Lean on your friends	Lean on his friends
Go to a new restaurant	Go to the restaurant where you had your first date

Drink wine	Drink and text
Take bubble baths	Hold your breath underwater for too long
Get acquainted with your DVR	Save anything you used to watch together
Watch a horror movie	Watch a romantic movie
Replace all photos of your ex	Replace them with anyone other than Ryan Gosling
Take a drive in your car	Don't drive by his house
Blast "Blank Space" on repeat	Blast "I Will Always Love You" on repeat

Lesson Learned: *Your outside need not match your inside.*

DAY 16. 10:05 P.M.

Daddy Knows Best

I just got home from dinner with my parents who, thankfully, live close by. My family has always been extremely tight-knit, but during a depressing time like this I notice even more just how close we are. However, that closeness comes at a cost and makes this breakup that much harder. I'm not the only one affected by all of this; they are too. I've pretty much suckered them into eighteen months of craziness by making out with multiple guys on national television and having them meet some of my suitors, which is ironic, considering I'm notoriously bad at introducing men to my family. Well, it's mainly just introducing them to my intimidating father. The epitome of a "man," my father has a strong six-foot-two frame, shaved head, and killer sharpshooting skills. He always wanted a son, but as fate would have it he got two daughters and decided, along with my mom, that going for a third child in hopes of getting a boy wasn't worth the risk. He's fiercely protective of my sister and me, and from a very young age, he cemented into our brains that when it came to dating, every boyfriend of ours should know three things:

1. Daddy has a shotgun and he knows how to use it.
2. Daddy owns a really big plot of land somewhere.
3. Nobody finds what—or who—Daddy buries.

Now that I think about it, it actually would have been pretty badass to invite a guy over and have my dad sitting on the porch cleaning his shotgun, but while I was in high school, this hypothetical situation terrified me enough to avoid dating altogether. As time went on and I had serious relationships, there was no more hiding boyfriends from my family, but I still felt panicked each time I introduced a man to them. Turns out, the guys usually ended up liking my scotch-drinking, cigar smoking, manly father more than they liked me.

When it came to dating on television, though, introducing a man to my father reached another level. It started with Number One, who came to Atlanta to meet my family and hypothetically asked my dad for his blessing to propose, but added that this would happen only if *he* decided to choose me in the end. Yeah, that conversation, albeit hilarious television, didn't go so smoothly. My father refused to offer this conditional approval and explained that if he chose me, and more important if *I* chose *him*, then and only then would my dad discuss giving his blessing. My father didn't give a shit that the entire conversation was being filmed and certain to grace the television screens of millions. When it came to his daughters, nobody was going to get his blessing easily.

Luckily for the remaining men, when round two of my journey to find love came around, my dad was a little less intimidating.

It was different this time; I was in charge and would be deciding which men stayed and went. And since my family had already gotten their first dose of how it felt to wear a microphone and be on camera, when the time came for Numbers Twenty-Five and Twenty-Six to meet them, they were much more relaxed.

With the overnight dates finished, my parents, sister, and brother-in-law arrived in the Dominican Republic to meet the two finalists. Because I'd had no contact with them during filming, they had no idea whom they were going to be meeting. I was ecstatic to see them for the first time in eight weeks, but also scared shitless to introduce them to my potential fiancé. I debated whether to introduce them to both men, or just the one I really saw a future with. The truth is, after the overnight date with Mr. Would You Rather, I was 99 percent sure that I was going to choose Number Twenty-Six—but would my family give their blessing? I knew they would recognize my favorite as my type, and their first assumption would be that this was lust, not love. But I felt love, and I needed my family not only to hear that from me but see it with their own eyes.

So, I selfishly decided to introduce Number Twenty-Five to my family first, in an effort to set the benchmark low. I knew I was using him, but I justified it by convincing myself that I still had doubts about which one to choose. In hindsight, I probably should have considered this a little more. Here I was feeling like I had to prove my love for Number Twenty-Six by showing them I wasn't in love with Number Twenty-Five. Why did I feel the need to prove my love in the first place? Why was I using one man to bolster another man's credibility?

Nevertheless, it was finally time to begin introducing the men to my family. First up, Number Twenty-Five. Nervous to say the least, I started my morning with a stiff screwdriver. My family arrived at my house and greeted me with hugs, kisses, and a few tears. I was so excited to see them, so anxious for them to meet my final two men, and most of all so ready for them to see me in love.

I greeted Twenty-Five outside and we walked into the living room where my family was apprehensively waiting. All was going well. The afternoon included lunch and various one-on-one private conversations. Having done this once before, my family and I knew the drill and basically said whatever we needed to say on camera to satisfy the producers, before talking about irrelevant nonsense and goofing off. I didn't know what my family had talked about privately with Number Twenty-Five, so when the day ended and he left, it was time for a family powwow.

"So what did y'all think about him?" I asked.

"He's very nice, " said my mother, "but I'm not sure if I see real sparks between the two of you."

"Really?" I asked.

"Oh, please! Not a fucking chance," my sister agreed. "When do we get to meet the next one?"

We laughed.

"Well, I'll tell you what, if the next one is anything like this, I would be very disappointed if you didn't come home single," added my father. (I told you he is picky when it comes to a son-in-law.)

Okay, so my family wasn't going to be fooled, not by the cameras, not by the men, and not by me. They knew I had sent in the "dud" in order to pump up the "stud." And though it certainly didn't hurt to set the standards low, it still didn't mean Number Twenty-Six was going to get a pass, but I had twenty-four hours to get through before that terrifying meeting happened.

The following day, it was time for round two, and time for

my family to meet the man I hoped would be my fiancé the next time they saw me. I greeted Number Twenty-Six outside. Already sweating his ass off, and practically pissing himself with nervousness, he walked with me into the lions' den, which happened to be the living room where my family was seated, yet again.

The vibe was immediately different this time; there was undeniable chemistry permeating the room as the two of us sat side by side across from my family, hardly able keep our hands off each other. The mood was lighter, looser, and more comfortable than it had been the previous day. As we ate lunch, I couldn't help noticing how easily he seemed to fit in with my family. It was as if he was already part of it. After we broke off into pairs and had more one-on-one conversations, the day ended with my sending Number Twenty-Six off with a kiss before a second family powwow.

"So . . . ?" I beamed.

"Spaaaarrrkkkss!" exclaimed my mother.

"Oh, yes, definitely different," my sister agreed.

As we talked in more depth about what I was feeling, my sister began to voice her concern that Number Twenty-Six was extremely similar to guys that I'd dated and consequently broken up with in the past. My father agreed and asked me whether it was lust or love, just like I knew he would.

I explained to them that I'd never felt this way about anyone before, and that my instinct was telling me this was absolutely love. We continued chatting away and making sarcastic jokes about various things. I felt a sense of relief that the day had gone so well. It was as if I had crossed the finish line a winner. I was ecstatic—until I met my father's eyes. He was sitting to the left of me, and as everyone continued to talk, he stayed silent. But the look in his eyes spoke volumes. I knew exactly what this look was . . . it was a look of caution. While my mother and sister may have taken my words as sufficient proof that I was in love, my father could see past the words, past the smile plastered across my face, and most important, past Number Twenty-Six's charm.

That's the thing with my father—nobody gets past him. All my life, I've known my father to be wise and intuitive when it comes to feeling people out. It's an art. The man can spend twenty minutes with someone and come away with an eerily accurate analysis of the type of person they are. And though he's never been wrong, I couldn't help in that moment but feel defensive. He didn't know this man the way I did; he hadn't spent eight weeks with him, met his family, and felt the butterflies around him the way I did. Or did he?

In hindsight, of course I should have taken that look in his eyes more seriously. But in the moment, no warning was going to change the way I felt about Number Twenty-Six. I was ready to get engaged to the man I had fallen madly in love with.

I thought I knew full well what I was getting into when it came to Number Twenty-Six. I found his little quirks endearing, from his excessive sweating regardless of the temperature to his penchant for talking with a mouth full of food. He wasn't the most intellectual man I had ever been with, but that didn't bother me because he made up for it in charm.

But as time went on, I realized that maybe I didn't know him so well after all. Maybe he didn't know me either. During our many conversations prior to getting engaged, he made it clear how proud he was of my legal career and my ambitious attitude. He told me he loved how opinionated and at times abrasive I could be. He had always wanted a strong, ball-busting type of woman, which was music to my ears because that's exactly what he got in me. Yet as the months passed, I realized that off camera my feisty attitude wasn't sexy, my ambition wasn't admired, and my smart mouth wasn't attractive to him. Instead, my role as his future wife was very different from what I had thought it was going to be, and as time went on it became downright terrifying.

THE IDEAL WIFE FOR NUMBER TWENTY-SIX

- is a domestic goddess
- supports anything and everything he does, no questions asked
- wants to bear his children

Being a domestic goddess would mean there was one place for me, and it wasn't in the courtroom. It was at home. When people asked if I missed my days of being an attorney, I would beam as I gushed about how much I longed to return to work. It was very clear, however, that he had no desire for me to go back to being an attorney. I believe "selfish" is the word he used. As in, it would be "selfish" of me to return to such a "dangerous job"; selfish to him, selfish to our relationship, and selfish to our children (who, mind you, were nonexistent at this point). He was adamant about filling the role of the "manly breadwinner" and paid the majority of our bills, although money wasn't an issue for either of us at the time. We weren't rich by any means, but we weren't worried about where our next meal would come from.

In addition to being a domestic goddess, I was expected to support all his ideas and ventures, no matter how ridiculous I thought they were. From suddenly trading penny stocks, to selling vitamins and weight-loss products, there was no telling what my fiancé's next venture would be. Though I never got into the penny stocks, I did help out with the weight-loss endeavor, despite not being into the whole sales thing. But, nevertheless, as a fiancée I attempted to support him by jumping on conference calls, going to meetings with him, and even helping him throw parties to boost sales. Hell, I even did a twenty-four-day cleanse thingy. You don't want to know the shit I had to drink in order to "cleanse" on that program. Oh, and let's not mention the fact that for twenty-four freaking days, I couldn't drink alcohol. I'm sorry, but if that's not support, then I don't know what is.

But it never seemed to be enough for him. And thus, I began to resent him. Truth is I resented him because he was doing something he enjoyed and I wasn't. I resented him because he expected support for his new career when he wasn't willing to support my old one. That resentment led to bitterness, which led to apathy, which eventually led to me wanting absolutely nothing to do with hawking the weight-loss products, and it became clear neither of us was supporting the other.

So I wasn't a domestic goddess, I wasn't supportive, what could I do? Oh, I know! Bear his children. He made no bones about the fact that he wanted to impregnate me as soon as possible. I decided that I'd prefer to be married before we had a child. I mean, look, shit happens, I get it, but I already had a ring on my finger, so I figured I'd finish out the drill in a way that wouldn't upset my father any more than I already had in the past year and a half. Plus, my family had an impressive 100 percent record of marrying before procreating, and I didn't want to break the streak.

At first his reasons for wanting children immediately were joyous ones, but later it seemed as though he saw it as a solution to our faltering relationship. He once said to me, "Let's just have a baby, it will solve all of our problems." First off, can we talk about how mother-effing deluded this is? What, did I miss some newfound fad where babies became the magical fix to any and all disasters? You just whip 'em right on up, put them in a pan, stick them in the oven (pun intended), bake some nice little fluffy baby muffins, and when the oven dings . . . all your problems have been baked away?

Day by day, conversation by conversation, it became clear that although I may have been the fiancée Number Twenty-Six desired, I was never going to be the wife he required. And I slowly began to realize there was a huge difference between people's wants and their needs.

Like anything in life, the need for something has to come before the desire. We all want wine, but to survive, we need water. We all want shoes, but we need to pay the rent. The needs in life are pretty obvious. The wants, well they're obvious too, but the problem is they don't always get you what you need. I've always known what I wanted in my life, whether it was my career, the people I surrounded myself with or my ideal relationship. I mean, this relationship is a perfect example of that. Twenty-Six was everything, and I mean EVERYTHING, I thought I wanted. From his features to his jokes to his hometown, all the way to the adoring looks he constantly gave me. I'd thought every box on the checklist had been marked when I found Twenty-Six. I thought my dream man had finally come into my life, and yet it still didn't work out. Satisfying every desire didn't mean shit, because we were miserable.

I guess what I wanted trumped what I needed, and as a result, here I am . . .

Lesson learned: *Having everything you want doesn't mean shit if you don't have what you need.*

DAY 19. 8:47 P.M.

Namaste My Ass in Bed

I've been up for twelve hours now. Yes, that math is correct Somebody got up before 9:00 a.m. today, and that somebody is moi! (Thank you, thank you very much.) Though I can't take all the credit, or really any, for that matter—I didn't wake to an alarm but rather to the sound of Kelly's Southern twang.

"Up, up, up!" Kelly says as she enters my room and turns on the light.

I moan and roll over to the other side of my bed, hiding my face. I want to tell her to get the hell out of my room, but I'm stopped by the fact that I am still living in her house, so my room is technically hers.

"Get your ass up, we're doing something today!" She announces.

"Whyyyyyy?"

"Because you need to get your ass out of bed and get out of this house."

"But *whyyyyyy*?"

"Because it's time."

"What do you have in mind, do I even want to know?"

"Probably not. I've booked us for yoga."

"Yoga?" I glare at her with my infamous death stare.

"Yes, yoga. It will be great, it will clear your mind, and you should probably start getting back into a workout regime," she says tactfully.

"On one condition," I state.

"What's that?"

"Can we go to lululemon first?"

"Do you even have to ask?"

Despite her subtle jab, I know she is right. Hadn't I just been saying the other day that I was going to get back into sexy single shape? Wait a second, has Kelly been reading my diary? The timing of this feels a little suspect . . .

KELLY, STOP READING MY DIARY.

YES, I'M TALKING TO YOU.

Since my clothes are still at Number Twenty-Six's house, and I haven't mustered up the strength to go over and get them, I decide I'll stock up today. We drive to lululemon and I head straight to the wall of leggings where I pull my usual size 4 along with a bunch of tops, which I find, once in the dressing room, no longer fit me. I'm up a size and down some pride. But with a fresh outfit I can make myself believe that this is going to be my stepping-stone to my new life and I think, *maybe this whole yoga-Zen-namaste junk is actually my turning point.* I've always secretly envied yogis for their auras of sophistication and inner peace. Maybe the new me will be a super-fit, granola-eating, flexible yoga knockout. This could be great!

We arrived at the studio where Kelly had thankfully booked us a private session. We enter the mirrored room, lay out our mats, and as the lights dim, the toned instructor begins our session. "Think about the powers that be. Wash away those fears by taking a deep breath in and exhale. And as you exhale, release all of those worries that have been on your mind. Find your inner space," she says in soothing tones. I breathe in and out so deeply that I feel moments away from fainting. I'm too concentrated on not passing out to be bothered by exhaling my worries.

"Breathe in the peace, exhale the fear. Letting go of all the worries. Inhale, exhale. Inhale, exhale."

Yeah, right. Does this chick really think that three deep breaths are going to wash away all the pent-up shit I've been dealing with? *Focus, Andi, focus!* Desperately trying to balance on one leg with my eyes closed and hands clasped together in what I learned was "prayer position," I sneak a peek to check on Kelly. Damn, she looks so peaceful. As I'm desperately praying I don't fall over and wipe out while I've got one leg in the air and one arm oddly pointing to the ceiling, all I can think about is the sadness of my broken relationship. Instead of an hour of Namaste-y clarity, I find this session filled with idle time, making my mind a devil's playground. It's been over two weeks and I can't concentrate on anything but my breakup. It doesn't help that with each new move, I realize more and more how unflexible I am.

What in the hell am I thinking, trying something new in this fragile state of mind? Not to mention the fact that I have absolutely zero chance of being good at it. I'm neither flexible nor well balanced, and it doesn't take me an hour of yoga to figure that out. I've known it since I was six years old, when my mother thought it would be an excellent idea to enroll me in an after-school gymnastics program. Two days a week she would drive me to class for an hour and a half of sheer humiliation as the other girls soared through the air, flipped on the mat, and did handsprings along the balance beam. They twisted and turned in ways my body could only dream of. All the while, I was the girl in the corner, alone, attempting to master the basic somersault. It took me three weeks to finally land one. And just like that, my gymnastic career was over before I knew it. This twenty-year-old memory must have slipped my mind when I agreed to a yoga session.

Plus, I have never been nor will I ever be a "calm" person. I'm high-strung and I know it, which makes the whole Zen idea completely unattainable for someone like me. So unlike Katniss Everdeen (my idol), the odds were never in my favor when it came to yoga. Sixty minutes later, and I actually feel worse than before. I quickly cross "Zen yogi" off my Possible New Identities list. Now I am not only sore, but feeling even more pathetic about myself. Note to self: when in a vulnerable state, you should stick to things you're good at.

After yoga, Kelly and I go out to lunch and I tell her how lost I'm feeling. She's been such a confidante for me during these difficult times, and I have come to not only crave but also value her advice. She's one of those friends who doesn't get competitive or need to one-up me or rub in the fact that she's happy and in love; instead she simply and genuinely just wants the best for me. As I tell her about my plan to overcome this breakup, she brings up a great metaphor.

"You should think of your life as a bunch of buckets," she says.

"What do you mean?"

"Well, you have all these buckets. Some of them are short term, some of them are long term, and some of them are forever. Every time something comes your way, whether it's a new project, an appearance, or any opportunity, you just place it into one of the buckets."

"But then what do I do with the buckets?"

"They just keep your life in perspective. You can't expect everything to go into the long-term buckets. Some things you just have to do to be happy now."

"So an appearance would be short term, and finding a steady job would be long term?"

"Exactly!" she exclaims.

"What would go in the forever bucket?"

"Something like finding love."

"Shit."

"But that's the thing, you don't have to worry about that right now, just focus on the things that are in front of you in the now."

"Where did you learn all of this?"

"Oh, please, you don't think you're the first woman to have her heart broken, do you?"

We both laugh.

Kelly's right—I have to start compartmentalizing my life. A lot has gone on in the past year to make me feel stuck in the chaos. But now that the cameras have gone away, now that my journey has officially ended, I'm finally able to pause and consider my next move.

I think about what it would be like to go back to being an attorney. I'm not one to toot my own horn, but when it came to my job, I was good at it. I had passion and I had a bright future ahead of me. But, my occupation was a double-edged sword when it came to participating in the show. On one side, it was a major reason that I was selected as a contestant in the first place, as it provided what producers called great "packaging material." While some women set themselves apart with tragic stories, dramatic pasts, or single-mother status, I had my job. Other than that, I was pretty much just your run-of-the-mill single woman. On the other side of the sword, my job invited a magnitude of opinions from fans who only knew me from the show. From the moment I finished the first season until this very day, the most criticism hasn't been over my love life, or the drama of the season, but rather my career.

Among the plethora of questions I am often asked, the top two have got to be: (1) Why would a lawyer *ever* want to go on a reality television show? and (2) Why haven't you gone back to your job yet?

I know they say you have to have thick skin to make it in this world, even thicker in the world of television, and though my skin is getting there, these two questions always remind me of just how penetrable I am. I find myself feeling incredibly defensive and insecure when these questions get flung my way. My mother tries to convince me that most people simply ask out of curiosity, and though she's probably right, I still hear a condescending tone in the questioners' voices.

What I *really* want to say in response is, "Fuck off. Are you still working at your first job? Oh, you're not? How dare you make a career change!" But I stop myself as I hear my mother's voice in my head saying, "If you don't have anything nice to say, don't say anything at all." I guess "fuck off" isn't exactly what you'd call nice. So instead, I reply with a canned answer such as, "Well, I left a great job to go on the show to find love, of course" and "I hope to return to work as soon as everything settles down."

Truth is, I wonder if anyone really cares about the real answer, or if the blanket bullshit answer I give satisfies their "curiosity." But nonetheless, here's what my real answers would be, without saying "fuck off" and trying really, really hard not to be defensive.

QUESTION 1: Why would a lawyer *ever* want to go on a reality television show?
CANNED BULLSHIT ANSWER: *I loved my job, but I wanted to find the one thing missing in my life: love.*
REAL ANSWER: First off, let me get something off my chest and then I can actually answer the question sensibly. What is so damn bad about a reality television show? We *all* watch them. I watch them, my friends watch them, doctors, scientists, teachers, politicians, housewives all watch them, and I bet if nuns had televisions they'd watch them too. Hell, I'm pretty sure as part of domestic relations, even POTUS watches them. I mean, come on, somewhere in that massive White House there has got to be a television on that just so happens to have a reality show playing in a room that happens to have a love seat with a lady who just so happens to be POTUS's wife (aka FLOTUS/Head Bitch in Charge), and her eyes just so happen to gaze at the television, right? The fact is, reality television is a huge part of our culture, and we can all try and pretend we don't watch it, but we do, so let's just own it. But it seems in the minds of opinionated strangers that my status as an attorney somehow made me superior to a reality show. As if being on television automatically makes you the dull crayon in the box. Let me tell you from experience, there are a shit ton of idiots on reality television, but there are also a shit ton of idiots in the legal profession.

Second, I realize watching is very different from partaking in it. At the risk of sounding cheesy, I actually went on the show thinking I would fall in love. Well, let me clarify. The first time, I didn't expect to fall in love. How could I? There were twenty-plus other women vying for one man, so the odds weren't exactly in my favor. But I knew the possibility was there. The second time around, I absolutely expected to fall in love. Now, I say this with a disclaimer because of-fucking-course the travel, clothing, and every other glamorous thing that came with the gig certainly helped to persuade me as well.

Last, the main reason I, "the attorney," went on the show was that, frankly, I was tired of always being responsible. I wanted to be a little reckless for once in my life. When it came to my career, I had always done the right thing in order to succeed. I graduated high school, then went straight on to college, law school, and right into my job as an attorney. I had always placed this internal pressure on myself to be a self-sufficient career woman, despite the fact that my parents would have been supportive of any career path I chose as long as I followed Dad's Three Golden Rules: (1) Don't embarrass him, (2) Don't embarrass my mother, and (3) Don't sell my body.

I abided by these rules for most of my life, give or take a few slip-ups in high school. For the most part, I was a decent teenager. Though not a genius like my older sister, I was smart enough to know how much fun I could have and how low my GPA could get and still guarantee me admission to a decent college. I had the same balancing mentality once I got into college, although I tried a little harder. Well, actually, I didn't try harder in college, I just partied harder, but I was smart enough (again) to find the easy classes. And when I say easy, I mean E-A-S-Y. Put it this way, I had one class where our final assignment was to teach the class a "how-to" of our choice. One kid taught the class "How to Chill a Beer in Less Than Two Minutes," I shit you not. Unfortunately, I knew those days wouldn't last forever, so during my junior year I began preparing for my future. I was hit with the panicky realization that at twenty-one years old, I had no idea what I wanted to do with my life. The economy was in crisis, nobody was getting jobs, and I was terrified of facing the real world or, as my father referred to it, "The Closing of the Daddy Bank," so I decided, why not try my hand at law school? A year later, I was a college graduate and headed to Wake Forest to become a first-year law student.

I thrived in law school more than in high school and college, which I admit isn't saying much. It wasn't due to intelligence but because I worked hard, I actually enjoyed studying (weird, I know) and, most of all, I had found my niche: the trial team. Despite being a communications major in college, I'd rarely done any public speaking. That all changed a month into law school when I, along with the rest of the 150 first-year students, entered the First-Year Trial Competition. After miraculously making it to the semifinals, I was offered a spot on the school's National Trial Team. My passion for performing in a courtroom led me to accept an internship at the District Attorney's Office in Atlanta. I loved my job. It gave me a feeling of purpose and challenge. It showed me a world that I never knew existed. I saw more of the world in my time as an attorney in one city than I did in eight countries on the show. My office wasn't just the courthouse; it was the most dangerous streets of Atlanta, where single mothers tried to support five children in one-bedroom apartments and prayed their sons didn't go to jail. I saw dead bodies, gangbangers, crackheads, and a broken system I never could have imagined. It was a far cry from the comfy suburban life I had grown up in, filled with tennis moms, Botox, country clubs, and high school student parking lots that looked like luxury car dealerships. Maybe it was the rebel inside me, but something about my new world intrigued me.

Looking back, I think that same rebel inside me was probably the biggest contributing factor to my going on a reality television show. I had gotten a taste of the extreme, and I was hooked!

Now for question number two. Hold on, I need to step off my soapbox, these stilettos are killing me. Okay, I'm back, barefoot.

QUESTION 2: Why haven't you gone back to work yet?
CANNED BULLSHIT ANSWER: *I've been distracted with press commitments and really want to be 100 percent available before I start back at work.*
REAL ANSWER: Honestly, I haven't gone back to work yet because although I loved my job, I didn't love making $57,000 a year working sixty-hour weeks. And as luck would have it, I didn't *have* to do that yet. I had an opportunity to travel, do fun things, and spend time loving up on my (then) fiancé. Let's be honest, if *anyone* had the opportunity to make money having fun versus fighting rush-hour traffic just to grind it out at work day after day, they'd choose the former. I don't care how much you love your job.

It's ironic that other than my friends and family, the people who never seem to ask me when I'm coming back to work are my former colleagues. I've kept in touch with them to this day, and every time I suggest my return, they ask if I'm crazy. See, despite loving their jobs, even my colleagues are smart enough to see the logical choice in this situation is to soak up the opportunity.

Besides, even my then fiancé didn't want me returning to what he deemed a "dangerous" profession, so it wasn't as if there was a ton of pressure from people whose opinions I value.

Plus, what's it to anyone? I'm a law-abiding citizen who made a decision to follow a winding road. Yes, I worked hard and spent money on my education, but that was my decision, and as such, it's my decision how I use that investment. Changes happen in life that make you veer off course. I never predicted any of this would happen. Not the reality show, not the engagement, and certainly not the breakup. But it did. It happened and here I am and I don't have all the answers right now, but I'm fine with that. There's something kind of beautiful about not knowing; there's something freeing about relinquishing control and going along with whatever life brings or throws your way.

What I'm trying to say is that nobody knows anyone else's secret to happiness. Nobody can dictate what you do with your life except you. Shit happens. Sometimes that shit breaks you, sometimes it makes you into the person you were always meant to be. And sometimes, that same shit makes you feel lost and question everything in life. But sooner or later, something will stick. You just have to keep trying stuff until you find it. Who knows? Maybe next year I'll become a yoga instructor. Oh, wait, we've already established that I suck at that.

But in all seriousness, I've realized that success has nothing to do with what people see on the outside. It's not about what others think you should be doing with your life; it's about what you want from your life. Success is measured by your own happiness. Because let me say from experience, the times that people probably thought I was the most successful were the times when I was the least happy.

Everyone feels lost at some point in their lives. I don't know when or how I will find my footing, and I don't know when you will either. But sooner or later you will. You have to. After all, nobody's ever died of a broken heart, and I don't think any of us plan on being the first one to do so.

Lesson learned: *You won't know unless you try.*

DAY 20. 6:10 P.M.

Will You Marry Me?

Thanks to yesterday's yoga session, my body is sore in places I never knew existed. As I lie on the couch, I find myself on my phone doing exactly what I shouldn't be doing, scrolling through old photos of my past relationship. There's a nauseating number of them documenting practically every moment of our relationship, from the first night I met Number Twenty-Six, to our first date at a castle in France, to the weekend I met his family, all the way to the day he got down one knee. They're pictures that luckily producers sent me once the show wrapped, since I wasn't allowed to have my phone during filming. And now, they're pictures I wish never existed. Looking at them is like taking a trip down memory lane, only it feels less like a happy stroll and more like I'm walking down my own plank. The worst comes when I see the photos of our first weekend after we got engaged. God, what an amazing weekend that was! I had just gotten my phone back after having gone the entire season without it, and the seventy-plus photos of the two of us together show that I was not only snap-happy, I was just plain happy.

It had been a long eight weeks, to say the least, but I remember the eve of the final day, lying in bed as I realized the journey was finally coming to an end. It was a journey that had taken me from Atlanta, to Los Angeles, to Europe, and now to my final destination of the Dominican Republic. Along the way, I'd gone on dozens of dates, played more tonsil hockey than I care to admit, visited hometowns, met families, dumped twenty-three men, and now there were only two left. Yes, finally two men and by the next day, there'd only be one.

It was a day I had dreamt about for so long, but with it right around the corner, I remember feeling a swirl of emotions. I was ecstatic for the exhausting journey to be over, but strangely saddened that the long days filled with difficult decisions, cameras rolling, and zero privacy were coming to an end. But most of all, I felt relief that without a shadow of a doubt, I was madly in love and wanted to spend the rest of my life with one man and one man only: Number Twenty-Six.

But before I could do that, I had to let go of Number Twenty-Five. It was only a matter of how and when. The first option was to go the normal route on the show, which meant waiting until he got down on one knee to propose or profess his undying love, only to dump him then. Or, I could defy the producers, play by my own rules, and end it before any more damage was done. The thing with Number Twenty-Five was that he was respectful (well, other than telling me he'd rather fuck me than make love to me), he was compassionate, vulnerable, and I liked him. He just wasn't Twenty-Six. Thus, I knew what I had to do, and allowing him to be humiliated by rejecting his possible proposal wasn't an option.

The next morning, I awoke to pouring rain, which eerily complemented the misery I was feeling. Leaving no room for debate, I informed the producers that I needed to see Number Twenty-Five immediately. They agreed, and I threw on some clothes and with cameras in tow (of course) drove over to the nearby villa where he was staying. I knocked on the door. His surprised expression meant I had caught him off guard, and it made the pit in my stomach sink even lower. I asked to come in and took a seat on the couch next to him. I swallowed hard. Choking back tears, I told him how great he had been to me for the past eight weeks, but knowing that he wasn't the one for me, I couldn't go through with letting him pick out a ring and, even worse, propose. He didn't ask why. He didn't even ask when I knew this. He just kept repeating "I did not see this coming." His shock turned to tears, which welled up in his eyes and threatened to stream down his face. He was upset, and rightfully so. But despite the anger in his voice and the sadness in his eyes, I knew this was the right thing to do, and I hoped that one day in the future he would see that too. I cried as I said my final farewell to him and headed back to my house.

It took a solid hour for my tears to dry up and for me to regain my composure. It was the last breakup of the journey, and with that came a sense of relief and, best of all, excitement. Now it was down to just one man. It was all in his hands now and, surprisingly, I enjoyed this power shift. All that was left to do was get my hair and makeup done, get dressed, tell Twenty-Six that I loved him, and watch him get down on one knee (hopefully) and propose. Oh, and practice my speech. Come on, you didn't expect me to chance flubbing the biggest moment of my entire life, did you?

Despite it being obvious to every single person on the show that I was madly in love with Number Twenty-Six, I hadn't said those impactful three words to him yet. Thus, the first time I said it, it had to be perfect. I spent the entire three-plus hours I was getting my hair and makeup done frantically writing and memorizing what I wanted to say on this final day. In an effort to stay true to my ball-busting ways, I decided my speech needed to make him sweat a little, one last time. My plan was to start by thanking him for making this journey so special blah blah blah, but then allude to the idea that I was going to dump him, and then of course, at some point, I would transition into my proclamation of love for him—and the rest would be history!

Everything was in place for this colossal moment: hair curled and pinned half up, makeup airbrushed but natural (except for the fake eyelashes), and to top it off, the most perfect ivory-colored gown. My stylist, who in eight weeks had become not only my friend but also my therapist, lent me diamond earrings and a matching bracelet. All that was missing now was a diamond ring. I took a deep breath as I looked in the mirror and saw myself as a single woman for the last time. It was go time!

With cameras rolling, I hopped into a waiting car and took a short drive to yet another mansion. There I walked down a cobblestone path to an oceanfront backyard where a dock had been constructed over a pool and adorned with flowers. I waited anxiously for Number Twenty-Six to arrive. He walked down the same stone path in an alarmingly snug navy blue suit that looked one deep breath away from splitting open. I greeted him with a kiss on his cheek and held his hands as he began his speech. And then I blacked out . . .

Next thing I knew, I had a diamond ring on my finger and I

was being driven, along with my new fiancé, from the spot of our proposal down the road to a sprawling mansion overlooking the Caribbean, equipped with a manicured lawn, pool, hot tub, and a full-time staff of no fewer than ten people there to serve our every need and desire. This would be our home for the next few days. In the mood to celebrate, we invited everyone from the show over for a cookout. Hours of laughing and reminiscing about the past eight weeks, along with polishing off dozens of bottles of wine, it was the picture-perfect celebration I had imagined as I sat on Number Twenty-Six's lap, intermittently kissing him and professing my love with a whisper in his ear. I couldn't get enough of my new fiancé. It was the first moment in my life where people were sickened by my display of love for a man. I'd never been one to openly gush about a beau or shower him with affection in front of others, but I was now. And I didn't care who knew it. It was a love beyond anything I ever knew existed and I couldn't hide it.

The next morning, I woke up next to my fiancé wearing nothing but a shit-eating grin, also known as the-woman-in-love look. For an entire weekend it would be just the two of us celebrating our engagement together. No microphones, no cameras, no worries, just pure bliss. It was the best weekend of my life. We spent the next few days basking in the Dominican sun while telling each other jokes and dreaming aloud about our future together. In between sips of champagne, we exchanged kisses and "I love you"s. Looking back, it's actually revolting how in love we were. We cuddled in the same lawn chair parked on our rolling green lawn overlooking the sea. Our biggest task each day was to decide (a) what we wanted the chef to cook for dinner that evening, (b) what cocktails we were sipping for the day, and (c) whether to dip in the pool, hot tub, or ocean. Real first-world problems right there. We were living in paradise, and every second reaffirmed that he was the man I was going to marry, the man my children would call Dad, and the man who was my soul mate. We reminisced about our love story in between conversations about our future and the wedding we couldn't wait to have.

As the weekend drew to a close, the realization of leaving him to head back to Los Angeles was unbearable. It was Sunday night and we were packing our bags when I lost it and began bawling uncontrollably. The fact that not only the weekend but also this entire journey was over dawned on me for the first time. Eight weeks of my life had been spent finding the man of my dreams, eight weeks of traveling, dating, kissing, and crying. And all of it was coming to an end, leaving me with a strange combination of relief and fear. Life as I knew it was changed forever, but in the best way possible. This is what I had come for, what I hoped and longed for. I had found it. I had found him.

And now, as a new chapter of our life approached, a chapter devoid of camera crews, microphones, and rigorously planned lavish dates, I began sobbing while packing my suitcases. I was terrified about our future. Would it be the same? Would everything be this great when we got home, or was this weekend the best weekend I'd ever have with him? Change was coming, and though I had every reason to believe it was a good change, still I feared the worst. Just like I had questioned his motives before the overnight date, I wondered if he'd be different when we got home. What if, when all of this went away and it was just the two of us, we had nothing to talk about? What if his family hated me, or mine hated him?

My fiancé was finally getting a glimpse of what he was getting himself into: He was engaged to an emotional, terrified, insanely in love woman. While I found my tantrum alarming, he found it endearing and reassured me that everything was going to work out. He told me how much he loved me, that I was his soul mate, and that nothing but happiness was in our future.

The following morning, the time had come for us to be separated. I was flying back to Los Angeles to embark on a week-long "press tour," whatever that meant, and he was flying back to Atlanta to embark on a week of getting his life back in order before I returned home. Before we left, several producers sat us down to tell us that *under no circumstances* were we allowed to be together, except on designated trips, which they would plan for us. Considering we were now engaged and living less than five miles apart, the odds of staying away from each other were less than slim to none—more like not a shot in hell. They also warned us that these upcoming months would be the most difficult ones yet. The secrecy, the rumors, the events that would play out on the show had taken a toll on relationships in the past, and they'd likely take that same toll on us. So much for bliss, huh?

I kissed my fiancé goodbye and headed off to the airport. Before even boarding the plane, I missed him. My producer and I landed in Los Angeles and began a rigorous week of promoting the upcoming season, which was days away from premiering. As if our hectic schedule wasn't daunting enough, the fact that I had to keep my engagement a secret was going to be painfully difficult given the joy which was plastered all over my face.

First up, *Jimmy Kimmel Live!* where I, yes I, would be a guest on the show. Can we just take a second to scream and say "holy shit!"? I mean, not only did I never in my wildest dreams imagine being on a reality television show, but now I was going on a late-night show with Jimmy fucking Kimmel! In a tight black dress that was one laugh away from busting, thanks to the three days of overindulgence I had just partaken in, I walked onstage and met Jimmy fucking Kimmel! As I plopped down on the infamous interview couch, I heard the worst sound a bloated woman on live television could ever hear . . . a pop. My zipper was DUNZO. I can hardly remember a single word I said during that interview because I was too damn worried that on my first live television show, I was going to have my first live nip slip. *Please don't let my boob come out. Please God, do not let my boob slip out. I'll do anything,* I silently prayed as I felt the zipper slide farther and farther down my back. What felt like hours later, the cameras finally stopped rolling and Jimmy motioned for me to stand up and take a photo with him.

"Umm . . . I can't."

"What do you mean you can't?"

"My zipper popped and there is absolutely no way I can move, let alone stand up without a nip slip."

He laughed. "When did it pop?"

"The second I sat down."

Mortified, yet relieved that I hadn't exposed myself on national television (which would definitely have broken at least two of Daddy's Golden Rules), I made my way back to my dressing room. It was over—I had popped my late-night-show cherry . . . and my dress.

Hours later, my producer and I hopped on a plane bound for Las Vegas for the next stop on our press tour, the Billboard Music Awards, where I would be introducing a musical act. Though I was still wondering who the hell I was and why I was even remotely worthy of being a presenter, I decided to just go with it. The plane landed and like every impatient passenger, I immediately stood up. Although unlike every passenger, when I looked behind me, my jaw hit the floor. That's because Lucy Hale, from *Pretty Little Liars*, was legitimately five inches away from me. My producer and I made eye contact and mentally communicated to one another the fact that holy effing shit Lucy Hale was sitting *behind* us. We giddily exited the plane and were greeted by a driver at the baggage claim who drove us to the hotel, where I took a hot bath and ordered room service. The following morning, I began the arduous task of getting ready for the award show, something I had grown to despise after having suffered through two months of being "camera ready" at all times. We arrived at the auditorium at the beginning of an actual red carpet. As I stepped onto the carpet, a wall of photographers began yelling "over here" and "this way" and "turn to the side," as the flashes of their cameras blinded me. I didn't know who to look at, how to turn, how to pose, or what the fuck I was even doing there. I just knew I didn't want to trip and fall on my very first red carpet.

After I successfully managed my introduction without falling or splitting my dress, the award show ended, and my producer and I were whisked away to a red-eye flight to New York in time for a live interview on *Good Morning America*. I arrived at 6:00 a.m. fresh off the plane and looking like a hot (Vegas) mess, much to the dissatisfaction of the hair and makeup team, who weren't exactly thrilled when I told them I desperately needed to wash my greasy hair. Annoyed, they handed me a towel and pointed me toward the bathroom. I looked around . . . no showers, certainly no bathtubs. Sink it is. There I was, washing my hair in a sink of *Good Morning America* as I imagine how many fabulous stars had washed—well, maybe not their hair, but at least their hands—in this very sink. After hair and makeup were complete, I made my way to the hallway before my segment was set to go live. And that's when I heard a shrieking, "YOOOOUUU!" I turned to see a bombshell brunette pointing at me. Lea fucking Michele! She gave me a huge hug and told me how insanely obsessed she was with the show. I, on the other hand, tried not to faint.

After *Good Morning America*, we were off to *Live! with Kelly and Michael*. This was one time that being really bad at drinking water was quite helpful, because had I been hydrated, I would have literally peed at the sight of Kelly Ripa and Michael Strahan. I had no business being on that stage, sitting in the same chairs that *actual* celebrities with *actual* talent had sat on before. But there I was.

While I was having out-of-body experiences left and right, I couldn't help feel an immense amount of guilt that my fiancé wasn't able to join in on the fun. The period of secrecy had officially begun, and I was already feeling the side effects. Finally, I was on my way back to Atlanta, alone for the first time in months, and I could not wait to be back in the arms of my new fiancé. The last time I was in Atlanta, I'd been single. But not anymore. Despite the warnings from producers that we were not allowed to see each other, I texted my fiancé as soon as I boarded the plane.

ME: I'm on my way home, baby!

26: Can't wait my love! Txt me when you land. I'll be waiting for u in the car at curbside.

ME: Sounds good, love you.

26: Love you too!

So much for keeping us apart, right? A few hours and a few screwdrivers later, I was stealthily slipping into my fiancé's sleek Audi. We kissed, and off he drove.

"Nice ride," I said to him as I examined the backseat.

"Thanks."

The fact that I was engaged to a man whose car I'd never seen, let alone his driving skills, was not lost on me. It was weird, and it was only going to get weirder. We arrived at his apartment, and I walked inside for the very first time. It was definitely a bachelor pad, but I figured we could fix that. We spent the next few weeks holed up in his place, cooking, watching movies, and being smitten with one another. Everything was perfect. We were going to make it—or so I thought.

Lesson learned: *All good things must come to an end.*

DAY 23. 8:09 P.M.

Restraining Order

I think I need a restraining order. Against myself. Seriously, I wish I were back in my ancient middle school days when my chunky Nokia phone was mainly used as a fashion accessory (bedazzled pink cover, of course) and to pass the time in math class playing snake (in black and white). This breakup would be so much easier if I didn't have a smartphone with every social media app ready to torture me at my very fingertips. It's been twenty-three days, and I'd be lying if I said I didn't look at Number Twenty-Six's profiles on a daily basis. I don't know why I do it to myself, considering it sends numbness running through my body every time I type his name in the search box and wait in anticipation for what will inevitably be a soul-crushing post. There are really only two possible outcomes: He posts nothing, which will leave me wondering what he's doing instead of posting, or he posts something, at which point I will see that his smile is getting brighter and he is clearly moving on much faster than I am.

The worst of all platforms has got to be Instagram. It's amazing how many hours I can waste using this app, but when it comes to the effect it has on a depressed single chick like myself, those hours go from entertaining to grueling. Last time I checked, nobody was posting photos of themselves with a hangover or eating sesame chicken while sobbing, or lying in a bed alone with puffy eyes and a red nose (not that I know anyone who's ever done that . . .). But you never see the real moments in people's lives, just the fabulous ones that show off their amazing lives, with their amazing boyfriends, on amazing holidays together. How amazingly nauseating! And having been that girl not so long ago, I now realize just how annoying my posts must have been for all the single chicks out there. If it makes them feel better, they should know that karma has come back around to me, and it's a bitch.

Despite knowing that nothing good will come of my psychotic stalking sessions, I still put myself through the hell of viewing not just his, but everyone's fabulous life. And as I scroll through my own Instagram posts from the past, I see those nauseating moments I shared with the world when we were actually happy, which often convinced me to stay in my not-so-happy relationship. I can see the genuine joy in my smile, the love I had for him in my eyes, and the pictures bring me back to memories that are now dead. But something keeps me holding on to them still. Something keeps me from erasing not just the photos on my feed but also the memories in my mind.

Today is no different. I've spent the better half of the morning stalking. I decide, in an effort to take a break and distract myself, to play a little Candy Crush. That lasts all of twenty minutes. It's such bullshit that they make you wait twenty-four hours for more lives if you won't pay for the upgrade. I think of other things to do, but as usual my curiosity about what my ex-fiancé is up to gets the best of me. I want to know who he's following and how much he's upped his selfie game in an effort to show the world that he is happy and single, but at the same time I want to resist the urge to stalk him, I really do. I'm scrolling through apps for other distractions when I come across the yellow icon for Snapchat, which I had forgotten even existed on my phone. I downloaded it only so the two of us could send stupid pointless photos to one another, as is evident by my dismal My Friends list, which consists of seven people.

I click on the yellow box, and as the home page comes up I see his name. Shit. I know I shouldn't click on, it but I have no self-control.

Number of Snaps: 397
Best Friends:
- Me
- Random screen name #1
- Random screen name #2

WTF? Who the fuck is this hussy? And that hussy? I don't know for sure they're hussies, but I assume. I go into madwoman mode and start a full-blown social media stalk session. I've always been a snoop, I admit it. I can't help it, I have to know the answer to things. Sure, it's gotten me into a shit load of trouble in the past, but nobody has to know I'm doing this, right? It takes me less than a minute to nail down who these usernames belong to . . . Chicks! Blonde chicks. Blonde "model" chicks. Both are now following him on Twitter, and he is following both of them back along with a bevy of other blonde chicks. FML.

With 99 percent of my dignity completely gone, I do the only thing I can think of to salvage the remaining 1 percent. I place my finger on the yellow Snapchat icon, hold it for three seconds, and click on the X that pops up. Yes, I'm sure I want to delete. I'm sure I want to delete all of it. Now, if only it was so easy to delete him as well.

Oh, wait . . . I can! If I can delete Snapchat, then why can't I delete every other form of social media, including Instagram, Facebook, and Twitter (or as my grandmother likes to call it, "the Tweeter") that I'm admittedly addicted to. I decide to take a closer look at his Twitter account, since clearly he's been active enough to follow those blonde hussies. I find myself at his main page and there I notice the Follows You icon is missing. This must be a mistake. I must have missed the first time I checked. I click on who he's following, scroll down the list, and don't see my name. I scroll through again.

Motherfucker! He's already unfollowed me. What the hell? I mean seriously, how immature can you be to unfollow your own ex-fiancée for the entire world to see? Fuck that! You wanna play that game, playa? Okay, let's play.

The funny thing is, he would shit himself if I had done this to him. I get that it's a little different now that we've broken up, but this is a man who was obsessed and controlling when it came to social media and whom I followed and what I posted. So many little arguments came out of these damn platforms. If I didn't post a "Man Crush Monday" of him, he'd get upset. If I posted a "Throwback Thursday" of my friends instead of us, he'd find it suspect. God, and don't even get me started on Twitter. That one could spawn a whole different fight.

Like that one time I followed another guy while we were

engaged. You would have thought an atomic bomb had dropped. I blame it all on Nikki—well, kind of. I had met Nikki on the first season with Number One, whom she actually ended up with in the end. I guess some would say she was the winner, but we all knew she had just gotten hit by the bullet the rest of us were lucky to dodge. Their relationship didn't work out, but our friendship did. She remains one of my best friends to this day. So one night or day, I don't even remember, she's telling me about some hot new country singer she's obsessed with. And by obsessed, I mean this girl would drive to any of this guy's concerts within a two-hundred-mile radius, plus she swore on her life that one day they would get married and in all likelihood had posters of him hanging above her bed. But, hey, if anyone could marry a country superstar she had never met, it was Nikki, the tall blonde bombshell who was a charming pediatric nurse by day and wore daisy dukes better than Jessica Simpson by night. So to make this marriage happen, I followed him on Twitter in an attempt to get his attention. Thanks to my completely undeserved "verified" status, which came with a cute little check mark next to my name, he would automatically get notified that I was following him, at which point, according to our plan, I would message him, introduce him to Nikki, and if all went well, be attending their wedding within a year. I'm pretty sure this delusional plan was hatched over some cocktails, and I say that because it wasn't until weeks later that I even remembered I had followed him in the first place. And I remembered only because one evening at home, as I was folding laundry, Number Twenty-Six accusingly asked, "Why are you following a country singer on Twitter?"

"Huh?" I responded.

"I'm just wondering why you would be following a country singer, seeing as you are engaged."

"I am?"

"Oh, please, you don't know who you follow?"

I scurried to my phone and logged on to my Twitter account, clicked on Following, and was reminded of that cocktail-infused night. Shit!

"Oh, yeah, I followed him because Nikki is obsessed with him and I'm trying to set them up."

He glared at me and asked, "Why are you so defensive if you're innocent?"

"What are you talking about?"

"I mean, innocent people don't have to defend themselves like you are right now, just saying."

Oh no, he fucking didn't! Not only did this make absolutely zero sense, but hot damn, did he just go lawyer on me? I should have let it go, but instead I lawyered him right back. While he argued that I was lying, I argued that it was clearly so insignificant that I truly didn't remember following the guy. It wasn't the first time I had used this trick for my friends, and it wasn't going to be the last, and I'm pretty sure, if I remember correctly, the singer never followed me back and I never got to set them up. (Sucks for me, because I would have been single by the wedding and he might have had hot groomsmen.)

But I guess now all bets are off. He can not only follow whomever he wants, but he can also unfollow me. I suppose all's fair in love and war. Hah! This guy has no idea who he's dealing with. I must respond. But I can't simply unfollow him. No, that's the obvious retaliatory move. It's way too easy. I need to step it up a notch.

Enter . . . Instagram! Oh, yeah, all those photos I had posted of the two of us so blissfully in love, those photos that I've been too sad and mortified to take down, well, guess what? BYE! I start with one, and damn it feels good. I delete another, and another, until I find that I've deleted five. I debate whether to just bite the bullet and delete all of them, but I know people will notice. I find myself at war with the public's perception and my own personal conquest. I compromise and decide five will do for now. Maybe I should give him a slow burn and delete them day by day until there is no more trace of a love that has died. Ahhh fuck it! Seeing his face on my account is poisonous and I quite frankly am ready to rid myself of him and everything associated with the couple we once were. I'm past the tears, past the negative feelings, now I'm onto purging him from my life forever. And just like that, I delete every single photo.

I'm in the midst of what I'd like to consider a detox. And by now, I hope you are too. You've successfully found your way out of the mounds of tissues and tears, so what's next? The clean up! You've felt the grief and sadness along with the anger associated with your breakup. Your body is literally a giant tank filled with emotions, and they need to be released. Enter, the breakup detox.

Yes, that's right, your breakup is just like one big detox. I know, you're probably thinking, *but those suck!* I agree, but I never said breakups didn't suck. Trust me, I've tried my fair share of detoxes. There was that one where all I could drink was a disgusting concoction of water, lemon, grapefruit, and cayenne pepper; another which consisted of eating only raw foods. Hell, I even tried to go vegan once, after J. Lo did an interview saying that's how she got her rocking body. Needless to say, I failed miserably at each of them. I made it hours on the juice, one whole day on the raw foods and about two weeks on the vegan diet before giving up and saying, "Fuck this!" But had I stuck with it, I'm pretty sure I could have overcome the initial days of torture, and I'd probably have a six pack instead of a three-inch pooch.

I bet I'm not alone in my unsuccessful attempts to detox. The reason we throw in the towel is largely due to how bad the concoctions taste, but also because we don't care enough to stick it out. But your breakup is different. Not only do we care about cleansing ourselves of this shitty breakup, but we *need* to.

So how do you compare a breakup to a detox? Well for starters, they both look disgusting. The sight of a sad glass of brown liquid is almost as bad as the sight of a lonely single girl crying in bed alone with snot dripping from her chafed nose. Almost. They also both involve phases. You've got the pre-detox phase, which consists of you ingesting various toxins and countless calories doing Lord knows what to your body, or in the case of a breakup, all the resentment, regret, irritability, and sheer hatred you feel. Next up it's the cleanse phase, where you rid your body of the toxins, followed by the balance phase in which you implement healthy nutrients to supplement the toxins you've said goodbye to. Until finally you find yourself in the adaptation phase, where you will have hopefully dropped a few pounds, but also found a new, healthy way of living so you never have to do this again.

Those last phases will come later. For now, think of this time as your cleanse phase. You've already ingested enough wine, chocolate, anger, and attitude. And now, those toxins need to be washed away. Your ex needs to be washed away. And it all starts with social media. Delete, delete, delete. When you think you're finished deleting every trace of him, go back and double check. Photos, gone. Following, not anymore. The social media war is on, and you are going to win it. Your moves will not be dictated by his, your blows will be deadlier, and you will emerge victorious. So push the Delete button, click unfollow, and de-friend that mofo. Welcome to Day 1 of your breakup detox. Keep Calm and Cleanse On!

Lesson learned: *Un-follow, un-friend, un-EVERYTHING!*

DAY 24. 10:45 A.M.

Mr. Regret

Have you ever done something bad and then waited on pins and needles to see how long it would take to get caught? This has happened to me plenty of times. Whether it was breaking curfew in high school and awaiting the moment my parents woke me up the next morning to ground me, or that time in college when I cashed in the meal plan my father paid for and bought Louboutins. Well, clearly some things never change, because I've been waiting in this all too familiar agony since yesterday, when I purged Number Twenty-Six from my social media life.

And just like I expected, I awake this morning to the sound not of my scolding parents but to a chime on my phone. I don't even have to look to know it is Number Twenty-Six and he's probably livid, because despite the fact that he unfollowed me first, there was no way he would remain silent. Though I must say, I am absolutely shocked that it's taken him a whole day to either notice my deletions or say something about them. I mean that takes some major self-control. I sure as hell wouldn't have been able to hold out that long. Nonetheless, the time has come. A pit forms in my stomach knowing that a nasty message awaits me. I figure on a scale of one to scathing, this message will be about a twelve. The temptation is killing me, but the sight of his name kills me even more. I can't read his message, I can't even see his name without wanting to vomit. Something must be done.

Part of me wants to block his number and never hear from him again. This would successfully eradicate any future seething messages, but what if he texts me something important, or there's some sort of emergency? I mean, what if it turns out that I left a pair of bomb-ass shoes at his house and he's trying to return them to me? What if he wants to tell me how sad he still is? If I block him, I won't know! Sure, the upside is a healthy severance, but I fear it might actually cause me to think of him even more, or else begin stalking him on social media (again), thus negating any progress I've made so far. I have to wonder . . . if I block him, will I become the cat killed by curiosity?

Yeah, perhaps it's better to delete his number but not actually block him. I decide to ignore the message for now and unlock my home screen, type in my password, and press the Contacts icon. I scroll through my list of contacts to find his name. I know as soon as I click on his name, I'll see his number, and as I have been both blessed and cursed with somewhat of a photographic memory, this just can't happen. Thus, I decide to squint my eyes just enough to see the corner blue Edit button but not enough to see the actual numbers. I tap Edit, still squinting, and miraculously scroll past his number until I find Delete Contact in red. With two taps, I have successfully deleted him. I silently chant, "na na na na na na na na, hey hey hey, goodbye!"

Thirty minutes pass and I've yet to read his message which is now from an unknown contact. I've also yet to delete it. I decide I need a distraction, so I call Nikki. She's the only person I know who, like me, doesn't have a regular nine-to-five job. Although, unlike me, she does actually have a job as a nurse, but that's beside the point. We gab for a solid twenty minutes about life before I tell her about the message and the fact that I have successfully deleted Number Twenty-Six from my social media, my phone, and my life.

"Well, that's a great step!" she says.

"Thanks, I feel good about it."

"Just one thing, though . . . I get that you deleted his number, but don't you know it by heart?"

"Whaddya mean?"

"I mean, you're saying you didn't memorize your own fiancé's phone number?"

Shit! She's right. How could I be so stupid? Of course I memorized my own fiancé's number.

I hang up the phone and frantically ponder my next course of action. This is pathetic. Why am I going to such great lengths just to get rid of a contact in my phone? Why can't I be strong enough to ignore a stupid text message? I guess the whys don't really matter. What matters is, I can't. Simple as that. And thus, something must be done.

If blocking, deleting, and replacing him aren't enough, I guess there's only one thing left to do . . . change his name. I've done this in the past plenty of times with men. Usually, once I decided I hated them, I replaced their contact name in my phone with some dirty word, so every time he called or texted (or I wanted to call or text), the name would remind me of what a sleazeball he was. It's worked quite well for me in the past, I'm not going to lie. It really makes you think twice before texting or calling someone with an offensive name. I'm not saying it's the high road, but whatever it takes, right?

With my game plan ready, I tap the contacts icon on my phone yet again. This time, I find + instead of Edit in the top right corner. Under New Contact, my curser is flashing, waiting for me to type in the first name. I stare at the keyboard on my screen before typing "Douche Bag." I type his phone number (which I accurately memorized) and smile as I click Save. But as I'm scrolling through my contacts to admire his new name, I realize he isn't the only "Douche Bag" in my phone, but rather one of four. Dammit, I really have done this too many times. There is "Douche Bag (original)"; I have no idea who it belongs to. There's "Douche Bag (LA)"; I know who that is. "Douche Bag #2," I think, is some tool I met out at a bar. And now just plain old "Douche Bag," which belongs to Number Twenty-Six. It's too confusing. It's not working for me—I have to go with something else.

Next I try "Mistake." Ehhh, it feels a little harsh and doesn't look very aesthetically pleasing. Backspace, back to pondering. "Don't Answer" isn't bad, but I realize, just like "Douche Bag," I already have several "Don't Answers" in my contacts. I go at it for a solid fifteen minutes, replacing his name with everything from "POS" (Piece of Shit) to "Never Again" to "Dumb Jock," until I finally settle on the perfect word.

Drumroll, please . . . "REGRET!" It means so many different things at the moment and is so perfectly ambiguous that I don't feel bad. Now that I've settled, it's time to face the elephant in the room. Do I respond to REGRET? And if so, what do I say?

I can respond to his message in a peaceful way, making it clear that I've moved on. Although, given the fact that I've just unfollowed him on Twitter, it's pretty clear I haven't. I could respond in a snarky way, making it clear that I am annoyed. But this would be stooping to his level, right? Or I could go the pure radio silence route. That'll really piss him off.

Ahhhh, why does this have to be so hard? I want to read the message, but if I do, there is no way I'll be able to bite my tongue. Thus, I'll be starting another civil war between us. If I ignore it, I am essentially taking back the power, but it's easier said than done. What I do in this defining moment could very well set the tone for the rest of time.

Be strong, be strong, be strong. Eenie, meenie, miney, moe . . . Option 3 it is! Pure radio silence, baby! Ah, I feel proud of myself. Not just for replacing his name but also for fighting the urge not only not to read the message but also not to respond. I must do something now where I can't use my phone.

"Hey, Kelly!" I shout from the guest bedroom. "Wanna go to the movies?"

We look up some times and decide on *The Hunger Games: Mockingjay Part 1.* Despite having seen this movie twice already, if there is one thing besides wine and chocolate that can cheer me up, it's Katniss Everdeen. I throw on some clothes, throw my hair in a side braid to pay homage to the girl on fire, and leave my phone at home.

Lesson learned: Don't answer it. And develop a colorful vocabulary.

DAY 26. 1:11 A.M.

Let's Talk About Sex, Baby!

As soon as the movie is over, Kelly and I head to a local wine bar for a drink (or two . . .). Without my phone, I feel naked as I sip my Cabernet. I wonder not only what Number Twenty-Six's first message said but if there has been a follow-up text.

"Why do you look so nervous?" Kelly asks.

"Not nervous at all. I just forgot my phone at home."

"So?"

I can't hide the truth from Kelly—she knows me well enough to tell something is on my mind.

"*He* texted me this morning, and I haven't read the message yet, and that's why I wanted to see *The Hunger Games* for the third time, because I needed a distraction to keep me from responding, and so I purposely left my phone at home and used you to go to the movies with me. Sorry."

"Wait, so you haven't read the message?"

"No. I'm sure it's bad, because the other night I deleted a bunch of photos of us on my Instagram and even unfollowed him."

"Haha, I like your style."

"Thanks." I roll my eyes. "Do I respond to his message, or what?"

"Well, for starters, you don't even know what it says."

"True, but it can't be good."

"Not a chance," she agrees.

"So what do I do?"

"What if you just never read the message, ever?"

"Please, if only I had that much self-control."

"Yeah, no one has that kind of control. Hmmm . . . Why don't I just take your phone and delete whatever message he sent?"

"But then I won't know what it says."

"Right, which is the point, and then you can't know how to respond, so hopefully you won't make an ass of yourself by answering."

"Hmmm . . . you raise a good point."

"Don't I always?"

"Yes, yes you do. Okay, so the second we get home, you walk in my room and take my phone off the nightstand. The password is 2850. Go to my messages and delete anything he said. Read it if you want, but you have to swear to never ever EVER tell me what it says. Deal?"

"Deal!"

We arrive home and Kelly does as agreed. I'll never know what that message said, but as much as my curiosity is running wild I know it's for the best. To distract myself, I decide to end my night in bed watching two episodes of *The Real Housewives* before changing the channel and landing on "why you should use a condom," also known as *Teen Mom 2.* Today's dilemma involves a high school girl with no idea who the father of her three-month-old child is because while dating one boy (and yes, I mean "boy") she cheated with another. Being the mature teenager she is, she decides to have sex with both of them, and whaddya know, nine months later, out pops a baby. As I sit on the couch judging the careless teen, I shamefully realize, "Oh, shit, I've done the same thing." Though, luckily, I don't have to worry about baby daddy drama (thanks to this often-forgotten thing called a C-O-N-D-O-M). But yes, just like her, I too had sex with two men in rapid succession. Although I wouldn't exactly consider myself a cheater. It wasn't as if they were on the same night, or even the same week, but they were definitely on the same show. Whoopsies!

To be honest, when it came down to having sex with two men in the situation I was in, I thought it was pretty obvious that (a) it was likely going to happen, (b) it did happen, and (c) it wasn't worthy of discussion. To me, it was just one of those parts of life that nobody talks (or even wants to think) about, like the fact that your parents probably still have sex, or that the bride doesn't deserve to be wearing white down the aisle. Or when your friend has a baby exactly eight months after her wedding and everyone plays along with the whole it's-a-honeymoon-baby bullshit. It's those harmless things that we all know happened, but in order to avoid any uncomfortable encounters, just accept and never talk about. Kind of like taking two different men to the fantasy suite.

There I was, a twenty-seven-year-old woman looking for a husband, I had narrowed it down to two men, and I was not a virgin. So when the option presented itself to bed these two men, of course I went for it. After ending up with my now ex-fiancé, I sort of forgot that I'd even had sex with anyone else. It was an out-of-sight, out-of-mind situation, and though I knew there was a possibility that the topic would arise, like a guilty teen I figured there was an equal chance it wouldn't. Why stir the pot? Maybe it's more that I just hoped it would never come up, and so I never brought it up. What a mistake that was.

About a month into our engagement, which had been going great, I was in Florida with my mom taking care of my grandmother, who was having surgery. Sitting beside my mother in the cold hospital waiting room, I received a text from my then fiancé.

26: Did u sleep with anyone else on the show? . . .

Three dots. He was still typing.

26: Because if you did, this is over. No way I can handle that.

Fuuuuuuuck. How could I think this day would never come? Paralyzed, I sat feeling like I had just been tased, not with a stun gun but with an ultimatum.

I looked up to see my mom reading a magazine. *Shit shit shit!* I wasn't surprised that the topic was rearing its ugly head, since the fantasy suite episodes were coming up the next week. But I *was* surprised by the ultimatum. What the hell was I going to do?

Option A: Tell the truth. *That would require admitting that I slept with someone else, which, if he meant what he said, would mean we were over.*

Option B: Deny, deny, deny. *This clearly is going to get me into major trouble, but maybe he would never find out. If I don't deny, it's over anyway, so does it really make a difference at this point?*

Option C: *Stall. Completely change the subject and deal with it at another time. If I tell the truth, it's over. If I lie, I live with regret, and when he finds out, it's over. Maybe I can buy some time.*

Talk about being stuck between a rock and a hard place. Not only did I have no options, but I was being faced with an ultimatum, which angered me. I mean, who the fuck gives an ultimatum over something that's already happened?

I had no options. Basically, it's over no matter how I slice it. In that moment I desperately wished I had a time machine so I could go back and tell him from the very beginning, but I don't, so Option C it was. I swallowed hard before typing my response.

ME: Nah.
26: Cool, just checkin. How is Florida?

And just like that, I had told my first lie as an engaged woman. I knew that at some point I'd have to tell him—when the time was right, or I guess when the time was more appropriate, because let's be honest, the time will never be right to tell your fiancé that you had sex with your other potential "fiancé" ten days before him *and* lied about it. But this was clearly not the right time to tell him. The selective optimist within me hoped I would get super lucky and he would forget about the entire thing and we'd continue to live in engagement bliss. A girl can dream, right?

Yeah, right. Two weeks later, the topic came up again, only this time I wasn't in a hospital waiting room. I was alone in Los Angeles, in a car on my way to film the reunion show where I would have to face all the sour grapes—aka eliminated guys other than

Twenty-Five and Twenty-Six—who had banded together and were ready to pounce. Each of them was armed with the same mission: either redeeming himself or getting his last precious moments of airtime by spouting whatever overrehearsed one-liners he'd been practicing.

Up until this point, our relationship had sailed rather smoothly through the airing of the show, which we pompously referred to as "our love story" (behind closed doors, of course). Since returning to Atlanta, we'd chosen not to watch the show together, which gave me a good excuse to indulge in a plethora of wine every Monday night with my girlfriends. We were an open and honest couple . . . except for this secret I had been keeping, which was now taunting me yet again. With only two episodes left, including the overnight dates and the finale, the promos were airing left and right, hinting at the scandalous details that would be revealed. Of course this had sparked his curiosity as to what really went down when no one was watching. Now he was on the other end of the phone asking the question again, and I knew if ever there was a "right time" to tell him the truth, this was it. Our relationship depended on it.

Ahhhhh . . . why did I not just tell him the first time? Was it the ultimatum that threw me off? Was it the feminist in me that made me feel justified and self-righteous about my right to have sex without apologizing for it? Or was I just a scared little pussy? Whatever, the secret had been weighing on me, so this time his question came as a welcome relief.

Though only Number Twenty-Five and I knew what had happened, and I knew I could probably get away with denying it all the way to my grave, my commitment and love for my fiancé made me realize he deserved to know the truth. He deserved to know my past and thus be spared any potential humiliation he would feel if, God forbid, he were to find out from someone other than me.

As I came clean during the call, a piercing pain shot through my stomach. I had to roll down the window in case vomit uncontrollably began spewing from my guilty mouth. He was devastated, angry, and hurt, badly. I apologized profusely for lying to him, and I didn't even include a "but." My mother had always told me, "Never use the word but in an apology because it means everything you just said is bullshit." Her advice played like a record in my head as I avoided the bullshit indicator.

He seemed to struggle over whether he was more upset by the fact that I had lied or that I'd had sex with another man. Several more apologies later, it became clear the issue was about the sex. Once I realized this, I found myself struggling as well; on one side, I was the sympathetic fiancée who felt terrible that I had hurt the man I loved, but on the other side, the independent feminist in me felt enraged that my choice was being called into question. I then started using the word "but" several times and went into full-blown lawyer mode as I defended my case for spreading my legs.

There were so many reasons I had done what I did, based upon emotions that ranged from uncertainty to confusion to fear. I could apologize for lying, but I just couldn't seem to genuinely apologize for doing something I didn't feel was wrong. Did I feel guilty? Yes. Did I regret it? Kind of. Did I feel slightly skanky for having sex with two men in a ten-day span? Yes. If I had the chance to do it all over again the exact same way, would I?

Yes.

Though I didn't outright say that to him (as my father taught me, you don't get to go through life saying whatever you want like an asshole), I did defend my romp. I wasn't defending it only to him, but to myself as well.

REASON 1: My head versus my heart

As hard as it is to remember my feelings about Number Twenty-Five during that time, now that I was so smitten with my fiancé, I can't deny that they ever existed. They had. I liked him, very much, actually, and it wasn't just because of the passionate kisses we shared. I liked him because he offered such a different future from that of Number Twenty-Six. A future filled with profound conversations, endless heated debates, and a cosmopolitan life. He offered me a future that excited me. It was as if my head was voting for Number Twenty-Five—but my heart belonged to Number Twenty-Six. So what was I supposed to do? Would he have been as mad if I'd had meaningless sex with Number Twenty-Four instead?

REASON 2: Hindsight is 20/20

It's easy to sit here and say, "Well, I shouldn't have done it because I found love" and blah blah blah. That may well be true, but it's also complete bullshit. I was absolutely terrified of being left brokenhearted by Number Twenty-Six. After our fight in Italy, where I had seen his ability to bring me to tears in an instant, I had my guard up. I wondered if he was really a raging lunatic behind closed doors, or if he was playing me like a fiddle this whole time and was going to leave after he got laid. There was no guarantee from his end, and I felt I had to protect myself by keeping my options open.

Plus, if I had picked someone else, it's possible I'd be in the same situation regardless. Whoever I ended up with would be mad that I slept with whoever I didn't end up with. So again, what was I supposed to do? Come on the show a virgin and leave a virgin? Umm . . . too late.

REASON 3: Drive before you buy

Thinking about a life with Mr. Would You Rather touches on another point: test-driving the car before you buy it. There's a reason everyone does this. It's a significant purchase and you'd like to make sure everything's in good shape and you aren't getting stuck with a lemon. And before you even get behind the wheel, you research it. You get your Carfax report, look at the odometer, find out the gas mileage, inspect for dings and dents, and then if all checks out, you take it for a spin. It's all about doing your due diligence before investing your valuable currency—whether cash or your heart. Metaphorically, a man is no different from a car. Your research is all the dates you go on, the dings and scratches are the foreplay, and taking it for a spin, well, that's the sex!

And I'm damn glad I did just that. Can you imagine if things didn't work out the way they did? I'd have ended up with Mr. Would You Rather for the rest of my life because, well, I had no clue that he was in fact Mr. Would You Rather, because I didn't bother popping the hood, let alone take it and him for a ride.

REASON 4: Screw the double standard (literally)

Call me self-righteous or a feminist or even a cold-hearted bitch, but I am so sick of the double standard when it comes to men and women and sex. It's the new millennium. I am a twenty-seven-year-old WOMAN, I shave my legs, I get a monthly Brazilian wax (where I get abused by an unsympathetic Russian with a heavy accent while in the "froggy" position), it takes me an hour to do my hair, and I cry for absolutely no reason three to five days of every month. Thus, I am a bona fide woman with a vagina, and I should be able to have sex when and with whom I want to, just as a man does.

I guarantee you that all guys in that situation are having sex, and not just with one or two girls, but all three! But nobody says anything to them, they just get a pat on the back and get called a stud. But when a woman does it, she is reduced to being a slut. A slut whose fiancé is mad at her.

REASON 5: You know what you signed up for

My last reason, I swear. Come the fuck on, dude! Eight weeks surrounded by hot men, them surrounded by one woman, and the first night alone with no cameras, guess what? You're in all likelihood having sex. Gasp! The lead knows this and so does every one of the contestants. It's the epitome of the statement I often roll my eyes at: "You know what you signed up for." Yes, we may all be plucked from obscurity and filled with naïveté that leads us to say and do things we later realize were all contrived, so we use the excuse that we didn't know what we were getting ourselves into, which is often true. But not when it comes to this, because no matter where we're from or how naïve we are to the ins and outs of reality television, we all come in with either a vagina or a penis. And unless you're the lone virgin of the season, if you last long enough, you're going to be using it. Every season it's the same format: You date, you kiss, you visit the hometowns, you meet the family, and then you have sex in the fantasy suite. It's all part of the weird "sister-wife" or "brother-husband" scenario you find yourself in. So he can't be that surprised that I had sex with more than just him, right?

With my case laid out, the conversation remained touch-and-go for hours. I didn't know the fate of our relationship, but at least it was all out there, finally. After we hung up the phone, I regretted not being more sympathetic. The truth is I had hurt someone I loved, and instead of swallowing my pride, I turned to my ultimate defense mechanism of justification. I thought about how awful and betrayed he must have felt, and even if what I did wasn't technically wrong, my reasoning couldn't take his hurt away. No amount of self-righteousness could mitigate his feelings of pain. To this day, only the pain he felt makes me wish I hadn't done what I did.

It took a lot for us to move on from the argument that by every indication could ruin our relationship. At the time, I was pleasantly surprised by his ability to accept my apology and agree to disagree on the merits of the situation. It was our first fight over something substantial. He had every right, though I would have thought it was immature, to walk away from the relationship right then and there. But he didn't. He handled the conversation and the issue like an adult, like a man. He handled it like a future husband.

And with the slate wiped clean, our love was going to be stronger than ever. The entire situation would just be a part of history that we agreed would stay in the past, where it belonged. Right?

Haha, yeah, right. Despite my belief that we had moved past it all, we hadn't. Or at least, he hadn't. I didn't know it, but in a matter of weeks, the subject of my sexcapade with Number Twenty-Five wasn't only going to reemerge, it was going to serve as a catalyst for a multitude of fights. Fights that would continue for months, all the way until our breakup. That one sexual escapade would become a power play used by my fiancé to justify his distrust of me. It would be an excuse to call me a "whore." And it would eventually lead to the demise of our engagement. I just didn't know it then.

Lesson learned: *Don't lie, don't deny,*
but do test drive it before you buy.

DAY 28. 5:45 P.M.

Moving Out

MOTHER*FUCKER!* You are never going to believe what just happened. I knew this day was going to be difficult. It's the day I've been avoiding like the plague. But I've officially run out of clean clothes, am tired of smelling like Febreze, and know I have only one option: get my belongings out of the old home Number Twenty-Six and I shared.

As if it isn't enough to have to endure a messy breakup, nobody tells you that eventually you have to clean up all that mess. It reminds me of those times when you go out on a Friday night (which I haven't done in weeks), and you search for the perfect outfit before rushing out of the house. You return in the wee hours of the morning after a raging good time, go to sleep, and awake to a tornado of clothes, makeup, shoes, and shit everywhere. Yeah, apparently my relationship was just an extended Friday night—a blast until I realized I'd have to clean it all up. Only this time my crap isn't strewn across my own floor but probably on the floor of the closet we once shared. Like a silly lost-in-the-moment engaged girl, I decided to make the big mistake of moving in with my fiancé.

The truth is, I should have never moved in with him in the first place. By the time November rolled around and my lease was up, our relationship had been on a steady decline. All normal couples have their fair share of fights, but with the breakups and makeups and plenty of tears, our relationship was anything but normal. Nevertheless, we were still engaged, which made my decision whether to renew my lease that much more difficult. I could either sign another yearlong lease in my current apartment (which felt odd considering I was engaged) or move into Number Twenty-Six's apartment (which felt odd considering we weren't happy). Obviously, I decided on the latter and chalked the decision up to being the "next step" in our relationship.

As I boxed up my apartment, I thought how different it would be to "officially" live with Number Twenty-Six, even though we had practically been living together for months. I was terrified as I wondered what it'd be like. Where would I go to get away when I needed "me" time? How would all of my clothes fit in the closet? Would he expect me to shut off the lights when I left the house? Good Lord, what if I have to go number two?

I quickly realized that despite a few minor glitches, including an overcrowded closet, extra loads of laundry, and the claustrophobia every time we simultaneously attempted to get ready in the same small bathroom, living with him wasn't all that different. We fought just as much, but we also had some hilarious moments while playing house. Little quirks, like how picky he was with his hair, quickly became apparent. He did have a great head of hair—dark, thick, always coiffed perfectly, and salted with a few stray grays above each ear. But that lush mane didn't come without a little blow-dry action and a white wall for a background. Oh, yes, a white wall! Apparently, it was the only way he could successfully make sure each of his dark strands was in place. At first, this seemed ridiculous to me, but it ended up proving to be comical when one day we were out of town and—cue the gasp—in a bathroom covered in magnificent blue tile. This sent Number Twenty-Six straight into a panic. Flustered, he called me into the bathroom to explain this dire situation.

"What if you hold this white towel behind me?" he asked.

"Really?"

"Yeah, really, just while I do my hair." He handed me a white towel that hung neatly on the rack.

Shocked, I grabbed the towel and looked around the bathroom for something to stand on so I could hold it high enough. I stepped onto the ledge of the bathtub, took a corner of the towel in each hand, raised my arms, and held that damn white towel behind him like my life depended on it. Now before you judge me, I should tell you that I didn't do this out of love. No, I selfishly did it because I knew this would make one hell of a hilarious story next time I found myself sipping red wine with my girlfriends. These and other comical moments made living together fun at times, but no amount of levity was enough to avoid the turbulent fighting.

That's the thing about living together that nobody tells you—it is undoubtedly the quickest way to find out if you'll make it as a couple. It's sink or swim, do or die, fight or flight. Yeah, the realness of living together can quickly ruin that happy-go-lucky, delusional bullshit fantasy life you dreamed about as a tween. There's no privacy; you know where the other is at all times. There's no escape;

you don't get to run and hide. You can't say, "Hey, babe, I'm going to stay at my place tonight," and then come back the next morning all lovey-dovey, with the I-can't-believe-we-spent-a-night-apart feeling. And there's certainly no sneaking in with wine-stained lips after dinner with the girls. And worst of all, nobody tells you that when it doesn't work out, you find yourself totally screwed, just like I am now.

I've been waiting for an ideal time to go get my stuff, so when he tells me he is going to be out of town for the weekend, I figure it's now or never. Knowing this battle will be difficult, humiliating, and time-consuming, I need help. I enlist an army consisting of one lone soldier . . . my mother. Lord knows I can't do this alone, and whether she wants to or not, she is officially drafted to serve. Bless her heart.

My mom and I decide to convoy over to my old apartment, armed with two SUVs and a let's-get-this-shit-done attitude. As we pull into the parking garage, I realize just how foreign the place I used to call home has become. So foreign that as I reach for my keys, I can't even remember which one unlocks the front door. I stand on the doormat, trembling with anxiety, until I finally find the correct key. Taking a deep breath, I turn the lock and enter the battlefield. And that's when I realize just what a spiteful asshole Number Twenty-Six truly is.

There in the living room lies a heaping pile of all my stuff. Not in boxes, not in bags, just scattered in random suitcases and on the floor like pieces of trash. WTF?

What fucking right does he have to mess with my stuff? I get that technically, it is his apartment, but didn't he learn in kindergarten not to touch what isn't his? Did he think he was doing me a favor? Some sort of charitable act by "gathering" my belongings for me? If he wanted to do me a solid, he should have stopped being such a pain in my ass all those months ago. But no. Instead, let's just rifle through my drawers, the closet, the bathroom, and every other part of the apartment we once shared and pile up everything I own. Because that's *so* helpful. Mounds of clothing, boxes of shoes, plastic bins of toiletries, stacks of picture frames, and stuffed suitcases all in a pile and shoved into a single corner. Enraged, and feeling an overwhelming invasion of privacy, I concede that he has gotten the first blow. Tears roll down my face as I look over at my mother standing shell-shocked in the living room. She is crying too.

"This is not right, it's just not right!" she repeats as she shakes her head in disbelief.

It crushes me to see her cry. I know she is sad about the breakup, but she never lets it show, at least not in front of me. She always stays strong and positive, but in this situation, she can't hide this pain, nobody could. There in the living room next to the pile of my stuff, we embrace as she sweetly tells me everything is going to be all right. My old apartment, once so filled with happiness and hope, now holds nothing but bitterness and anger. It takes a few minutes for us to regroup and decide that this is no time to wallow.

"Let's just get this done and get the hell out of here," I say.

"Agreed. I never want to see this apartment again."

"All right, here we go . . . This goes there, that goes there, bag that up, trash that," I direct my mom. The mess he created for me only gets worse when I head upstairs and see yet another pile on the landing. What, did he get lazy after too many trips down the stairs? I mean, if you're going to start the job, at least finish the damn thing, right?

On my second trip down the stairs, I'm beginning to break a sweat when I pause and chuckle at the idea that it had to have taken him hours to pile all of this up! I can only imagine how many times he asked himself, "How much crap does this woman have?" I would have paid big bucks to see the look of disgust in his eyes. Serves him right, if you ask me. In between chuckles, tears, and the occasional shouted "Bastard!" my mother and I go into full beast mode. After sorting, stacking, trashing, and packing, finally it is time to load up our cars.

"I hope nobody sees us doing this," says my mom.

"Like who?"

"You don't think there will be any paparazzi, do you?"

"Oh, wow, I didn't even think about it."

"Okay, I'll go first, scope it out, and pull the car around to the front door."

"Text me when it's all clear."

The thought of paparazzi snapping a photo of me moving out, though unlikely, has me waiting in panic for the go-ahead text from my mom.

MOM: All clear!

ME: Doors unlocked?

MOM: Yes. Ready, set, go!

With the car outside the front door and no signs of any paparazzi, I begin hastily shoving bags and boxes into the backseat. Having no regard for where anything goes, what breaks, and whether it is mine or his, I accomplish the move-out in record time. I take one last look around the living room and spot a small stack of framed photos of Number Twenty-Six and me.

"He can keep 'em," I say, tossing them onto the stairs to ensure he would see them when he returned home. I open the fridge, steal two bottles of Powerade Zero, jack a couple of unopened bottles of wine, and slam the door behind me. Locking the door, I vow not only never to see this apartment again but also never to see or speak to him again.

As I drive to Kelly's with my belongings piled so high in the back of my SUV that they obscure my rearview mirror, I realize what all of this really means. It is so much more than my possessions being thrown in a pile. It is beyond the feeling of being disposable. It is the feeling of disrespect from someone who had once promised to love and protect me. And I think most of all, deep down, the fact that he could treat any woman this way disgusts me even more. Chalk it up to a fit of rage or immaturity or whatever you want, but no real "grown-ass man," as he commonly referred to himself, treats a woman like this.

And now here I sit sweating yet again because as grueling as it was to load my belongings into the car, it was even worse unloading them. The casualties of war now cover the entire floor of my bedroom at Kelly's, which I've officially declared a disaster zone. Suitcases burst at the seams with clothing, wire baskets overflow with my toiletries, a laundry basket is spewing stilettos and sneakers, and random blue Ikea bags with Lord knows what in them fill every corner of the room. Basically, everything I own except my furniture, which I put in storage when I moved in with Number Twenty-Six, is lying on the floor before my sad and irate eyes.

And being that this isn't technically my room, I have to clean it up before Kelly returns from her ski trip tomorrow.

Suitcase by suitcase, bag by bag, I begin taking out the various pieces of clothing (many of which still have tags attached), and hang them in the closet. I'm about an hour in when I come across a navy blue striped V-neck shirt that doesn't belong to me. No, this striped shirt belongs to none other than Number Twenty-Six. Well, I bought it for him, so legally it's mine, but I did technically gift it to him. I toss it in the corner and continue digging through the rest of the debris. I come across the black leather Prada booties I bought when I was shopping with him, which he said were sexy. I toss those next to the striped shirt. The more I dig, the more I find things that remind me of him. I toss each one into the corner: the green dress I wore to our last red-carpet appearance, his stained white basketball shorts (gross), and some random articles of his clothing.

The pile of reminders is getting bigger and bigger when I come across a Prada box, which should have been housing my black booties. My heart stops. Not because the expensive booties aren't in them, but because I know what is in that box. I take a deep breath as I open the lid. Damn! There on the very top is a picture frame with a photo of us, the photo we took and I had framed from the day we got engaged. My ring is blinding, but it pales in comparison to the sparkling smiles we both have. As I go through the keepsake box, I find more pictures of us along with copies of magazines we were in, and even the poem he wrote me and read aloud on our first date. A tear wells up in my eye as I reach for the bottom of the box and find the baseball card with my picture and his last name on it. It was the card he had made and gifted to me the night before we got engaged.

I feel as though I could vomit. Never in my life did I think I could hate a Prada shoe box. I can't stand the sight of these mementos. Each picture, each trinket, carries with it an old memory, causing my blood to curdle. I need a drink. Is it 5:00 yet?

Lesson Learned: *If it's broke, moving in won't fix it.*

DAY 29. 9:17 P.M.

Burn, Baby, Burn!

Phew! I've accomplished the daunting task of cleaning up my room enough to avoid annoying Kelly, but the pile of Number Twenty-Six's shit in the corner remains. As I look at it, the pit of sadness that has nestled in my stomach all day begins to turn to anger, and I realize there's only one thing I can do—get rid of it. Like a store closing, EVERYTHING MUST GO! I remind myself that it's all part of my cleanse phase. I am removing the toxins from my body, and now literally removing them from my bedroom as well.

This isn't my first time dealing with an ex's belongings. I've been in plenty of relationships before and certainly collected my fair share of mementos along the way. You know, the typical T-shirt, gifts, love letters, and, in my case, lots of athletic shorts. In my younger days I would typically hold onto the items, especially the clothes, not because nothing made me feel closer to a man than sleeping in his T-shirts, but because it freed up my sleepwear budget to spend on shoes instead. I'm all for sentimental value, trust me—just look in my parents' attic and you'll find every yearbook, trophy, and third-place ribbon in swimming I ever won (no, I never won a first-place ribbon, swimming wasn't my thing, okay?). But those mementos are different. They are reminders of joyous times that I can still look back on fondly. Despite some of the trinkets and photos in the Prada box that do carry with them good memories, the rage inside me makes me want to purge them. When it comes to my former engagement, memory lane is nothing more than a dead-end road leading me to only one place: Land of Depression. It's not as if I am going to put on his T-shirt, go to sleep with sweet memories while covering myself in his scent, and wake up next to him. Nor do I want to. So why should I hold on to things that remind me of good times that will never be again? Those times are long gone.

Instead of doing the normal thing, which would be to fold his clothes neatly, place them in a box, and return them to him, I decide to take the childish, psychotic, and, let's be honest here, the more satisfying route. I never claimed to be sane—I am a woman scorned, after all. My new motto: When in doubt, throw it out. I dump the contents of the shoebox on top of the mounting pile of his other belongings and head to the kitchen in search of a trash bag. But as I pass the living room, the fireplace catches my eye. I see a stack of logs piled up to the left, matches on the mantel, and a shiny silver turnkey sticking out of the marbled floor. *This is perfect,* I think. I'll burn it all!

I figure he isn't going to miss this shit anyway, and if you ask me, this is a huge favor to him. I'm allowing him the opportunity to finally get a much-needed new wardrobe. After all, it's 2015, and in case he missed the memo, Air Jordans and stained basketball shorts are no longer in style. This is my first act of charity in a long time, and I feel like a fucking saint.

It takes me a solid two minutes to examine the fireplace and how it may or may not work. I'm assuming I set the logs up first, turn on the gas, and then light the match. But the lighter fluid next to the stack of logs has me questioning whether I need to douse his belongings first. Will that burn the house down? Shit, I don't know how to do this. Isn't that why I had a man in the first place?

Fearful of burning Kelly's house down and blowing myself up, I decide better to be safe than sorry and engage in a quick Internet search. Now I think I've got it. First, logs; second, put lighter fluid on logs, NOT on belongings; third, gas followed by dropping the match in. I think? I start by building a cute little teepee with logs. Dammit! Doesn't anybody desplinter these things? I've got the pile ready, the lighter fluid out, and now I've got a damn splinter the size of my false eyelash stuck in the palm of my hand. Hold on, gotta find tweezers.

Okay, I'm back. Splinter-free, logs in place, and the room reeking of lighter fluid. I'm pretty sure I poured way too much, but whatever. I turn the pretty silver key to hear the sound of the gas flowing, strike the match, drop it in, and voilà! Ladies and gentlemen, we have FIIYAAAHHHH!

One by one, I examine the articles before I drop them into the blaze. First up, the striped pima cotton T-shirt I got him from that cute boutique in L.A. I hold it out to admire my taste in men's clothing when I see the tag still on it. Asshole! This was an expensive shirt. On to the next . . . A few hideous oversize T-shirts, some mismatched socks, and old magazine articles go into the fire. I'm feeling accomplished as the pile gets smaller and smaller until I come across the purse he bought me as an engagement present. I debate as I pet the beautiful black leather Céline bag I had always dreamed of owning. My eyes shift from the pristinely crafted bag to the blazing fire, which is now a little too large for comfort. Like a tennis match, I glance at the fire, then the bag, then back to fire, then back to bag. "Nah . . . this one can stay." I'm already the crazy chick sitting here burning his stuff, and despite the satisfaction I might get out of it, I'd be absolutely pysch-ward-worthy to burn a $3,000 bag. Let's be honest, come hell or high water, this purse is coming with me all the way to my silk-lined coffin, where I hope to be buried in an extravagant Gucci gown many, many years from now, of course. I continue on my parade of psychosis as I turn proof of our love into ash. The pile may be getting smaller, but the flames are getting bigger, and I find myself needing to regroup. I decide to make a list.

SAVE, SELL, OR SET FIRE

Save

- The Céline bag. Obviously!
- The Prada booties he thought were "sexy." Italian leather being set on fire is simply against my fashion morals.
- His toothbrush. This will now be used to scrub the dirt out of my toenails. Can you say "resourceful"?
- Naked photos of him I wisely printed out at the local CVS. He's got them of me, I'm sure, so I'll need these as blackmail just in case.

Sell

- The Tiffany necklace he bought me. No sentiment left in that one, but it is real diamonds (at least I think). Plus, the thought of burning a diamond, no matter how spiteful I may be feeling, seems sacrilegious. I'll take the cash.
- Those naked photos of him I printed out? (Just kidding, at least for now.)

Set Fire

- Everything else.

The way I see it, nobody said you had to go through this breakup taking the high road the entire time. That's impossible. Sometimes you just have to get pissed and burn some shit in order to feel better. And in doing so, you haven't just enjoyed watching as every item goes down in flame and up in smoke. You haven't just gotten rid of those memories and cleared out some extra storage space. No, my dear, you haven't *just* burned his shit, you've done something far more significant. You have burned the bridge. I know, I know, they say you should never burn a bridge. While this may be the "rule" of life, if nothing else, breakups are entitled to a little exception. Think of it as a "Bridge to Hell." A bridge that brings you back to that asshole; back to a world of fights and tears, a world of misery. Do you want to go back there? I know I sure as "hell" don't want to. So imagine every item burned is just one more piece of the bridge burned as well. Until finally, there is no bridge, there is no way to go back. Even if you wanted to, you can't. That's how it should be. Sometimes, you've got to burn the bridge to stop yourself from ever crossing it again. And dammit, if that means you have to literally set it ablaze, then so be it. And while you watch it burn, laugh a little, feel a little psychotic, but know there is no going back. There is only going forward, toward a new bridge (which hopefully won't need to be burned as well).

Lesson Learned: *When in doubt, add more lighter fluid.*

DAY 31. 10:18 A.M.

The Moment I Knew

Despite my vow to never speak to Number Twenty-Six again, I just can't help myself. I refuse to allow him to think piling up my belongings has gone unnoticed, much less will be tolerated. Thus, in true ex-fiancée fashion, I decide to fire off a text, making it crystal clear that (a) he was an asshole, (b) he had no right to touch my shit, and (c) he was never to speak to me again.

The image of my possessions piled high to the ceiling like garbage has engrained itself in my memory. I haven't felt this infuriated since . . . when *is* the last time I felt like this? Maybe after the fantasy suite with Number One? I don't know, I was pissed, but not like this. Hold the phone—I got it. I know *exactly* the last time I felt this infuriated. In fact, it was the first time I truly realized Number Twenty-Six and I weren't going to make it.

It was late October, and Sarah and Phil were getting married in Charleston, South Carolina. I couldn't be more thrilled for the two of them, and the wedding was sure to be the shindig of the year, considering Sarah was having Jo Malone candles as centerpieces, lobster roll appetizers, and a top shelf open bar complete with a signature cocktail. As if that wasn't enough, I was the maid of honor leading the charge with Leslie and Caroline as bridesmaids, and we were all staying together in a beautiful downtown mansion along with all our beaus. Okay, truth be told, the candles and cocktails were pretty appealing, as was getting to see my girls, but the real reason I was so excited for the upcoming nuptials was because for the first time, I wasn't going to be the token single girl forced to stand in a sea of women eager to catch the bridal bouquet. I finally had my very own fiancé as my date. I'd been waiting to show him (and my giant diamond rock) to the girls, and the time had finally come. After all, these women were the reason I'd met him in the first place, and now it was time for all of us to gloat about it.

As the maid of honor, it was my duty to be the bride's right-hand woman, which I surprisingly enjoyed. This is largely due to the fact that I can be quite bossy and slightly OCD, but mainly because Sarah was hands-down the easiest bride in the world. With the big weekend ahead, I decided to drive from Atlanta to Charleston a few days early to help Sarah tie up any loose ends, while Number Twenty-Six planned to make the trip the following day. Despite not having met any of my friends or their significant others yet, I knew he'd get along just fine with the sporty bunch.

The festivities were in full swing, starting with a Friday afternoon bridal brunch at a restaurant around the corner, where I found myself noshing on Belgian waffles and sipping mimosas in between checking my phone for status updates from my fiancé. It was just the beginning of what promised to be a fun-filled weekend, and the champagne was already flowing! Fast forward and I'm in between mimosa number four and five, or perhaps five and six, when I peer at my phone to find twelve new messages, three missed calls and myself in hot water, already. I'd lost track of time, which I obviously blame on the champagne, and my now-agitated fiancé had arrived at our rental house before me.

I frantically power-walked (in stilettos) back to find him waiting in his car in the driveway with a scowl not even a mother could love smeared across his face. "Hey, babe, I'm so sorry," I said as I pecked him on the cheek rather than the lips, in hopes that he couldn't taste the champagne still lingering on my breath.

"Why are you so late?" he asked.

Ooooopsies, Papa Bear's mad, I laughingly thought to my giddy buzzed self. Operative word being "thought." Yeah, let's just say I made sure to hold my laughter in. I had to. Twenty-Six was not the type to get upset, hear an apology and be over it, nor was he the type to find such a "serious" blunder the least bit comical. No, he would be over it when he decided he was over it, and there wasn't a damn thing anybody could do about it. So, like a guilty toddler caught drawing on the living room wall, I lowered my head and marched upstairs to our room, where I'd spend the next hour or so sleeping off my buzz.

Later that evening, I began getting ready for the evening's events, which consisted of a quick run-through of the next day's ceremony followed by a rehearsal dinner. While primping, I couldn't help but notice the salty mood Number Twenty-Six *still* seemed to be in. Though I wished it was due to his long day of travel, I knew in actuality it was due to my long day of boozing on champagne. Nevertheless, an application of fresh makeup later, I was grabbing my clutch and my fiancé and heading out the door, bound for the evening.

After the run-through, we were shuttled to dinner. I found my name at the table and took my seat. To my left was Leslie, followed by Wade while Twenty-Six was to my right, next to another bridesmaid, KK, and her husband. KK, who was now six months pregnant and could no longer fit in her bridesmaid dress, was a longtime friend of Sarah's who had often visited us in law school. A ball of fun, even while pregnant, she was a social butterfly who had the unique ability to make you feel like you'd known her your entire life. So, in true KK fashion, she immediately whipped up a conversation with Number Twenty-Six.

"So tell me everything. How was the show? How is life? Are you happy?"

Let me just say, thank goodness KK wasn't even close to full-term, because his reaction to this question was jarring enough to make any woman's water break.

"Umm . . . what kind of question is 'Are you happy?' Has someone been telling you I'm not happy or something?" he snapped back at her.

"No, no, not at all. Just the opposite. I was just asking how everything was," she replied, nervous and utterly confused.

His head swiveled. My eyes met his accusatory glare, which I had nicknamed "The Death Stare." Uh oh. I'd become all too familiar with this look, and even happened to have one of my own, which I'd perfected during my terrifying teenage years, but Twenty-Six's gave me a run for my money. His was fierce, laced with pent-up anger. Steam practically protruded out of his eyes, and there was no question that once it was used, I was S-C-R-E-W-E-D.

Ohhhhh, fuck . . . here we go again, I thought. And even worse, poor KK! I could see the panic in her eyes, she was like a deer caught in the headlights, unable to run and hide, and even worse, unable to drink it off. Twenty-Six leaned in and rhetorically whispered into my ear, "So, how much shit have you been talking about me to your friends?" With an eye roll, and a hefty dose of annoyance, I "whispered" back, "Stop! She's just asking about your life, like are you happy? Are you happy with life, with being engaged. And she's pregnant."

The bickering between us continued, as I found myself attempting to explain the lack of malice behind her question. It was like I was teaching a toddler something but failing so miserably that I was beginning to question who was smarter, the teacher or the tot. He'd made up his mind that I'd been bad-mouthing him behind his back, and no amount of explaining was going to change it. That was the thing about Number Twenty-Six—he had the ability to carry an entire room, for better or worse. His mood was contagious, rapidly spreading from person to person: If he was happy, everyone else could be; if he wasn't, everyone else was doomed. So, I did what any doomed girl in this position would do . . . ordered another glass of wine and started gulping.

The next morning was the wedding day, which meant a total takeover of the house. The hair and makeup team arrived, and within minutes commandeered virtually every inch of the downstairs portion of the house. While blow dryers were blowing, curling irons were curling, and airbrushes were working their makeup magic on each of us bridesmaids, the men sat on the couch in the adjacent living room drinking beer and watching college football. While the other men were thrilled that their wives were occupied so they could watch football unmolested, mine kept asking me when I'd be done and able to hang out with him. I have to admit, though many would have seen this as a red flag as well as slightly annoying, in the moment I found it oddly endearing.

"Once the ceremony is over, I'm all yours," I'd reassuringly say as I gave him a small smooch and pretended to be in denial over last night's mortification.

Several hours later, next thing we knew, the sun was setting and the bride was walking down the aisle. And there, underneath an enormous oak tree, I watched as my best friend said, "I do."

A few bridal party photos later, and it was finally time to get the party started. I made my way through a sea of guests and into the cocktail party to find my dapper fiancé dressed in my favorite Hugo Boss suit waiting for me near the bar. Damn, did he look good in a suit! Almost good enough to make me completely forget about the night before. Almost. We sipped on cocktails as we made small talk with some of the guests and bridesmaids. Everything seemed great until he surveyed the crowd, which happened to include many of Phil's former baseball teammates, and yet again leaned close to my ear. Out came yet another rhetorical accusation, "So just how many of these guys have you hooked up with?"

Dear Lord, not again, I thought as I rolled my eyes. While I may have been able to get past the meritless accusation from last night, this one was more difficult to ignore. In fact, it fucking pissed me off. He'd gone from lashing out at a pregnant woman to insinuating that I was a whore. Who says that to someone, let alone their fiancée? And the funny thing is, I hadn't even dated, let alone slept with, let alone touched with a ten-foot pole, a single one of them. Even if I had, did he have the right to bring it up?

I remember feeling as if he just wanted to pick a fight with me. I questioned whether he was mad that he wasn't the center of attention or if he truly was this jealous a person. Whatever it was, the joy of the ceremony and the excitement of the party had evaporated. His mood was already saltier than the Charleston air and it was only going to get worse.

With the cocktail hour over, you could cut the tension between us with a dull knife. We entered the reception hall, where under a clear tent festooned with hydrangeas, peonies, and Jo Malone candles, we found our assigned seats—mine in between Sarah and Leslie, Twenty-Six's across from me, along with the other husbands and fiancés, something he obviously took offense to. Some snarky comment from him about how "strange" it was that couples didn't get to sit next to each other, and he'd racked up yet another strike in what had to be the longest at-bat in history. I'd gone from the point of embarrassment to annoyance and was teetering on the brink of being flat-out repulsed by my own fiancé. I was tired of walking on eggshells with him, I didn't want to get in another fight and couldn't promise restraint if he decided to accuse me again of sleeping with someone. Basically, I was over the drama and instead of dealing with it, I decided to run away. Well, really I decided to skip away with Caroline and Leslie on each arm as we made our way to the scenic dock where we proceeded to snap selfies and giggle. When we returned to the tent to bust out some dance moves, I couldn't find my fiancé. Not that this was all that bad of a thing at this point, but after ten minutes went by and he was still nowhere to be found I decided to text him:

ME: Where are you?

26: You were ignoring me, I left.

ME: You left? What? Come back, we can dance.

26: Nah, I'm waiting for a car outside.

Cut to me stumbling down a gravel driveway in my five-inch stilettos, where I find him in the parking lot waiting for a cab. I pleaded with him to stay, less because I actually cared about him staying at that point and more because I didn't want to create yet another embarrassing scene. After promising to pay more attention to him and even dance with him, he agreed to rejoin the party. I led him back down the driveway toward the tent where the music was blaring and the party was jamming. We had almost reached the end of the driveway before he made yet another snarky comment. I don't even recall what he said, because in a five-minute-long argument, all I remember was when he called me a "bitch." I froze.

It wasn't the first time he'd called me this name, but it was the first time he'd said it in public, loud enough for a slew of guests and the wedding planner to hear. My humiliation had hit an all-time high,

"Is everything okay?" the wedding planner interjected.

"Yes, totally fine," I replied with a fake smile.

But it wasn't fine. Not even close. It was the third and final strike; he was out. I'd finally been pushed to my breaking point—I was tired of the snark, tired of the childish behavior, tired of the accusations, and now I was tired of him. It was bad enough that someone who supposedly loved me was calling me a bitch, but that he was doing it in front of a hundred people at a snazzy event made my biggest fear of public embarrassment come true. It was one of those weekends where I just couldn't please him, no matter what.

I wasn't completely innocent, I get it—I was inattentive, to say the least, as I spent the better part of the weekend focusing less on Twenty-Six and more on insuring Sarah's dress was perfectly fluffed and her teeth were lipstick-free. But that's what I was there to do. It wasn't my weekend to be the perfect fiancée but rather the perfect maid of honor. This wedding wasn't about me, or him, or us; it was about Sarah and Phil. I'd had enough and finally blurted what I'd wanted to say all day, "If you don't want to be here, then just leave."

Immediately, his eyes widened as if he'd been waiting to hear those magic words. Before I had even finished my sentence, he'd turned around and was headed straight back to where I'd found him, at the end of the driveway waiting to get a cab. I could have chased after him (again) and had it not been for strikes one and two, maybe I would have. But as I stood there, mortified, with blistering feet and a long gown now dredged in dirt, I didn't take a single step. Instead, I watched him make his way down the driveway until he was out of sight. I gathered myself for a minute and then walked right back into the party. This would be handled later; for now, I was going to grab some champagne, take my heels off, and dance the night away with my best friends.

When the party was over, I called to let him know we were on our way home. I wasn't surprised that he didn't answer and assumed I'd find him snoring in our bed when I returned to the house. But I didn't. Instead, all I found was an empty spot in the driveway where his car had been parked. Dozens of unanswered calls and texts later, complete with shedding drunk girl tears to my friends and their husbands, I finally called it a night. In bed alone, I asked myself, *How in the hell did this go so terribly wrong?* This was supposed to be a fun weekend, a weekend to show off my new love, and instead it had become a complete disaster. Was I right to avoid him during the reception? Probably not. Was he immature about it? Probably so. But still, those minor details shouldn't result in anyone leaving a wedding, let alone leaving town. As I sobbed in bed, I looked at my phone one last time, saw all of the attempted calls to him, and in that very moment I knew deep down in my soul that this relationship was never going to work.

When I awoke, the realization that he wasn't there hit me once more. I called him, but no answer. I packed my bags and said good-bye to my friends and began the lonely four-hour drive back to Atlanta. About an hour in, I still hadn't heard from him, causing me to go from pissed off to now terrified that something horrible had happened to him. I called again and again, like a crazy fiancée, until finally he answered.

"Where are you?" I shouted.

"I drove back home last night."

"Why? Why would you do that?"

"You told me to leave, you kicked me out, Andi."

Now that I knew he was alive and safe, my worry turned back to fury.

"First off, I didn't *tell* you to leave," I explained. "I told you, after several snarky comments and you calling me a bitch in public, that *if* you didn't want to be there, then leave."

The lawyer in me says that what I told him wasn't a direct order to leave but merely a conditional statement: *If* you want this, then do that. He still had a choice, right? But it didn't matter. He heard what he wanted to, and with his departure had made me feel a way that could never be forgotten. I spent the remainder of the drive crying and wondering what to do. I knew the way we treated each other wasn't healthy. I knew I didn't want a life filled with fights like these and public embarrassment. I wanted to be done with him, but something inside of me just couldn't let go.

That night I slept alone at my place. The next morning, I did what I always did with him . . . made up. I had gotten into a routine of not only tolerating these situations but accepting them as part of our toxic relationship. It was as if I was addicted to this man and the destruction that resulted in loving him. Being in such an unpredictable relationship was foreign to me, but so was the intense love I had for him, and I figured, maybe this was just the price I had to pay for finding the spark I had longed for all these years.

Lesson learned: When you know, you know.

DAY 32. 2:15 P.M.

The Master Asshole List

It's been about four days since I moved my stuff out of our apartment and the rage within has yet to subside. I keep playing back the fact that he actually had the nerve to pack up my things—no, not pack, *pile* them—in the corner of the room. It triggers so many other angry moments like Charleston and our fight in Italy. I know, I need to get over it, but it's hard to when I feel so much ill will toward someone I once loved. Right now, there's no better adjective I could use to describe my feelings toward Number Twenty-Six than *hate.* Despite being taught by my parents to never use that word, I feel justified in saying that I HATE him!

I've hated very few people in my life, in fact, probably only two or three people ever. One was the bitch who slept with my college boyfriend because her only goal in life was to be a home wrecker, the other was another ex-boyfriend's sister-in-law because her only goal in life was to make me miserable, and the third is probably Number Twenty-Five, because his only goal in life was to humiliate me. (That's a whole other story I'll tell you about later.) Each of those bitches/assholes deserved hatred from me. And right now, so does Number Twenty-Six.

I think about the reasons I hate him so much, and it seems there are just as many why I once loved him so much. I hate him because he took a part of my heart and stomped on it. I hate him because he made me fall in love with something that wasn't real. The man I fell in love with was funny, compassionate, and protective. He was outgoing and cared only about family and me, not the cameras and certainly not the fame. He adored the fact that I was a career-driven woman with a feisty personality. But, now I feel as though that man didn't exist, not beyond the lights.

No, when the cameras stopped rolling, he couldn't sustain the persona of the man he was trying to be. He was funny at times, as long as the joke wasn't on him; compassionate when he was in a good mood. And while I genuinely think he liked the idea of being with a career-driven, strong-willed woman, ultimately that wasn't what he really wanted. It's not to say that I think he was faking who he was, but instead, he just presented himself as the man he *wished* he was. I get it. Why would anyone go on national television and not put his best face forward? Maybe if the setup of the show had been different, or I hadn't let my infatuation for him blind me, I could have seen this side of him, the real side. I hate him for packing my stuff up. (I promise this is the last time I will mention it. Bible!) I hate him for holding my past over me, for the names he called me. I hate him for ever having met him. Something that isn't even all his fault. If I had never laid eyes on him, I would have never wasted that first engagement and, with it, my dream of having done it only once. I hate that I will always be and always have an ex-fiancé. But most of all, I hate that I hate him so much.

How is it possible to hate someone you loved beyond all reason? Was there a memo I didn't get that says the more you love someone, the more you'll hate him when it doesn't work out? I used to go to bed and wake up every morning crying, but lately I seem to go to bed and wake up every morning just thinking of how much he revolts me. I never knew how much energy it takes to feel this way. If only disgust could burn calories. As it consumes me more and more, I realize that hatred might be even worse than sadness.

But what can I do to relieve the hate? There's nothing I can force myself to think about to rid this feeling, but it's got to go. It's consuming me, infecting me like a disease that's spreading rapidly throughout my body. I don't want to vent aloud to anyone, because even though ripping him a new one might make him look bad, it would also make me look bitter and stupid for staying with him so long. Plus, I'm running out of therapy sessions with Kelly, who is at work right now, because unlike me she has a life. It's only so long before she understandably reaches the breaking point and says enough is enough, and I'm not ready yet to be cut off cold turkey. The online self-help articles, which I've come to despise but also obsess over, tell me to try to see the positive in my relationship, learn from the negative and begin to move forward. But I say, FUCK that noise. The way I see it, I'm a ticking time bomb that is bound to go off at a moment's notice.

And then, it dawns on me . . . These feelings are just like his belongings that only days ago were scattered across my bedroom floor. They too are memories. Memories that belong to a dead relationship. And if I can burn his belongings, can't I burn this hate as well?

I grab a pen and a piece of paper and immediately my hand begins to uncontrollably scribble words and memories of hate onto the lines. And I realize, this is my ticket out, my final step in completing the cleanse phase of my breakup detox. This is my very own Master Asshole list.

THE MASTER ASSHOLE LIST

Step 1. Make sure no one is home.

Step 2. Gather the following: pen, paper, pissed-off attitude. (Oh, wait, I already have the last item.)

Step 3. With pen, on paper, and keeping in mind my attitude, write down every bad memory I can think of. This should include words such as "narcissist," "selfish," "prick," "douche bag," and "tool."

Step 4. Keep writing.

Step 5. Smile as I glance at the beautiful list of what I avoided.

Step 6. Burn the list.

Step 7. Tell no one I did such a thing. What list?

As I watch the yellow notebook paper burn in the fire, I have to admit I feel amazing! Not just because I successfully made a fire, again, but also because I bashed him in the quietest way ever and in doing so, I can physically feel the hatred leave my body. It's one of those accomplishments that feel better knowing that I am the only one in on the secret. It's a power trip. And as the paper turns to ashes, it takes away not just part of my hatred but also my desire to be connected with him in any way. I realize at last that I want nothing to do with him, ever again. We are, as Taylor Swift would say, "never ever ever getting back together," but we will never ever be friends either.

Why does everyone want to stay friends with their exes anyways? If you ask me, it's total bullshit. We only say it so we can end the awkwardness of the breakup conversation, right?

The truth is, the second you decide to take the plunge and be in a relationship is the second the "let's be friends card" goes out the window. There should be a hard-written rule that once you see each other naked, the friendship is dunzo—no ifs, ands, or, pardon the pun, butts.

It's impossible, not to mention completely pointless. I mean, seriously, what the hell is the point in staying friends? What are you going to do, stay in each other's lives so you can do what? Keep up with one another, hear about the next girl he's dating, send a wedding gift when he gets married, be on the family Christmas card mailing list each year? No thanks, I'll pass. The reality is, your friendship with your ex was over long ago. It's why you couldn't make things work. Now, you have to accept that you will never be friends with your ex.

But what about the friends you shared? This is when shit gets dicey. The reality of a breakup is that you don't just lose your relationship, you lose friends too. I know, sorry. Mutual friendships that you made while you were a couple are now in question.

RULE #1: FRIENDS ARE PART OF A PRENUP

Like property, your friends are part of the prenup that will dictate your post-breakup future. This means what he came in with remains his and what you came in with remains yours. Yup, doesn't matter if you became the best of friends with his childhood friends, he gets them. But you get yours too.

RULE #2: LET THEM COME TO YOU

You'll have mutual friends you both met during the relationship, who aren't covered in the breakup prenup. These people are fair game, but let them come to you first. It'll feel like they get to be the captain of the kickball team, but the truth is, you don't want to be on a team with someone who doesn't want you anyways. It also relieves the possibility of you a) looking desperate, and b) being labeled a friend snatcher.

RULE #3: SET BOUNDARIES

If you do get picked to be part of the team and your friendship remains intact, set boundaries. Don't vent to them about your ex, because remember, once upon a time they were friends with him too. It's disrespectful to your ex, to your friend, and it's uncomfortable for everyone. Instead, you are Switzerland; you don't take sides, you don't start wars, you are just a pretty little country everyone wants to visit. Besides, you have plenty of friends you can vent to who aren't associated with your ex—use them!

RULE #4: DON'T TAKE IT PERSONALLY

Don't be offended if you find that you not only lose a man after a breakup, but lose some friends as well. It's normal. You'll feel abandoned, but remember if a mutual friend chooses your ex over you, it might be out of loyalty and obligation, not out of desire. It's the classic "chicks over dicks, bros before hoes" rule. The truth is, just as much as people don't like ending relationships, they don't like ending friendships either. The end of your relationship puts them unwillingly in a tough situation, so cut them some slack and if need be, leave them in the past, right where you've dropped your ex off.

RULE #5: FIND COMMON GROUND

Friendships form from common bonds, and now that you are single, some of those bonds no longer exist. Couples like to be friends with other couples so they can talk about "couple-y" things. Don't be surprised that you are no longer invited on weekly double dates. Trust me, you don't want to be surrounded by happy couples right now anyway. Instead, make a concerted effort to strengthen the relationships with your single friends. You'll find comfort in commonality, and just like you, they'll have the freedom to party all night long.

Back to your list in the fireplace. Take a deep whiff and smell the burning scent of relief.

Lesson Learned: *You swore you'd stay friends till the end? Well, this is the end.*

DAY 34. 3:13 P.M.

The Dreaded Text

It happened today. I got the dreaded text I knew I would receive at some point but would never be fully prepared for. It wasn't from Number Twenty-Six—we haven't been in contact since I fired off a text regarding the moving-out situation. It was from one of my girlfriends, Tay.

Deep exhale—this one sucks . . .

TAY: So I have to tell you something and I don't want you to be upset at me.

ME: Umm . . . not a good way to start a convo, but shoot.

TAY: I saw your ex last night.

ME: Which one?

TAY: The latest one.

ME: Oh Lord, where?

TAY: In Buckhead, out at a restaurant.

ME: There's more to this, isn't there?

TAY: Yes. I don't know how to say this.

ME: Just say it.

TAY: He was on a date with a girl.

ME: I had a feeling that's what you were going to say.

TAY: Please don't be mad at me, but as your friend, I have to tell you.

ME: No I know, I'm glad you did. One question . . .

TAY: Yes . . .

ME: Was she blonde?

TAY: Yes :-(

ME: Motherfucker!

TAY: Haha! Hang in there! Love you, girlie.

ME: Love you too.

Dagger to the heart! I want to vomit. I wish I were numb right now so I didn't feel this bone-chilling, soul-curdling, gut-wrenching pain. I wrestle back and forth in my mind over whether I am hurt, jealous, or just fucking angry. I think it's all three.

The jealous part of me realizes that while I sit here and wallow, feeling unmotivated and hopeless, he's doing what I desperately wish I could, moving on. Trust me, I wish I could find it in me to rebound with the future Number Twenty-Seven, but I can't. I don't get it! Why do men always seem to move on faster than women? Here I am, reeling in pain that has yet to subside long enough to even begin to fathom seeing another man. Not only would I fail to hold it together for the duration of a romantic dinner, but I don't even want to. I was engaged for nine months, that engagement ended only thirty-four days ago, and I'm not ready to start dating again. And to make matters even worse, of course, he's with a blonde! I swear to God, I should have read those lie detector test results . . . I would have known he preferred blondes.

In all seriousness, though, is it fair to put a timetable on your ex? It's not as if there's any chance of resolving our irreconcilable differences and making our way back to one another. We passed the point of no return long, long ago. And though he's moved on quicker than I find to be in good taste, isn't this what all men do? Avoid having to feel these foreign things called emotions and instead grieve by getting right back in the game as quickly as possible? This is where it sucks to be a woman. We grieve by curling up in a ball and crying while getting fat on red wine and sesame chicken and Thin Mints while men pull their pants down and screw anything with a vagina. Or at least take her out to dinner in hopes of later getting to pull his pants down and screw her. If women do this, we are branded crazy psycho skanks, whereas men are just being, well, men.

Maybe I'm not so much jealous as I am pissed. I'm certainly not jealous of the blonde—she has no idea what kind of mess she's about to get herself into. I'm angry at the message he's sending by doing this. It's one thing if a man wants to mend his broken little heart by hooking up with a chick so that he doesn't have to actually feel the pain of a breakup. But it's a whole different ball game when you take a rebound chick out in public. There's only one reason someone does this . . . so the other person knows about it. Oh, and in the city I live in, no less. What if I had been in that restaurant? What then? The fact that he was willing to take that risk shows he has zero respect for my feelings or our relationship.

And what angers me the most is the contradiction of it all. Throughout our entire relationship, Number Twenty-Six was so self-righteous when it came to members of the opposite sex, especially when it came to infidelity. Don't get me wrong, I know this doesn't rise to the level of infidelity, considering we are broken up, but hear me out.

His insecurity started very early on in our relationship when he told me about the time he was twenty and his girlfriend of about a year (which at that age is more like ten minutes) had kissed another guy while they were together. It tore him apart and scarred him not just for the next decade, but for life. He called it "cheating," though I'm hesitant to categorize it so definitively. Personally, I called it bullshit (in my mind, of course).

For starters, it was a decade ago—let it go! Not to mention the fact that if that's what he thinks cheating is, then bless his heart. Here's cheating: when your boyfriend of a few years *actually* cheats on you. Not just "Oh, he kissed a girl and he liked it," no, full-blown penis-inside-vagina cheating. Nevertheless, he constantly made a point of reminding me of his fear of being cheated on. I wondered if it was really baggage for him, or if it was just an excuse to mask his jealousy. There seemed to be no other reason for this "insecurity" other than that one girl *ten years ago.* I tried to determine if maybe something about his family triggered this fear, maybe something from his childhood, but nothing.

Regardless of why he was insecure, it didn't really matter because as I explained to him, it was completely irrelevant. I'd never been a cheater and didn't plan on starting now. I've always believed that while we may not be able to control our minds and the dirty and tempting thoughts that run through them, we can refrain from acting on those thoughts, and I have always been a person of self-control (except when it comes to red wine and Thin Mints, obviously). Aside from cheating being too much of a bother, not to mention the guilt that comes with it, the chance of ruining an entire relationship with one sexcapade has never seemed worth it. Plus, it wasn't like I had given him any reason to suspect that I had cheated or was planning to. This insecurity wasn't the problem, though. Everyone has insecurities; my family members do, my friends do, and I certainly do. But you love those people regardless. The problem was that his insecurity had manifested itself into a method of control.

The first example of this that I remember was at my parents' house one Sunday evening. We had continued my tradition of Sunday family dinners anytime we were in town, even when we weren't supposed to be seen in public together. While we sat around the dinner table, my mom brought up *Dancing with the Stars.* Rumors had been circulating that I was going to join the cast, but they were just that, rumors. First of all, I hate dancing and I suck at it, and not in a cutesy way but in an embarrassing and nauseating way. Not only would it have been agony to have to dance all day long, but it would have been pure torture to make others watch me. My mother always wanted to stay up to date on the latest rumors, I think in part because so much was going on and she felt out of the loop, though I often reminded her she would be the first to know if anything was ever true. So when she asked if I was going to do the show, I emphatically replied, "Hell, no!" Should have been the end of the conversation, right? Not even close. Number Twenty-Six decided to give his two cents by voicing his opinion—or, rather, his *ruling*—that I was not going to participate "in a show like that."

"Why not?" my mom asked.

He explained to her that the show was all about sex and how totally inappropriate it would be for *his* fiancée to be dancing and sweating on another man. In his defense (I can't even believe I'm saying that), my family has always been very open. We would often engage in debates on anything and everything at our weekly dinners long before Number Twenty-Six ever made his way onto the scene. So it wasn't the fact that he voiced his opinion that surprised me, or my mom, for that matter, but the way he said it. There was so much animosity and intensity in his tone.

"It doesn't have to be all sexual, you know," said my mother.

"Well, we've already discussed it and it's not going to happen."

I looked at my mother's face, and I don't know who was more mortified, she or I. But worse than the look of mortification was the worry I saw in her eyes. It was a familiar look, one I had seen just months ago when I looked into my father's eyes the day he first met Number Twenty-Six. I was angry over the way he spoke to my mother, but I decided not to make a big deal about it at the time. Like his fear of my cheating, *DWTS* wasn't something I was interested in doing anyway, so why have an argument?

And it wasn't just these proactive little tantrums. As time went on, it felt as though Number Twenty-Six would look for ways to accuse me of cheating, almost as if he wanted it to happen. It was a Twitter fight here, or me talking to a guy there, or him accusing me of secretly being at dinner with men instead of with the girls like I told him (which was never true). The more ridiculous his accusations were and the more disproportionate his reactions, the more I wondered if all of this was less about his fear of cheating and was his way of exerting control over me. And even worse, was this the way the rest of our lives would be, stupid fight after stupid fight, accusation after accusation?

Perhaps my anger and jealousy really stem from the hurt I

feel deep down. His hasty rebound makes me feel discarded and replaced, yet again. First it was the packing of my belongings, and now this. Am I that disposable?

But, as much as something like this hurts, it's a blessing in disguise. It's a free pass to move on without being the one that looks like the jackass. Thank your ex (silently). You've been drowning in your misery because you loved someone and it didn't work out. You don't want him back, but it's difficult if not impossible to let him go. Well, now, you don't have to, because he's let you go first. He's given you the jolt you needed to finally cut the cord.

Though the idea of cutting a cord sounds terrifying, we've all done it before. In fact, the cord was cut from you before you even realized you had arrived in this world. You'd barely made it out of the womb before *snip snip,* and just like that you'd gone from nine months relaxing in your mother's stomach to out on your own. Sure, you weren't completely left to fend for yourself, but you didn't know that. And that's exactly what you did—you survived. Which is exactly what needs to happen now. He's let you go, and now you must do the same. The time has come to cut the cord from your relationship and begin to survive on your own.

Lesson learned: *Snip snip, clip clip.*

DAY 35. 6:54 P.M.

Revenge

Well, I woke up this morning, and though the tears have disappeared, my dislike for Twenty-Six hasn't completely vanished just yet. I guess that takes time. But I've made progress! I have my stuff, I've purged my hatred (well, most of it), and after learning of his date, I, too, feel ready to take the step of moving on. And with the jolt of knowing that he's begun the process by physically replacing me, I'm beginning to move on myself, by replacing him and the toxins he brings me with new healthy nutrients. Yup, I'm ready for the "Balancing Phase" of my detox. Woohoo!

However, I have a slight dilemma. As much as I am ready to move on and start substituting the negatives with positives, I also want him to suffer as I do it. Is that bad? Basically, I want revenge. I want him to pay for all the shit he put me through, both during and after our relationship. I want him to suffer just like I have. Shit, maybe I'm not done with the cleanse phase after all.

While I debate how to exact vengeance, I have an epiphany

that I think healthily embodies my desires to get even *and* get better. What if my ultimate revenge could actually be beneficial to myself? Like killing two birds with one stone!

If you're anything like me, when the tears finally dry up and every memory of the past has been burned to ashes, you wonder, *What's next*? Naturally, what's next is to get even. I blame this feeling on human nature. Part of you probably wants him to royally fuck up for all the world to see, right? But the softer side of you wants to spare him any pain, considering you did love him at one point. Then there's your selfish side that figures, if he fucks up, then I look like a fuck-up for having been with well . . . such a fuck-up. But the overwhelming desire, all softness and rationality aside, is to give him a dose of his own medicine. To even up the score. Because it's become clear that you have undoubtedly drawn the shitty end of the heartbreak stick. And in all fairness, you deserve some retaliation.

There are a variety of ways to go about this. You could . . .

- slit his tires
- accidentally leave a voice mail of you hooking up with another guy
- send him a text saying you're pregnant and it's his
- go over to his house wearing nothing but a trench coat and thigh-highs
- send yourself flowers from a mystery man . . . to his address
- tell everyone you broke up because you found out he's gay
- do a drive-by (not shooting, just surveying)
- hook up with one of his friends, in public

Okay, so you're not going to actually do any of those things, but don't deny that they've crossed your mind. (Although the voice mail would be great.) You don't want to hook up with one of his friends and become, not the one who got away, but the skank who screwed herself away. You don't want to spread rumors about him because it'll make him think you still care, which even though you obviously do because you want vengeance, you don't want to give him the satisfaction of knowing that. Ultimately, deep down, what you really want is to get revenge so you feel better about yourself. You want him to miss you. And though no amount of missing will ever make you want him back, you still want him to want you. So what do you do? How do you get the revenge you need without looking insane?

The answer: You be mother-effing awesome!

Even though you aren't "the one," that doesn't mean you can't be "the one . . . who got away," right? That's the kind of wound that never heals. It's the slow burn that haunts him, that keeps him up late at night. It's the lethal dose of his own medicine. But it's also, in the most selfish way possible, the best thing you can do for yourself. You give up trying to make him miserable, and instead make yourself invincible.

It'll be easier said than done and will require a heavy dose of self-control, but you are a warrior, there's nothing you can't do. So get ready, vengeance is right around the corner. And here's how you'll find it:

OPERATION BE MOTHER-EFFING AWESOME

Step 1: **The pity party is officially over!** You've wallowed enough, drunk enough, cried enough, pouted enough, and pitied yourself enough. No more. You've had your hall pass long enough, it's time to turn it back in. So box up the wine, throw away the remaining chocolate (if there's any left), and do whatever else you need to do to wrap this party up. You can't be the one who got away if you're a train wreck.

Step 2: **Kill him with kindness.** Next time he sends you a rude text, you will either ignore it or kill him back with the sweetest words you can grudgingly muster up. It's time to pretend to be the prim and proper sophisticated woman you were born to be.

Step 3: **Refrain from talking shit to anyone and everyone.** You have officially done all the shit talking there is to do to your family and closest friends. Your side of the story is out there. It has been heard probably to the point of exhaustion. It's the end now. If someone asks you what he's really like or what went wrong in your relationship, you will respond with only positivity and a screwed-on smile. You can do it, I know you can!

Step 4: **Get your ass in shape and flaunt it.** Say goodbye to those post-breakup pounds. Though this probably should have started long ago, it's officially time to hit the gym and get slim, baby! Time to get your ass in shape. And while you're at it, you will make sure to maintain shaved legs, clean underwear, and shampooed hair. Box up the breakup uniform, break out the heels, and look like you're ready to play. You wanna be awesome? Start looking awesome.

Step 5: **Don't fuck up.** This doesn't mean you have to go out of your way to appease him. Hell, that was reserved for when you were in a relationship. You really don't have to do anything when it comes to him, except not fuck up. Don't give your ex a reason to deny the fact that he loved you, or to call you a skank or a drunk fool. No flirting with his friends, no dancing on bars, no photos of you looking a hot mess. Basically, anything that draws negative attention to yourself is to be avoided.

Step 6: **No Stalking.** All the places the two of you used to go? As far as you're concerned, they went out of business. Yeah, no more frequenting the restaurants, bars, stores, or parks you used to go to with your ex. Consider these places casualties of your war. As much as you might find yourself yearning to run into him (now that you're looking all hot and everything) you can't. Sorry, it's just the price you pay of being awesome. Think of this as a chance to explore new places, new things, rather than waste time claiming the old. Besides, only bitches pee on their territory.

Step 7: **Bring on the social media.** Let's be honest, nobody, myself included, posts bad photos on social media. The whole point of Facebook and Instagram is to brag about your picture-perfect life. And though it's borderline narcissistic and pathetic, it does tend to succeed in making others envious. So from now on, your posts will be fabulous. The vodka bottle will be replaced with the champagne bottle, the Chinese food will now be the finest sushi. Your weekend posts will not be of the bed but of the beach. Not sure how you'll find the time or money to do this? Two words . . . FAKE IT. Fake it till you make it, girl. Wouldn't be the first time you did . . . wink wink.

The plan is set. It's finally time to move on, time to get revenge by being the one . . . who got away. It's time to be mother-effing AWESOME!

Lesson learned: *The sweetest revenge has nothing to do with him, and everything to do with you!*

DAY 36. 4:15 P.M.

Mayday

Holy hangover. Last night, my girlfriends decided it would be a good idea to drag me out of the house and out on the town. In all likelihood they did this out of pity and because my bedroom badly needed to be aerated of the stench of red wine, depression, and homeliness, but I'm going to assume that as true girlfriends, they just wanted to help me get back on track. Plus, I figured this was a good way to maintain my balancing phase. Replace nights home alone crying with nights out with the girls partying!

Being that it was going to be my first time since the breakup going out in public, I was nervous and reluctant. But nevertheless, as part of Operation Be Mother-Effing Awesome, I had determined to start being, well . . . mother-effing awesome. This meant, I needed a mini-makeover, aka a well-deserved trip to the mall! Despite knowing that retail therapy will provide only temporary happiness, these days I'll take what I can get.

First stop, Bloomingdale's, where I make my way to the sale rack and begin pulling random items, including some silk blouses, pants, and even a faux fur vest. With my arms weighed down by countless bargains (hello, 40% off sale!), I finally make my way to the dressing room where I slip off my yoga pants and slip into a pair of size small black faux leather leggings—make that I *attempt* to slip them on. When I finally get each leg up to my thighs, I grasp the sides of the waistband and go for the power tug. That's when I hear the dreaded sound of a rip. *It's just the tag being pulled off, or maybe a seam stretching,* I think. The elastic waistband is around my belly button now as the leggings snugly encase the rest of my lower half as I turn and do what no woman going through a breakup should do, examine my rear in the mirror.

"Fuck!"

Either these black leather leggings have a teal lace and flesh-tone pattern on the ass or I have just fallen victim to the dressing room disaster every woman fears most. That seam is not stretched, it's *split.* I quickly roll the leggings down my thighs and, in an effort to hide the evidence of my mortification, hang them back up and slip them in the middle of the rest of the hanging pants, before sprinting out of the dressing room without trying on another item. Then I do what every woman does on a fat day at the mall: I ditch the dressing room and head to the makeup counter.

I mosey around the different cosmetic stations as I collect a handful of paper strips with different spritzes of perfumes, handed out by the overzealous salespeople. I stop by the SK-II counter, pretending to be interested in purchasing some products, but really I am just looking to score a free sample of their expensive eye cream. Finally, I make my way to Dior where a row of colorful lipsticks in pristine silver cases grabs my attention. I try on the latest line, first a nude, then a light pink. But then the row of bright reds catch my eye. *Do I dare?* I pick one up and swipe it across my inner wrist. "Holy shit, this is bright."

"That would be fabulous with your skin tone," says the consultant, who has emerged out of nowhere.

"Ehh . . . I'm not sure, I'm not really a red lips kind of girl."

"Honey, every girl is a red lips kind of girl."

"I usually just stick to the nudes and pinks."

"Well, sounds like you need a change! Sit, sit."

She directs me to a white leather stool.

"Do you mind if I apply some foundation, just to even you out a little?"

"By all means. I can use any help I can get."

With my skin now even and slightly dewy, it is time to take the plunge into the red lip pool.

"Pucker up," she ordered.

I close my eyes and purse my lips as I feel the consultant drawing liner around my pout, before applying the lipstick.

"What do you think?" she asks as she holds a mirror in front of my face.

"Holy Satan Red!"

"Girl, you are too much!" She laughs.

"No, this red is too much!" I joke back.

"I think it's amazing. You seriously look sexy with red lips."

I pucker my lips some more as I turn to each side, examining my reflection in the mirror I am now holding.

"It's actually not so bad."

"With a black dress and some heels, girl . . ."

"Fine, whatever, I'll take it."

"Great! It seriously looks amazing on you! Do you need anything else, some foundation, blush, a liner?"

"No, I'm good. Just Satan's lips in a stick, I guess."

She directs me to the counter as she rings up a fresh tube of lipstick.

"What's the name of that color, anyway?"

"Oh, this one is called Mayday!"

Of course the red lipstick I pick is Mayday.

"That comes to thirty-three dollars even."

"Thirty-three dollars? For lipstick?"

"It's Dior . . ." she says with a shrug and smile.

"Well, Dior better get me laid."

I swipe my credit card and immediately feel buyer's remorse. Thirty-three freaking dollars for one tube of lipstick! Never did I think I would be that woman who shells out $33 on something I'll likely lose within a week. I mean, do you know what I could buy with $33? An entire outfit from Forever 21, two sushi lunch specials, three thongs from Victoria's Secret, the list is endless. But all of those things I guess either get me fat or remind me I've gotten fat, so lipstick it freaking is. Plus, the girls' night out planned for the night gives me a small dose of justification for this otherwise ridiculously reckless purchase.

I turn the corner so the Dior lady can't see me and use a tissue to wipe off the red stain on my lips. If I'm going to take the challenge and wear red lips, it's certainly not going to be at 1:00 p.m. while walking around the mall, by myself. I meander through the quiet mall, clutching my small brown paper bag, which is now worth $33. I stick to window-shopping in an effort to avoid making another impulsive purchase and steer clear of mirrors and dressing rooms. After an hour or so, I call it a day and head home. The shopping trip has put a dent in both my self-esteem and my wallet.

When I get home, I decide to play with my new purchase as I

sit on top of my bathroom counter and get ready for the evening. I twist the bottom of the tube to reveal the bright red waxy Mayday. I pucker and apply the color to my lips. As I stare at my reflection, I have to admit that this could be worth $33 after all. It's the gaudiest shade of red you ever did see, which would make Twenty-Six absolutely squirm. He hates red lipstick, just like every other man in this world does. Part of me understands their hatred; red lipstick is messy, showy, and without a doubt the number one way for a woman to mark her territory on a man. One make-out session with a girl in red lipstick, and a man can literally kiss any chance of two girls in one night goodbye.

But in my opinion, the real reason men hate red lipstick is that it's freaking fabulous! This Mayday shade is no different. Call it a cry for freedom, a well-deserved splurge, or a complete and utter waste of $33, but it feels damn good to pucker up with these red lips. It not only makes my teeth look pearly white, but I feel rebellious and sexy for the first time in a long time. I want to scream "Va-va-voom" as I glance at myself in the mirror.

I'm on a roll! I dig through my closet to find the sexiest dress I own: a black bandage Herve Leger. I slip into the slinky black dress (thank you, Spanx) and take a deep inhale as I fight with the zipper. It finally makes it up to the clasp without breaking, thankfully. I go back into the closet, open a shoebox, and slip my favorite stilettos onto my unpolished feet. I close the closet door and take a glance at myself in the full-length mirror.

"Damn, I still got it, kind of."

As I admire my accomplishment of stuffing myself into the dress and rocking some red lips, I wonder how the hell Number Twenty-Six and every other man out there, for that matter, could not like this look. The plunge is just deep enough to see a hint of cleavage while giving my handful-sized boobs an alluring mystery. It's tight enough to give my white-girl ass a much-needed boost, but not so tight that it reveals the dimples on my upper thighs, or splits right down my caboose. The sky-high stilettos add length to my pins, and the red lips just put the freaking cherry on top of it all.

This outfit makes me a tad excited for the evening's outing with the girls. And I'm not gonna lie, as shallow as it sounds, this is the best I've felt about myself in quite some time. I throw on a moto jacket and I'm ready to go!

The girls arrived at Kelly's house—where I'm still living, by the way—and enjoyed a pregame cocktail before we called an Uber. We headed to our favorite swanky Atlanta bar, where we found a corner table before the waitress takes our first of many drink orders. I glanced at the cocktail menu thinking, *Why didn't I wear leggings?* My Mayday lips were awesome, but my dress's zipper is one vodka and soda away from bursting. Hoping to avoid a carbonation-fueled wardrobe malfunction, I settle on a glass of wine instead. (Which, now that I think about it, actually has more calories than vodka, but whatever.)

Truth is, I loathed being out in public. I felt as though complete strangers were staring at me and thinking, "Oh, my, I wonder how she's doing after the breakup" or "Oh, wow, I can tell the breakup is really taking a toll on her." In reality, odds are that not a single drunk ass looked my way or gave even an ounce of thought to my breakup or me, but regardless, my paranoia was in full force.

Despite the worry, I have to admit I felt glimpses of happiness throughout the evening. I was feeling like a human being for the first time in a very long time. I was finally wearing makeup and heels outside the confinement of my bathroom. It felt like it had been forever since I was "allowed" to be with my girlfriends. This was another thing that always seemed to bother Number Twenty-Six. He'd say things like, "I love how you and your friends don't care about guys when you go out, you just like having fun with each other." But when it came to actually going out with just my girls, he'd forget that sentiment. Like that one time I wanted to go to Mexico on an all-girls getaway. When I told him about this, he was perplexed.

"Why would you go on a girls' trip to another state?" he asked.

"Well, actually, it's another country, but what do you mean?"

"I just think it's weird that you feel the need to go on a girls' trip at all, let alone in a completely different state."

"Umm . . . well, that's what girls do."

"I've never heard of that."

"Well, it's perfectly normal."

I ended up going on the trip, mainly because I had already committed to my girlfriends, but also because it was in December and our relationship had been on the rocks for months by then and I was tired of feeling controlled. And I wanted to fucking go to Mexico the *country.* I'm glad I did, because we had a killer time, and I'm even more glad now because I don't have to get permission or ask forgiveness anymore. I am a free woman, who can go out with my girlfriends and even other men—and even to another country—if I want!

Speaking of other men, the more I drank last night, the cuter they seemed to get. I found myself actually wanting to flirt. Though I wished I could just go balls out and be the confident girl who struts up to the bar, flips her hair, and gives a come-hither look to the hottie in the corner, I couldn't. Instead, I waited for them to come to me. And waited, and waited. *Fuck this noise*, I thought as

I whipped out my phone. I scrolled through my contacts, determined to find a man for the evening. Someone low-key, someone I'd hooked up with in the past, someone hot . . . I continued to mentally list traits as I scrolled through name after name. No one in A, nobody in town in D, don't know anyone in the I's . . . I kept scrolling until I hit Z. I scrolled back up in disbelief. Shit! Had I been so out of the game that I had literally had no game anymore? Was there seriously not a single man in my phone that I could booty-call? I mean, I know I was engaged and occupied, but that's over now. FML.

Despite being a little let down that I couldn't find a single man to cure my loneliness, the fact that I survived the night feels like progress. I had built up so much anxiety about going out in public for the first time as a single girl, and at the end of the day (or should I say night?) nobody even noticed.

Ordinarily, it sucks to think nobody cares about you. But when it comes to a breakup, it's a welcome relief. It reminds you that the sun doesn't rise and set on your ass. The fact that my breakup wasn't the forefront thing on everyone's mind proves just how ordinary I am. I remember having this same realization when it came to breaking up with all the men from my show. Having to dump them was the hardest thing I'd ever done. I was so worried about hurting them, so insecure about having the power to look someone in the eyes and tell them I didn't want them. It was hell. The guilt lingered with me for months and months after the show wrapped. And it didn't abate until I finally saw some of the men while on a trip with Number Twenty-Six to L.A.

As we sat around the bar, there was the immediate awkwardness that one would expect when seeing their exes—let alone seeing five or six of them at the same time! Finally, after several whiskey shots had been slung, I was buzzed enough to finally blurt out how sorry I was to have dumped them. I went on and on about the guilt I felt and how I hoped I didn't ruin their lives. I was expecting forgiveness, but what I got was a heavy dose of humility.

"Are you kidding me?" one asked.

"Getting dumped on television was the best thing ever!" another chimed in.

"Do you know how many chicks we slay now?"

"I mean seriously, we pull girls who are way out of our league."

"I've become the most eligible bachelor in my city, and look at me."

I burst out laughing. Here I'd been agonizing for months over the possibility of having broken hearts and ruined lives when, all the while, they were living it up. How had I been so narcissistic?

It was easy to get caught up in myself throughout the journey to find love on television, considering the entire experience revolved around me, from the twenty-five men competing for my attention, to daily hair, makeup, and wardrobe styling. I chose who I went on dates with, who stayed, and who left. Everything was about me and, despite being the baby of the family, I'd never had that type of undivided attention in my life. I didn't think I'd become self-centered, but seeing how delusional I was about the impact I'd had on the men's lives makes me wonder if maybe subconsciously I had drunk my own Kool-Aid. The more we laughed about the entire situation, the more I could feel my conscience shedding chunks of guilt. My former suitors' lives actually were better than mine! They were single but happy. And though I had served them with walking papers, they had served me a heaping slice of humble pie.

And last night's outing did the same. It made me realize that

I've been so consumed in the world of my breakup that I thought everyone else was consumed in it too. When really, they've got their own lives to live.

None of us are the first people to go through a breakup, and we certainly aren't the last. We've all got a past, and a present, but we've all got a future too. And I guarantee you, you won't like your future if you spend it sitting at home alone. So, do yourself a favor and take a night out and leave the baggage behind. You don't have to necessarily jump back into the dating game, but at least force yourself to get back in the game of life. Be the fun girl you used to be, who can sip wine with her friends, in public, instead of curled up in bed. Throw on some makeup and heels and even if just for a night, get back to living instead of just existing.

Lesson learned: *Grab your girls, get dolled up, and get over yourself. Everyone else has.*

DAY 38. 6:11 P.M.

Cupid Is Stupid

Despite having no viable booty-call candidates, I think my night out has put me on the path to reclaiming my life. That is until this morning, when I wake up to a calendar alert on my phone reminding me that Valentine's Day is in less than two weeks and I have no Valentine. I must have set this calendar alert back when I was in love, because why else would I have alerted myself two weeks before?

Dammit, I really thought 2015 was going to be my year. Last year was quite the whirlwind, but it was all worth it because it led me to this year, where I was supposed to get married, start a new life, and most important, not have to spend Valentine's Day alone. And with the dreaded holiday approaching, I wonder if I will ever have a Valentine again. Or am I going to be the single girl whose girlfriends force their kids to make Valentine's Day cards for "Auntie Andi" because they feel sorry for Mommy's only single friend?

This blows. I've never really been a fan of holidays. If you ask me, they're anticlimactic, overrated, and basically a way for retailers to prey on cheery nostalgic consumers. The only reason I celebrate a holiday is so I don't feel like a loser for not celebrating. And Valentine's Day has got to be the worst of them all. Holidays like this just seem to remind us single girls that we are, well, single. We get it! We don't need a special fucking day to remind us! All Valentine's Day really is, is a judgmental holiday that lumps every human being into one of three categories.

Category 1: The lovebirds. *These are the women in relationships that use this day to brag to the world about the fact that they are in love. They post pictures during the day of the beautiful flowers they received at work from their "sugar bear sweetheart." Then they post another picture of their shitty price-fixed dinner followed by yet another vomit-worthy post at night of them kissing their "amazing" boyfriend. The caption usually reads something to the effect of "Thank you to my amazing boyfriend for being my better half today and every day. Thanks for making this #ValentinesDay one I'll never forget. #love #blessed #Cupid." Gag me! These people suck because they're happy, they know it, and they make sure we all know it too.*

Category 2: The drunks. *These are the single ladies who are so distraught by their status that they head to the bar, even if it's Tuesday, to celebrate Valentine's Day by hating on Valentine's Day. These are the girls who get plastered, look around the bar to see other single ladies, and feel better knowing they are not the only ones. They toast to their friends over kamikaze shots and dance to Beyoncé's "Single*

Ladies" a minimum of four times in one evening. They end up getting drunk, then screwing someone they think is a 7 and wake up to the reality that he is actually a 4. They're usually late for work the next morning.

Category 3: The ice cream tubbers. *These are the depressed women who don't want to be seen in public on Valentine's Day because that would mean the jig is up. (That, or they are just responsible employees who know the Wednesday after Valentine's Day is not a recognized federal holiday.) Instead of drowning their sorrows at a bar, they sit at home drinking wine with their two boyfriends, Ben & Jerry. These women indulge in not just food but also self-pity the entire night. Though they wake up on time for work the next morning, they're still single.*

I can easily eliminate category 1 because that whole happily-in-love ship has clearly sailed. So basically my options are to be either the drunk, desolate bar rat or the drunk, desolate girlfriend of Ben & Jerry. Neither sounds particularly appealing, nor do they fall within Operation Be Mother-Effing Awesome.

As I'm debating, I get another alert on my phone. Luckily this one isn't reminding me of the worst day of the year but is a text from my hot, blonde, single friend Christy, whom I also met on my first journey to find love.

"What are you doing for Valentine's Day?" I text her back, completely ignoring the subject of her original message.

CHRISTY: Nothing. I'll be in Chicago, single and drunk.
ME: I'm coming.

CHRISTY: Do it!

ME: I'm serious. Do I fly into Midway or O'Hare?

CHRISTY: Midway.

ME: Done. See you on the 13th!

CHRISTY: Can't freakin' wait!

And just like that I've booked a flight to Chicago. Hey, if I can't get ass in Atlanta, maybe I can get some in Chi-Town.

I thank the love gods above that at least I don't have to be alone on Valentine's Day. That's one thing I've really been grateful for during this breakup, friendships. Maybe it's that I'm on my period and feeling extra emotional right now, but I can't help getting sappy when I think about how supportive, reliable, attentive, and downright loving my friends have been in these tumultuous past few weeks.

It's interesting how sometimes it takes a tragedy, whether it's death, divorce, or something as simple as a bad day, to see who your true friends are. My breakup is no different. Some of my friendships have been strengthened over the past weeks, while others have been exposed as flimsy. I've certainly lost some friends now that I'm no longer one half of a pseudofamous couple, but I guess those people were never really my friends in the first place.

It's become more apparent than ever who my real friends are. They are the ones who ask, "How are you?" rather than "OMG! What happened?" They love me unconditionally, even when I can't do anything for them. They are what I like to call my "bury-the-body friends." You know the type, we all have them—the ones you call in the middle of the night and say, "Oops, I did something bad, and he's in my trunk." And all they ask is, "Where are the shovels?" and "How far down are we digging?" I'm realizing that no matter how alone I feel in this world, I'm not. I have friends and family whom I love and who love me back, and who save me from my own self-destruction. I get emotional thinking about it. I don't deserve such love and support, yet I am indescribably thankful for it. It's the only way I've managed to make it to this point, because let's be honest, there's no chance in hell I'd make it if it were up to me alone.

Ironically, many of the friends that I've counted on in these past few weeks are competitors from my first "journey to find love." I know it sounds weird. Everyone thinks it's bizarre that women can come out of a situation where they are all dating the same man and actually be legitimate friends in the end, but it's not as complicated as it sounds. First of all, you're sharing an unbelievably weird, cringe-worthy, emotional, and yet awesome experience. It's like going to study abroad with a group and you come back all best friends because you shared experiences that nobody else did. You have stories, memories, inside jokes that only you and the people you were with could ever understand. You speak your own secret language. It was that way when the show ended, and it's that way even now that my relationship has ended. Forget the passport stamps, first-class flights, helicopter rides, and private concerts—those are just memories. My friends are still around, and never have they been more present than right now.

And I know every season someone says, "I didn't come on the show to make friends"—usually the villain in the house, who says that only because she didn't make friends—but it's not an either-or thing. Granted, the girls from my season and I got pretty lucky considering none of us fell in love, except Nikki. But as time went on, she realized what the rest of us had already known, that although she may have "won" our season, in the long run, she ultimately "lost" when she was picked by such a tool. Oh, shit—I wonder if my friends are thinking the same thing about me right now.

In all seriousness, I consider myself one lucky girl to have the friends I do. A friend like Kelly, who opened not only her home to me but her heart as well. How many people can say they have a friend who without hesitation tells you to come over and stay as long as you need, without asking anything in return? Where would I have gone that night had it not been for Kelly? I don't know, but I don't even have to think about it, because I have a friend like her.

And a friend like Nikki, who stayed on the phone with me anytime I needed her, even if it was in the wee hours of the morning and she had just finished a twelve-hour nursing shift, telling me everything was going to be all right. And friends like Sarah, Leslie, and Caroline, who signed me up for the damn show in the first place—who are now forever indebted to me considering how this fiasco turned out—who on a moment's notice drop everything they're doing just to talk to me.

And a friend like my mom, my "person," as I like to call her, who tells me every day how much she loves me. Who helped me gather my stuff from my old apartment. Who holds back tears in a show of strength as she hugs and consoles me as only a mother can.

It's not lost upon me that all my friends literally saved me. Their overwhelming kindness and generosity inspire me to be better myself—a better friend, a better daughter, and a better person. When my girlfriends call and need a sympathetic ear, I think about all the times I blabbed on and on to them, and now I just quit my bitching and start listening. Or when I don't feel like answering when my mom calls because I just talked to her an hour ago, I remember how she was there for me through every step, and I pick up. And I will continue to do so.

If you'd asked me during the early days of my breakup what I would gain from all of this, never would I have thought it would be recognizing the simple yet impactful meaning of friendships. The more I think about those nourishing, positive relationships in my life, the less I think about the negative one that brought me to this realization in the first place. There are so many more positive things in this world that wash away the negative—sometimes I guess you just have to be willing to open your eyes and see them.

Lesson Learned: *Think about the positive relationships that surround you, not the negative one that you escaped from.*

DAY 42. 3:00 P.M.

The Interview

I've just boarded a flight back to Atlanta from Los Angeles, when I am greeted by the familiar blonde flight attendant with a friendly, "Hey, girl!"

Five minutes after I take my seat, she brings me a screwdriver.

"You still like screwdrivers, right?"

"Yes. Perfect. Thank you."

"I made this one a little light for you, we'll make them stronger as we go."

"We know the drill, don't we?" I chuckle and she laughs back.

I'm buckled into my seat for what feels like the hundredth time in the past year. I've made this same cross-country voyage from Atlanta to Los Angeles and back enough times to achieve Platinum Status on Delta and be deemed a "regular" among the attendants. Come to think of it, I should have gotten some damn wings out of it, but, hey, at least they're prompt and generous in their vodka pours. I've gotten into quite the routine with all the traveling I've done. I start by picking the big planes with the pods and flat beds (thanks to networks with deep pockets flying me first class). When I board the plane, I have exactly two screwdrivers before the meal is served, at which point I switch to a glass of red wine before polishing off a few packs of Biscoff cookies while I watch either *The Hunger Games* or *Frozen.*

Unlike most of the previous flights, this one feels different. I feel lighter, calmer, and though the screwdriver has me slightly buzzed, I know the feeling that has come over me is a result of what I did yesterday. I purged—figuratively, not literally. I should clarify: Yesterday I purged my heart by doing my first sit-down interview since my breakup.

Despite my family and a handful of my closest friends knowing the gist of why my engagement ended, there's been so much that I have kept to myself. My feelings have been bubbling up inside me like carbonation in a bottle, shaken and ready to explode at any point. I may have burned every memory of my relationship, but outside spectators don't know that, and thus the questions seem to become more plentiful by the day. Every time I check an email, a trashy tabloid request awaits me. And though I wasn't interested in dishing the dirt on my breakup, especially not to reporters whose sole job is to twist people's words, I've been searching for a way to answer the persistent questions. It had become clear that my silence wasn't going to make the storm pass, and so long as the dark cloud of everyone's curiosity hung above me, I'd never be left alone.

And then, a few days ago, I found my opening, when I got a call that both startled and intrigued me. It was from my producer asking if I would be interested in doing a sit-down interview with the host of our show, Chris, who had also become a close friend of mine. He explained that it would be whatever I wanted it to be and would take place in Los Angeles, where this entire adventure/shitshow/life maker/life breaker all started. My initial reaction was similar to when I was asked to do the show in the first place, "Hell to the no." But the more we talked about it, the more I began to wonder if this was the way out of the slump I was in.

I thought about it, and thought about it, and thought about it some more until finally deciding I needed to bite the bullet, rip off the Band-Aid, splurge on new stilettos, and pray I don't get hit with an overdraft fee. Basically, I needed to suck it up and get the hell over all of this because clearly whatever I'd been doing hasn't worked (at least not fast enough) and my jeans that now give me six ass cheeks and are missing the button are proof. I figured if this was the way to close the chapter titled "My Disastrous Breakup," at least I was going to do it with people I knew, people who had seen it all and in a setting in which I'd become weirdly comfortable.

Within twenty-four hours, I was booked on a nonrefundable round-trip flight from Atlanta to Los Angeles. I had debated whether to tell Number Twenty-Six, whom I hadn't spoken to in at least a week. Regressing back to my teen years, I decided to go the better-to-ask-for-forgiveness-than-permission route and keep my plans to myself. Truth be told, I was scared shitless of what his reaction would be, as well as all but certain he'd go on a Twitter rant or something equally embarrassing and damaging. The bitter part of my hardened soul didn't care if he embarrassed himself for the world to see, but my sad broken heart oddly did. Though I didn't know what questions I'd be asked, I knew I wasn't going to divulge the real and disturbing reasons our relationship had spiraled from enviable to torture so quickly. My love for him kept me from wanting to hurt him, but I couldn't bear my own pain any longer. I needed closure.

The morning of the interview, I took a deep breath as I exited the sedan and entered Hartsfield-Jackson Airport. I rolled my suitcase up to the check-in counter, where I was greeted by the familiar faces of the employees I'd come to see more often than some of my friends.

"Hello, Ms. Dorfman. Where are we flying to today?" said Anne, the sweet middle-aged blonde and self-proclaimed fanatic of the show.

"L.A."

"All checked in. By the way, I'm sorry about the breakup. So sad."

As I walked to the security checkpoint, I didn't dread taking off my shoes to reveal my mismatched socks, or having to remove my laptop from my carry-on, or getting my larger-than-three-ounce perfume confiscated. Those were small inconveniences compared to the panic I felt about what was wrapped in an envelope and zipped in the small inner pocket of my purse—my treasured eighty-some-odd-thousand-dollar engagement ring. That was the catch with the interview; I wasn't just going to give up the details of my split, I was also going to give up my engagement ring.

I placed my belongings on the belt, all the while thinking, *God, if I have to have my purse hand-checked and they ask about this ring, I am going to have a TMZ-worthy breakdown in the middle of the world's busiest airport.* With a pounding heart, I looked suspicious as I anxiously waited for my purse to come out on the other side of the belt. With no purse check, and thankfully no meltdown, I headed toward the gate. I boarded the plane and was quickly greeted by the familiar face of Kate, a tall strawberry-blonde flight attendant who always seemed to be in a perky mood.

"Welcome aboard, Ms. Dorfman!"

"Thank you, Kate!" I gave her a hug. She was one of my favorite flight attendants and I always got excited when she was on my plane because she (a) made the best screwdrivers, (b) dated a super-hot young European guy and always showed me shirtless photos of him, and (3) always gave me an extra serving of dessert, which luckily was the Belgian chocolate gelato. I figured if ever a day to need two scoops, this was it.

Throughout the flight I continued to check the inner pouch of my purse to ensure that the ring, which was worth more than my life, was still there. I even went so far as to take my purse with me to the bathroom, which in hindsight probably looked extremely sketchy. The plane touched down in Los Angeles and, disheveled and tired, I made my way to the baggage claim, where a driver waited to take me to the interview. I arrived at a hotel and was greeted by my producer with a comforting fatherly hug. As we talked about the logistics of the night's interview, he looked at me with agonized eyes and asked for the ring back. I dug out the envelope, took one last look at the sparkler I had admired every time I looked down at my hand, and placed it in his open palm. I waited to feel something, perhaps sorrow or resentment or even humiliation, but I felt absolutely nothing. It was as if the ring had become a burdensome reminder of a love that was no longer there. The sentiment was gone, and so was its beauty.

During the few hours of getting my hair and makeup done, I wondered what questions would be asked and what my responses would be. Would I cry, or would I be consumed with anger and bitterness? How should I respond to the tough questions I haven't been ready to face in private, let alone in front of cameras? I needed advice from someone I trusted. I needed to call my mom.

"Just be honest about your feelings," she suggested.

Yeah, right. Honesty would mean I call him an asshole who called me a bitch among other things, tell the world I'd been drowning my endless tears with wine, and that I made the biggest mistake of my life, all of which would confirm the fact that even after a month, I'm still a bit of a mess. No, thanks.

"I will. Thanks, Mom, love you," I lied.

It was time for the interview. I arrived at the host's house. The last time I'd been there was under even worse circumstances if you can believe that. It was the night when I, along with the final four men of my season, sat on the couch and were told of the death of one of our cast mates. It was a horrible kind of night, life-changing. This house was forever filled with sadness as far as I was concerned. As I walk into the kitchen to grab a glass of water, I had yet another vivid flashback of that evening—the conversation I had with Number Twenty-Six following the news. I'd found him alone perched on the kitchen counter processing the tragic blow we'd just been dealt. I leaned against the adjacent counter and asked if he was okay, to which he responded with a shrug. Nobody was okay in that moment, but it was the only thing I could think to say. There we were, just the two of us, with no cameras or microphones, when he suddenly looked me straight in the eyes and said, "Let's just leave. Let's be done with this, go home and start our lives together in Atlanta."

I looked at him, completely speechless and terrified that the next word out of my mouth would be, "Yes." Images of us playing with his dog in the yard, cooking dinner, going to movies, and living happily ever after flashed in my mind. My heart wanted to accept his invitation and ride off into the sunset, but my head knew I had to keep going. Despite my intense yearning to be with

Number Twenty-Six for the rest of my life, I had to see this "journey" through to the end.

As I stood in that same kitchen once again, I wondered if he had been right. If we had left it all behind and just gone back to Atlanta that evening, would things have been different between us? Would we still be together if I had just said yes? I guess I'll never know. At this point, nothing could change the fact that I was back in this city, in this house, about to do what I hoped would be my final interview and get the closure I so desperately needed.

A small microphone was placed on me, and I took my seat in the living room across from Chris. Cameras and producers crowded every available space, which made the once mild room uncomfortably hot. A curious silence permeated the air as everyone, including myself, eagerly waited to see what the next thirty minutes would bring.

"How are you?" Chris asked.

I opened my mouth to respond with the answer I had rehearsed, but when I tried to say, "I'm doing all right, given the circumstances," the words refused to come out. Instead, my jaw began to ache. I knew the tears were imminent. I stared blankly in an attempt to delay the inevitable, but I was no match for them. The breakdown had begun.

During the interview, everything I thought I'd say seemed to vanish from my memory. My heart ached and I didn't have the strength to hide it anymore. I felt like a failure, an idiot, and an emotional basket case. I felt raw. There I was at the lowest point of my life and to make matters worse, I was admitting it to the world. After thirty minutes of questions and more tears, the interview was finally over. I don't remember what I said and, to be honest, I don't think I want to watch the interview, which will air next week. All I remember is standing up to exit the room, taking off my microphone, and feeling something I hadn't felt in eighteen months since this journey first began. It wasn't sadness or anger. It was relief.

Lesson learned: *The truth shall set you free.*

DAY 44. 7:43 P.M.

If I Show Up Dead, Tell the Cops He Did It

I told Number Twenty-Six about my interview today. Guess how he felt about it? Two words: NOT HAPPY. I thought about not telling him at all, considering the bad blood between us. But then I put myself in his shoes and imagined what it would feel like to find out about what I'm sure will be promoted as a "jaw-dropping, bombshell, tell-all" interview, through a commercial or on the Internet versus from me. Yes, as much as I hate my ex, I hate being a cold-hearted callous bitch even more. Bummer! So, I bit the bullet and sent him a text telling him I did an interview regarding our breakup and that he had nothing to worry about. Unsurprisingly, no reassurance was enough to appease his anger. Instead it was just "How could you do that to me?" and "What a betrayal."

I wanted to say, "How could *I* do that to *you*? Get the fuck over yourself!" I mean, I am so sick of everything being about this man. My relationship felt like it was all about him, my breakup has felt like it's all about him, and now he's making *my* interview for *my* show all about him too? Yes, I picked him and he picked me, but still, it was my show to begin with and if I wanted some closure for *myself* by going back to it, then so be it.

That was one of the many red flags in our relationship: It became so much about *him* and *us* that I lost *me* along the way. I don't blame Number Twenty-Six for this, I actually blame myself. I laid the groundwork in the beginning by catering to him and taking care of his needs like a Southern woman is taught to do. The truth is, I was so happy to be someone's fiancée that my world revolved around him. And not only did my world revolve around my relationship, but my livelihood did as well. The show had afforded us ample opportunities in the form of public appearances, sponsorships, or hosting charity events. But we were a package deal—there was no me without him or him without me. We were living our lives as a couple, both socially and professionally. And now? I was no longer me, I was one half of a couple.

Even through both seasons of the show, I'd done well in maintaining my identity. I had started the first journey secure with being a twenty-six-year-old walking contradiction, still young enough to be naïve but mature enough to embrace the contentment of knowing who I was deep down. And despite having been plucked from a normal life and thrown into a foreign world full of cameras, fancy hotels, and manipulation, I found a way to stick to my beliefs and be myself, for better or worse. Perhaps it was a heightened awareness of my surroundings, or maybe just plain luck, but I learned very quickly that the moment anyone showed even the slightest sign of weakness, he or she was a goner.

I knew when I embarked on all of this that my life would change at least a little, and as the exposure grew, so would the magnitude of this change. But it was all supposed to be for the better; my *life* was supposed to change, not *me*. I resented the change, because I wasn't happy, and felt like I had to pretend to be for the sake of my new identity.

What people didn't know was that after two shows, I had become a twenty-seven-year-old woman who walked on eggshells in her own home. What they didn't know is I was trapped with someone who, in my opinion, often behaved like an emotional abuser. Yes, I said it, and I'm not taking it back. He was good-looking, with an electric smile and the ability to charm anyone, and his affection in public made people believe that he was a loving partner, but by the end of our relationship, it was just a mask covering the control he exerted in private. He had an uncanny way of manipulating situations and conversations to make me feel like the worst person in the world. In his own words, I was not only selfish and unappreciative, but the "most miserable person he'd ever met." If we didn't get invited to a red-carpet event, he'd say it was "because of my actions with Number Twenty-Five." If I talked to another man, I was a "whore." If I disagreed, I was "argumentative." If I defied him, I was a "bitch."

The more he said these things to me, the more detached I grew from myself. I stopped fighting back and instead started not only accepting his words, but actually believing them. And in doing so, I became an equally shitty person. Though I didn't take it to his level, I wasn't nice to him either. I wasn't happy around him, I wasn't supportive and adoring. I was resentful. And it extended beyond him. My parents and friends could see the change and often told me I looked stressed or tired. I'd snap at the slightest critique, which proved that not only was I someone different, but I was actually morphing into Number Twenty-Six. I operated at only two levels: silent or angry. I was either empty or mad, and no amount of makeup, gowns, photo ops, or public displays of affection could change it. I had let my relationship turn me into a person I didn't like.

Ironically, it wasn't what he said to me that made me truly realize this, but rather words that came out of my own mouth. You know how there are certain conversations in life that you never forget? The kind you remember exactly where you were, who you were with, and what you were doing when it happened?

Mine happened at the mall (no surprise there) on a Wednesday, when I was desperately on the hunt for a dress to wear for the live premiere of the current season of the show in Los Angeles, which was only two days away. Everyone was going to be there, including us—who as far as the viewers were concerned, we were still a happy couple planning our wedding. Frantically combing through the racks at Bloomingdale's, I found myself pulling anything that was in my size, no matter how ugly or expensive it was. The saleswoman started a dressing room for me as I continued my search, and then my phone rang. It was Nikki.

"Hold on, walking into a fitting room."

I found my dressing room marked with an ugly dress that I had picked out on the outside of the door and entered to find a plethora of dresses hung neatly by the saleswoman.

"Okay, I'm back, sorry—shopping for a stupid dress for this premiere."

We gabbed about how excited we were to be seeing each other in a few days and about what Nikki was wearing, since she already had a dress picked out. As I tried on one ill-fitting dress after another, I unloaded to her about a fight I had just had with Number Twenty-Six.

I remember standing there in the dressing room examining each dress and bitching to Nikki about how fat I was, how awful the dresses were, and how shitty my relationship was, when I said something so surprising that it jarred even myself.

"Well . . . if I show up dead, tell the cops he did it."

Immediately after saying it, I could see in the mirror my oh-shit-did-I-just-say-that? face and I quickly giggled in an attempt to sweep it under the rug, but Nikki knew me too well to leave it at that.

"What did you just say?"

"I said if I show up dead, tell the cops he did it." I gasped and covered my mouth. Shit, I said it again! "No, I'm just kidding, I know he would never actually kill me."

I quickly changed the subject as I continued trying on ugly dresses and asked her what she was wearing to the premiere, despite the fact that she had already told me. We gabbed for a few more minutes until she had to go to work. I don't even know what we talked about, because to be honest, I didn't hear a single thing she said. I was still in shock at my own word-vomit.

I was baffled about why I'd said that—and twice. There was never any type of physical abuse in our relationship. Emotional, yes, verbal, absolutely, but it never got physical, nor did I ever think it would. Partially because he knew that if he did, my dad would finally get the chance to dust off his shotgun and use the three-acre plot of land in the middle of Bumblefuck, Georgia, he had bought "just in case."

But still, I had actually just said to my best friend, "If I turn up dead, tell the cops he did it." Where was this coming from? Even in jest, I'd never said anything like that before. Had I really reached the point of leaving clues from my grave?

It was the fact that I didn't take it back that really cut me deep. That's the kind of stuff crazy women say about their crazy boyfriends. Had I become that crazy woman? Had he become that crazy man?

There I was in a brightly lit dressing room, barefoot, wearing a red cocktail dress, one hand clamping the back as I stood on tiptoe and envisioned walking the red carpet. I was paralyzed when I gazed into the mirror and saw a pair of brown eyes belonging to a woman I didn't recognize. The eyes looked weak, hopeless, completely lost. There, in the mirror, was a woman so far gone she was joking about her own murder. They were the eyes of a stranger, yet they belonged to me. They belonged to the woman I had become. It was the first time I had truly seen this woman, and I *never* wanted to see her again.

This became the single most vivid moment of my relationship. I realized just how much of myself I had lost in the past nine months. I was trapped in a relationship that made me feel utterly worthless and dismally defeated. I had experienced so many moments where I knew in my heart that the life I was living was unhealthy, but it took standing in a dressing room and joking about my own death for me to truly hit rock bottom.

How had I become this woman? I used to be a woman who didn't take shit from anyone, let alone a man, and who certainly didn't feel subordinate. No, once upon a time I was sassy yet considerate, abrasive yet understanding, assertive yet self-deprecating, and most of all, just me.

I'd seen this scenario play out a thousand times during my days as an attorney—time and time again when I'd walk into a courtroom and see women with broken bones and bruised faces standing next to their partners. They'd tell the judge it was all a misunderstanding, but the proof was written on their faces—in black and blue. Same story, every time, and no matter how routine it became, I'd watch in utter disbelief. *How the hell do these women stay in these relationships?* I wondered. I wasn't naïve. I understood perfectly why gangbangers killed rivals and dope dealers robbed convenience stores, but I couldn't get past the mystery of why these women stayed with their abusers. To cope with the disappointment and disbelief, I'd make excuses for them: They don't have a job so they stay with their abuser for stability, they don't know any better, or they have no way out. But no matter how much I justified their decisions to stay, I never fully comprehended them until I was forced to ask the very same question of myself.

I wasn't being beaten and battered like these women, but I was staying in a relationship that I knew was lethal. Unlike them, I had a way out, but just like them, I stayed. Why? Was it because I believed there was a chance that we would wake up one day and be transported in time back to the days of happiness? Our pure and undeniable love had gone from being a blessing to a curse. It attached strings to me that even the sharpest scissors couldn't cut. Until now.

Because now I am free. We all are. Yes, shitty things have happened to all of us in the past. We've put up with things we never should have, we did things we wish we hadn't, but we don't have to be damaged because of it. Not anymore at least. What's the point in being ruined by something as minor as a man? It does no good, not for you, not for your future. I always wondered why people come out of relationships and say they are "damaged." I guess the prime example I always think of is cheating. I've seen it so much with my girlfriends, the typical douche bag who can't keep his pants on, goes out and hooks up with someone, leading to the demise of the relationship. And you know what my girlfriends say? (Other than "he's an asshole.") They say, "I'll never be able to trust anyone ever again." Same goes with heartbreak—we all say, "I'll never be able to love again." I know I've said it during this breakup, probably a dozen times or so.

But here's the thing, what good comes out of being damaged? So an asshole cheated on you, or broke your heart. Are you going to let that affect you for the rest of your life? Are you really going to let someone else's actions be a detriment to you? Call me narcissistic, but there is no way in hell I am going to let someone else's mishap steer me down a damaged road. If I'm going to carry baggage, it's gonna be my own. Think about it—if someone's cheated on you, or broken your heart, isn't it *their* fault? Shouldn't you only suffer from your own actions, not someone else's that you can't control. You can't control that you broke up, you can't control the feelings that you've had, you can't control who you fell in love with in the past—but you can control whether or not you're stringing them along with you. The choice is all part of your newly found independence. So repeat after me, "I will not be damaged, I will not be damaged, I will not be damaged." Say this to yourself every time you brush your teeth or wash your face. Say it in the car, say it while you grocery shop, say it all the time until you believe it.

Lesson learned: *Being damaged is a choice. So is being happy. Choose wisely.*

DAY 45. 4:25 P.M.

Running Away

In order to begin reclaiming my independence, I decided to make my very own breakup bucket list. I figure, it can't hurt to write down everything I wish I was doing instead of dealing with this breakup. I ask myself what I want to try now that I've dropped off some baggage and am free to do whatever I choose without being weighed down. I ask myself, what do I *wish* I could do . . .

THE BREAKUP BUCKET LIST

- Find a place to live
- Take a girls' trip
- Volunteer at a charity
- Learn a new language
- Lose 5 pounds
- Clean out my closet
- Take a road trip

- Get a tarot card reading
- Learn about wine
- Go to a sporting event
- Travel abroad
- Perfect my carrot cake recipe
- Watch *Game of Thrones*
- Go to the Kentucky Derby
- Visit my sister in San Diego
- Visit Nikki in Kansas City
- See Taylor Swift in concert
- Maintain shaved legs and armpits
- Try 5 new restaurants
- Move to a new city
- Make out with a hot man who's the opposite of "my type"
- Buy an expensive purse
- Learn how to sew
- Learn to forgive

In making this list, I realize a few things. First of all, damn, there's a lot of stuff I haven't done. Secondly, I hope I live a long time because this list is going to take quite a while to complete. And most importantly, I haven't even crossed off the first thing, which right now is the most important: finding a place to live.

Yes, in order to get back to living, the first step isn't finding a new man, but finding a new home. This breakup feels like a natural disaster; it has crushed my soul, made me lose faith in love, and taken with it my home, leaving me physically displaced. Well, not really, thanks to Kelly, but in my mind I am homeless. Though Kelly's house is nicer than anyplace I've ever lived in and fancier than most hotel rooms I've ever stayed in. And although she constantly tells me I can stay as long as I want, I know that I can't. Yeah, I guess you could say that I'm starting to ease into my big-girl thong, which means it's time to move out.

So I decide to check out a few apartments around town. Those that I see are nice, really nice, in fact—affordable, in superb locations, and with plenty of space for a single girl. But I just can't seem to sign on the dotted line. Even when I run out of excuses, I still can't do it. Something doesn't feel right. My reluctance gets me thinking that maybe the reason I can't commit is that I'm not supposed to be here anymore. Not in this emotional state and not in the state of Georgia. I wonder if what I really need right now is to once again ignore the self-help advice and just *run.* Run far, far away. Run to a place where my past doesn't haunt me with memories of my former relationship every time I pass a favorite restaurant. To a place that doesn't carry with it the risk of running into my ex or hearing about his wild nights out. Run somewhere away from it all.

The fact of the matter is, I have no lease, no job, and no real life plan right now. It's not fun to admit that, but when your world revolves around a relationship, and it doesn't work out, that's what happens. You find yourself lost. Yeah, it's hard, but I have to face the fact that I have no idea what I'm doing with my life and I need something to push me to figure it out, because right now, I can't do that for myself.

And thus I've begun to think about moving to a new city where I can start fresh. It's scary leaving behind not just my hometown, family, and friends, but ironically also the sad memories that this city holds for me. It's hard, but necessary.

I think about where I can go, what I can do, and who I can be. The second two are far more long-term decisions (as Kelly would say, should be dropped into the long-term buckets). And in my still somewhat frazzled state of mind, they probably shouldn't be answered right now. That leaves me with where to go.

I have always wanted to live in a big city like New York or Los Angeles, but found excuses not to. First, I wanted to stay close to home for college. Then I fell in love with law school in North Carolina. Then I passed the bar exam in Georgia, so I would stay there to practice law. The latest excuse was that Number Twenty-Six didn't want to move to a big city. The fact was that *our* home was Atlanta, and while I could dream of living in a big city, he was right, it was just a dream.

The reality was that sharing a home extracted every ounce of independence I had. Growing up, I was pretty autonomous. Though my parents were always around and hands-on, there was a part of me that liked doing stuff on my own. I joined a sorority in college and was often asked by my "sisters" if I wanted to go grocery shopping or to the gym with them, but I never obliged. The very notion of the buddy system repulsed me when it came to things I could do much more efficiently on my own. And to this day, I still feel the same way. While I love being social with others, I love my independence equally.

But living with Number Twenty-Six had changed that. The longer we lived together, the more I was desperate to be alone. Every time I returned home from running errands, or traveling, or dinner with the girls, I would find myself overcome with anxiety. I wasn't excited to walk in the door and shout, "Honey, I'm home!" but rather reluctant as I'd slowly turn the doorknob in hopes that maybe he'd be gone and I wouldn't have to account for my whereabouts. Knowing this feeling wasn't normal, I assumed it was my sense of independence that was the problem. But, normal or not, I was struggling.

It actually took a shopping spree, of all things, to make me realize just how much of myself I had lost. I remember vividly pulling into the parking space outside our home and looking over at the passenger seat to see the retail damage I'd just done. Without thinking, I reached into one of the bags, pulled out a new lacey bralette, took off my shirt, and layered the lingerie over the underwire bra I was already wearing. I reached into another bag, removed the new Rag & Bone plaid scarf, and ripped off its price tag before wrapping it around my neck. I continued pulling out various items from dozens of bags and condensing them into just two before tucking them behind the passenger seat. As I pulled the key out of the ignition, I glanced in my rearview mirror and asked myself: Who am I? Why am I hiding purchases I made with my own money in my own car like I'm a teenager hiding a handle of Mr. Boston vodka from my parents? Have I really become the type of woman I grew up despising, who was so scared of a lecture from her husband or fiancé that she is layering clothes on her body and hiding shopping bags?

That was then. Now I don't have to feel that burden anymore. I'm single, and with that my dream of living happily ever after is gone, but it's left room for the dream of a big-city life to swoop in. Silver lining, perhaps? Not gonna lie, it would be the ultimate fuck-you to Number Twenty-Six, right? Although it might also end up biting me and my bank account in the ass. Oh, well, I can deal with those details later. For now, I'm just dreaming about where I could go. Hmmm . . .

1. **LOS ANGELES**

   Pros: *Sunny days all year round, sandals, maxi dresses*

   Cons: *The traffic, "industry" people*

2. **CHICAGO**

   Pros: *City life, summers, which I hear are to die for*

   Cons: *Winters, proximity to Number Twenty-Five*

3. **AUSTIN**

   Pros: *Bring on the weirdness, the culture, the weather, the hot cowboys*

   Cons: *Who the hell do I know who lives in Austin? What the hell would I do there? Why did I even write this down?*

4. **NEW YORK**

   Pros: *Living in the best city on earth, pretending to be Carrie Bradshaw, the ultimate fuck-you*

   Cons: *Living in a shoebox, getting eaten alive*

Making this bucket list and a list of places to live makes me feel something I haven't felt in months—motivated. It's the first thing I'm actually excited about. Life in a new city! Though it's still just a dream, I can at least envision it coming true. What if, at the end of the day, it wasn't a man or the search for love, or even my little Operation Revenge that was the key to my happiness. What if it's all just a bunch of signs pointing me in the right direction to my final destination?

Now all I've got to do is follow through with these genius

ideas. Anywho, Valentine's Day weekend is here, which means I'm off to Chicago in the morning, so hey, who knows, maybe I'll just stay there for life.

Stay tuned . . .

Lesson learned: *Take advantage of having nothing and no one tying you down.*

DAY 48. 1:40 P.M.

Chi-Town and the Ex

I've just gotten home from Chicago and I might as well have taken acid (which I've never done in my life) because that was quite a trip. It was my first time in Chicago, and like an idiot, I chose to go in the middle of winter. Let me tell you, people are not lying when they say the cold is effing brutal there. But sitting at home alone on Valentine's Day was out of the question, so I probably would have gone to Siberia just to avoid feeling any more like a loser than I already do. But it wasn't the cold that made it a shitshow, it was Number Twenty-Five.

After taking me to my first-ever hockey game, Christy and I decide to meet her friends at a local bar. No big deal, right? In a dimly lit dive bar with Maroon 5's "Sugar" blaring in the background, I found myself on my second vodka soda of the night, when all of a sudden, who walks in the front door with a gaggle of his bros? Drum roll please . . . the asshole himself, Number Twenty-Five. I swear, this guy is like a case of herpes that won't go away. Just when you think the agony is over, there's another flare-up. (Not that I know from personal experience, mind you, but it's such a fitting analogy that I can't resist.)

Before you judge my harsh name calling, let me just say, I feel as though I have good reason to call him an asshole. He did, after all, ruin what was supposed to be one of the happiest nights of my life. It was the live finale, which meant it was time for the world to finally know that I was happily engaged to Number Twenty-Six and very much in love. We'd been living our relationship in secrecy for two months, and I couldn't wait for everyone to know that I had chosen him. But, before that could happen, I had to jump one last hurdle: a live televised conversation with the last man I dumped, Number Twenty-Five. We hadn't spoken since the day I said goodbye to him in the Dominican Republic, and I had no idea what he would say, though normally, the runner-up cries a little bit, asks why it didn't work out, gets his closure and leaves single but with the sympathy of millions of viewers. And while I hoped this would be the way it went down, something in my gut warned me I wouldn't be so lucky.

Number Twenty-Five was the designated villain of my season, whom nobody really cared for, so I didn't expect him to go down without a fight. Plus, he had tried multiple times to confront me prior to this live finale, including once when I was with my then fiancé in Mexico on one of our secret rendezvous and once when he "unexpectedly" showed up at the reunion he wasn't invited to. Each instance had been on camera and felt like an ambush, thus I declined to speak with him, knowing this time would come and there'd be no shying away from a long overdue confrontation.

As I walked onstage to greet him, a wicked stench pervaded the room. I gave him an emotionless hug and sat on the couch next to him. I could instantly see in his eyes that he meant business, and I braced for impact.

Instead of the typical "what went wrong" question, he began mumbling. And then there was a long pause. I knew something bad was coming, but I couldn't stop it. It was like I could see the car stopped ahead of me, but my foot just wouldn't hit the brake. I couldn't stop what was coming, I was frozen. And that's when he asked, on live television, "Why would you make love to me if you weren't in love with me?"

The audience gasped. My heart stopped. Everyone was stunned. The bomb had been dropped and no one had time to make it safely to the bunker. This motherfucker! Really? You want to confirm to the world what they probably already know, which is that two consenting adults who had been dating for seven weeks spent the night together without any cameras and whaddaya know, had sex? Not that I cared that people knew I wasn't a virgin, but I could have done without my grandmother, and more importantly my father and all of his golf buddies, having it waved in front of their noses. But it was, in my opinion, a subject that shouldn't have been talked about so publicly without the other's consent.

Oh, and to not only confirm we had sex, but call it "making love?" Every part of me wanted to go all Georgia girl cray on his ass and fire back with some snarky response like, "Oh really? Is that what you're calling it now, because I'm pretty sure you called it 'fucking' when you were on top of me." But I didn't. Instead, I held back for one reason and one reason only: my fiancé.

Embarrassment aside, I couldn't help feel an overwhelming sense of relief that I had told Number Twenty-Six the truth prior to this. I knew we had gotten through it and vowed never to bring it up again, but I didn't know this live revelation would erase all of that progress instantly.

When the cameras went away, it was as if Twenty-Six's humiliation began to manifest itself in outbursts and a hatred for the show we once adored as the documentation of our love story. In an instant, my fiancé went from a disappointed but accepting partner to a humiliated and emasculated one, all because of one man's revelation. The fact that now people knew about my past had somehow changed his outlook on it, even though the facts hadn't changed. It didn't matter that he was the only man I had said I loved, the only man I let pick out an engagement ring, and the only man who made it to that final proposal day. All that seemed to matter now was that he was the fiancé of a girl who had once had sex with another man. In a moment that was supposed to be filled with bliss and freedom, that one nasty question triggered a downward spiral that would end a relationship.

According to him, my indiscretion had ruined the entire experience for him. Whether it was an offhand comment telling me we were no longer a "marketable" couple, not trusting me when talking to another man, or flinging the word "whore" in my direction, he always made sure that I never forgot what I had done and the damage it had caused him. Though the facts hadn't changed, the fact that people now knew changed everything and I couldn't help but wonder if Twenty-Six was more worried about his own perception than about me.

What was once just a skeleton to be locked away in a closet forever, had burst forth now that people other than the two of us knew about it, and it made itself a permanent home in our volatile relationship. My past was never going to be forgiven, much less forgotten, and it was all because of that asshole Twenty-Five.

Anyhoo, back to the asshole—where was I? So I'm at the bar, and he walks in. He's about five yards away from me, but I squint and hope that I *am* drunk and hallucinating, but no such luck. Granted, I am in his town, and he is actually friends with Christy and some of the other girls I'm with. Thus in the turf war, I guess he kind of wins.

I turn to the bartender and order emergency rations. "Straight whiskey, honey."

Shit, he's walking this way.

"You don't want another vodka soda?" she asks.

"I've changed my mind. Whiskey, neat please!"

"Are you sure?"

"Positive."

As I take a gulp of the whiskey, he's mere feet away from me and panic is setting in. He's greeting my friends and I don't know whether to get up and say hi, or shake his hand or give him a hug, or just ignore him. I decide to be cordial and say hello, but remain planted firmly on my barstool. Everyone tries to ignore the burgeoning awkwardness, but it's an impossible feat. An hour later, and he's still here! WTF? I can't take it any longer and decide to pretend to be way drunker than I unfortunately am, and convince Christy to take me home.

The next morning, I wake up next to Christy with a pounding headache. I roll over to grab the glass of water that sits on the nightstand along with my phone. It's almost noon and I have a text message from a number I don't recognize. I swipe right.

Shit! It's from Number Twenty-Five.

25: Hey! Hope you don't mind that I got your number. Just wanted to say it was good to see you last night and I would really really like to clear the air with you. I want to apologize for everything I did in person. I understand if you don't want to but it would really mean a lot if you could spare a few minutes and let me explain myself.

My headache gets worse as I read the message. Fuck, why did I come to Chicago? I decide not to respond yet, I need to eat first, then think through this mess later. Christy and I go for pizza, of course, and as we chow down, I find myself distracted by the unanswered message on my phone. I begin typing a response . . . then delete it. Type and delete. Fuck, I hope he can't see the three dots that indicate I am typing. Finally, I think I've come up with the perfect nip-it-in-the-bud response.

ME: Hey, good to see you too. Honestly, I don't know if there's anything left to say. I don't feel like holding a grudge, I'm going through a lot right now and this is kind of the last thing I'm worried about. Let's just consider it water under the bridge.

Send.

Three dots. Shit, he's responding.

25: Well, that's very kind of you. I still would like to talk to you, please, it will only be a few minutes. I can meet you or you can come over.

Come over? What the hell? This has got to be a setup . . . He's either trying to redeem himself or he's called TMZ and they're waiting outside his door ready to snap a picture of my freezing-cold ass standing in front of his apartment.

Several text exchanges later, I tell him if I am free later I will let him know. I honestly don't care what he has to say, not out of bitterness or anger but because I genuinely, flat-out do not care. But I also wonder if perhaps after one final flare-up he'll go away forever.

Hours later, Christy and I are enjoying happy hour when I get another text from him.

25: What time do you want to meet up?

God, this is getting annoying.

ME: Not sure, we are having a drink right now.
25: Where at?

I ask Christy and respond.

25: That's literally on my block.

Fuck. I should have lied, but it's not like I know where he lives. He sends me his address and I tell him I'll let him know when we're done. An hour of agony and a few drinks later, I—for some insanely stupid and ridiculous idea—agree to meet him at his place.

I arrive at his building, thankful that there are no paparazzi creeps outside, check in with the doorman under a false name, and head to the elevator. I push the button for his floor, and think, *What the FUCK am I doing?* This is perhaps one of the stupidest things I've done all year. No, not perhaps—this is *absolutely* the stupidest thing I have done. And worst of all, as I'm on what has got to be the longest elevator ride in history, I'm not wondering how the conversation will go or what he will say; I'm wondering if I'll have sex with him again.

I know, I know! That's a terrible thought, and I don't know why my mind even goes there, but it does. Having sex with him would not only take the cake as the worst idea I've had all year, but probably as the worst idea I've had in my entire life (and that's after I agreed to not one, but two reality shows). There's a *ding*, the doors slide open, and I'm on his floor. Here goes nothing but my dignity.

I knock on the door and he opens it right away. As I walk into his apartment, I feel . . . completely unimpressed. Not that it's bad—trust me, it probably costs double any rent in Atlanta—it just isn't what I was expecting when he'd gone on and on about his cosmopolitan and "sophisticated" lifestyle while we were on the show. I had envisioned high ceilings, exposed brick, a view of downtown, a bike on the wall, and contemporary artwork, but it's just a garden-variety bachelor pad. And in the shallowest of ways, being in his apartment gives me relief that the fantasy I had envisioned isn't reality. And along with the relief, it squashes any ounce of sexual attraction I might have felt.

He offers me a glass of water, which I accept, and we sit on opposite ends of the chunky leather couch.

"How are you today?" he asks.

"I'm fine, little headache." I laugh.

"Me too." He laughs back.

"So, let's just get to it."

He starts off his speech with an apology, not for his behavior but for my breakup. I annoyingly say thanks and tell him we aren't here to talk about my breakup.

"I'm sorry," he says again. "Also, I'm sorry for what I did."

He goes on to tell me that he had never planned to say on live television that we had sex and how it was a reaction to my coldness toward him. With an eye roll, I tell him I understand and half-heartedly apologize for "coming off cold." Next we get into why he decided to tell the world we had sex—or, should I say, "made love"?

"I'm just wondering why you would ask how I could make love to you when I wasn't in love with you, considering you certainly didn't call it making love at the time."

Instead of an actual explanation, he just gives me another bullshit apology. Tears well up in my eyes as I say, "I don't care if people assume we had sex, I'm not ashamed of it. But my father watches the show, my grandmother watches it—hell, your eight-year-old sister watches it. I just didn't think it was right to take a private moment and make it public without my consent. Not to mention the fact that you certainly didn't call it making love in the fantasy suite."

Seeing the hurt in my face, he tells me he was angry that he had tried to reach out to me so many times before, and he felt hurt that I refused to see him. This was true—he had, and I had refused both times and told producers that he would have his chance to talk to me at the finale. Turns out that had been a terrible idea on my part, though I think the conversation would have been the same no matter where we had it.

"I even wrote you a letter that you got at the reunion show."

"You are right, and I should have given you the chance to talk, but you never contacted me privately, it was always when the cameras were rolling, and that didn't feel genuine."

"Well, I wrote the letter in an email to the producers first."

"So you emailed the letter, and then rewrote it by hand so it could all be filmed?"

"Yeah, I guess."

"See, that's what bothers me about all of this. Everything was always on camera with you. You didn't email *me* the letter—you emailed it to a producer and not only that, you rewrote your letter by hand for a prop. So can you see how that comes off as very disingenuous?"

"Yeah, I didn't even think about it that way."

"How could you not think of it that way?"

"I don't know, I guess I just didn't."

As the conversation continued, more tears start to well up. I feel an overwhelming sense of frustration. I'm frustrated because the statement was embarrassing and unretractable, because of the effect it had on my relationship and most of all because he just doesn't seem to comprehend the consequences of his actions, and no amount of explanation or tears will change that.

"Look, I don't want to argue anymore. It's in the past. I don't have any desire for you to feel guilty about this. It happened. You say you're sorry, I say I'm sorry. We both hurt each other in different ways. And that's all there is to say."

He agrees and thanks me for forgiving him. But, it wasn't about forgiveness. Sure, I was mad at him, but I never felt like he owed me anything. Did I feel betrayed by him? Absolutely. Did I think that his revelation caused my breakup? At times. But the truth is, while what he did had a damaging effect on my relationship, *he* wasn't to blame. If it wasn't his revelation, it would have been something else down the road. God knows Number Twenty-Six always seemed to find plenty of ammo for our fights.

The conversation wraps, and I know that I am never going to trust him, never going to be friends with him, and never ever going to believe that he hadn't orchestrated the entire thing. But, I also know that I'm not going to hate him or blame him anymore. I had hurt him and he had hurt me back. Giving him closure was the right thing to do. And in all honesty, though I didn't think I needed any closure in regards to him, the conversation ends up freeing me not just from Number Twenty-Five but ironically from Number Twenty-Six. It puts both of them, along with the entire ordeal, in the past, leaving me not with a feeling of bitterness or anger or even regret, but with a feeling of peace.

I have to say, it's astonishing what closure can bring to your psyche, in life and in a breakup. You search high and low for closure so you can feel at peace, move on, and be happy again. You've suffered a massive wound, and you are ready for it to heal, so you can too. You think maybe if you can just find a bandage large enough, you can cover the bleeding wound and it will magically be fixed. But it's not that simple. Because the gaping gash of your heartbreak can't simply be bandaged up. No, in order to stop the bleeding, the wound requires stitches. Like loose ends, with each stitch you tie up, you find that the bleeding subsides a little more, until finally it stops and you can begin to recover.

Sometimes in life, you find yourself with one of these big wounds and if you want to survive, you've got to do something about it before you bleed out. But how? How do you fix heartbreak? The same way you fix a wound. You start with stitches. You tie up the loose ends; the people you've been avoiding, the unresolved issues. In my case, it was Number Twenty-Five, whom I was still blaming for part of my breakup. And you fix those little things.

And little by little, one by one, you find that the big wound starts to feel less painful, that the bleeding starts to subside, and the wound starts to become manageable. You physically feel the guilt, the anger, the regret begin to leave your body. Until you get to a point where you've tied off every hanging thread, and you're ready to finally begin to heal. . . .

Lesson learned: *A single bandage can't fix a broken heart, but a lot of stitches can.*

DAY 50. 2:10 A.M.

The Empty Proposal

Can't sleep. Again. Nikki arrived in town a few hours ago to celebrate Kelly's engagement party. She's staying here, in my bed (of course). In fact, she's snoring as I write this. Well, not snoring, but sweetly purring, I should say. A few other girls from our season are all arriving tomorrow to join in the celebration, which should make for one hell of a weekend. However, I find myself slightly nervous because I haven't seen any of them since the announcement of our breakup. I wonder if they will ask me any questions. It's not as if they don't know about my breakup—hell, the whole world knows—but isn't it funny that no matter how long it's been, there are still people you haven't personally told? It's the one instance where having a lot of friends feels like a disadvantage.

But the impending arrival of my friends and questions isn't what's keeping me up tonight. Instead, it's this weird sensation I feel. And it's all because tonight, for the first time ever, I actually watched my entire proposal.

What started off as a casual night in for Nikki, Kelly, and

myself, complete with Thai food and red wine (of course) turned rather eventful sometime between finishing off the chicken pad thai and my second glass. My phone chimed, notifying me that I'd been tagged in a Facebook video. Curious, I click it. What I see is the last thing I am expecting . . . my proposal video. It's so random that I can't help but be intrigued.

Nikki catches a glimpse of my phone, glares at me, and asks in a motherly tone, "Umm, what the hell are you doing?"

"I've never seen my entire proposal," I reply.

Despite it being filmed and viewed by millions, I have never seen the happiest day of my life. I'd seen bits and pieces, but never all of it. Sure, I witnessed it firsthand, but with all the nerves, I only remember parts of it.

"Uh, okay, but I don't think now is the time to see it for the first time."

"Why not? I'm fine."

"I know you're fine, but I don't think you should."

"I agree," chimes in Kelly. "It's pointless."

"Seriously, it's fine. I'll be fine. I want to see it."

"Totally unhealthy," warns Nikki.

"I'll open another bottle. I have a feeling you're going to need it," says Kelly, who always seems to know the right thing to do.

They both know I'm going to be stubborn and watch the damn thing. But being good friends, they are trying to protect me from the turmoil it is likely to cause. That, and their warning will allow them to say "I told you so" afterward.

And so I click the link and watch myself take that stroll down the stone pathway in my floor-length cream gown. There I am, standing nervously surrounded by flowers, waiting for Number Twenty-Six. It is exactly how I remembered it.

"How are you watching this right now?" asks Nikki.

"I'm fine. Really."

I continue watching.

His hands are gripping mine as he begins his speech, which seems memorized. It starts off with baseball and love, blah blah blah. And I have to admit, his tone is rather preachy, making the speech sound borderline cheesy. Not that it mattered. I was in love and no cheesy speech was going to change that.

When it's my turn to speak, I begin by regurgitating my own memorized speech. It starts off as rehearsed, expressing my gratitude followed by my concerns and fears when it came to him. My plan to make him sweat it out one last time works and I can see his grip on my hands slowly loosen. This was supposed to be the part where I threw a curveball and told him how much I loved him, at least according to the plan, but I've clearly forgotten the rest of my speech, so I just repeat over and over how I knew this was too good to be true. His hands begin to pull away more, and panic radiates from his eyes. *Shit, screw the speech,* I remember thinking and instead professed my undying love for him.

Life makes its way back into his eyes at the sound of those three words he had been waiting for weeks to hear me say. He drops to one knee and opens a little black box, revealing the most beautiful, round, haloed diamond ring I had ever laid eyes on, and utters the four magical words every woman dreams of hearing: "Will you marry me?"

I look so happy. I've never seen myself smile like that. I am literally watching myself be in love. Moments later the clip ends, and I put the phone down.

"Are you okay?" Nikki asks.

"Yeah . . . surprisingly, I am."

And I really am. As I watched our proposal, it was as if I was watching a stranger. I don't recognize the man who had professed his love for me as he got down on one knee and asked me to marry him. I don't recognize the smile on his face. I don't recognize the smile on mine either. It's like I don't know those two people. Instead, I'm watching the proposal of two strangers who would never have a wedding.

Ugh, that damn wedding. It was all the rage for a hot minute. Within hours of the public announcement celebrating our official engagement, people started asking about our wedding plans. *When are you going to get married? Where? Have you picked out a dress yet?* Though we had been secretly engaged for two months at that point, it had been only a hot second before everyone wanted to know the details. Part of me wanted to tell people to settle down and remind them that we had dated for only eight weeks before getting engaged, but the polite part of me smiled and said, "Hopefully soon, maybe even next spring," which was the short-lived truth.

The moment we got engaged, we started thinking about when and where we would get married. It was so obvious to us that we were going to live happily ever after that the chance of *not* making it down the aisle never crossed our minds. We had gotten engaged on May 9, which happened to fall on a Saturday the following year, and decided what better way to celebrate our love story than to get married on our anniversary.

I had been in the early giddy phases of planning our wedding between the time the show ended and our engagement was announced. I spent hours each day scouring Pinterest and various bridal websites. I was fixated on the wedding gown the most, but flowers, venues, bridesmaid dresses, and even the cake were also priorities. I remember one particular day, we were both sitting on the couch. He of course was watching sports, I of course was scrolling through wedding photos on my Pinterest app.

"What are you looking at over there?" he asked.

"Oh, nothing," I replied with the type of giggle that was a dead giveaway that I was up to something mischievous.

"Haha, what are you looking at?"

"I may or may not be looking at wedding ideas."

I didn't know what his response would be. Would he think I was getting ahead of myself? Would he freak out that I was already in planning mode despite having known each other for a total of two months?

"Awwww, I love that," he said.

"You do?"

"Yeah, I love that you are so excited to marry me that you're already planning. I think it's cute. What kind of dress are you thinking?"

Wow, definitely not the answer I was expecting! From what I hear from all my married friends, the grooms never give a rat's ass about things such as flowers and dresses. But not my man, he was ecstatic. In hindsight, I shouldn't have been all that surprised—turns out he was ecstatic not because I was planning our wedding, but because I was "excited to marry *him*."

About four months into our engagement, we actually went and looked at a wedding venue together. It was a fancy hotel that sat along a beautiful lake an hour outside of Atlanta. Posh, with sprawling green lawns, a golf course, and an infinity pool, the place was extravagant but also cozy and charming. The hotel's event planner took us on a tour of the property and showed us different options for the reception and ceremony, including a beautiful barn—which I despised. Don't get me wrong, it was gorgeous and the Southern girl in me had no qualms about getting married in a barn, but it just didn't feel right. Something was off. Our families weren't there, the excitement wasn't there, and for the first time, I feared that my heart wasn't there. Things had already begun to change, and the strain on our relationship was making me question if I was ready to spend forever with him. The excitement I once felt about getting married was fading in the harsh light of reality. That would be the only wedding venue we ever looked at.

As the days and months passed, my searches on Pinterest became scarce. Talk of our wedding was practically nonexistent by the time we hit the five-month mark. It wasn't that we deliberately avoided the topic; we just weren't ready to be married, and we knew it. By November, it was clear that the only way we were getting married was if I got knocked up (a prospect that mortified me but enthused him beyond words). Eventually, the wedding wasn't even on our radar. Our families wanted updates because even they noticed the planning had stalled. I remember telling my mom over lunch one day that I didn't think we were ready to get married yet.

"Good. I think you need to take plenty of time and make sure this is right for you," she said.

This statement kind of caught me off guard, and though I know she meant it kindly, concern was plastered across her entire face like a bad spray tan. She wasn't the only one concerned. I was too. The fact that we had gone from ecstatic about planning a wedding to completely ignoring that a wedding was even supposed to happen was another indication that our relationship was on the rocks—as if the constant arguments weren't enough. But despite the pit of instinct buried in my stomach, still I remained engaged.

But that was long ago. Now, having watched my actual proposal, I'm able to see who we were in that moment compared to who we are now. It makes me understand not just how wrong my intuition would end up being but, more important, how wrong we were as a couple. And though it brings a sense of sadness, it also, oddly, brings a sense of relief.

In all honesty, I made a mistake when I trusted my heart. I fell in love with the wrong guy for me. It's not the first time my picker was off, and probably won't be the last. When it comes to life, and especially love, none of us do it perfectly. We go with what we feel, we make a choice, and sometimes we realize we were wrong. There's no debating it, it's not subjective. We just flat-out got it wrong. It's kind of like missing a few questions on a multiple-choice test, but getting enough right that you still get a passing grade. One wrong answer doesn't amount to complete failure. Relationships are the same; we can look back and see all the wrong answers we gave, but don't forget the one you got right—the decision to get out; to swallow your pride and accept that you were wrong, and by getting that answer right, you get your passing grade and the class is over. You've passed, and now you move on to the next course, the next part of your life . . .

Lesson learned: *Mess up, fess up, and move on.*

DAY 53. 3:37 P.M.

Start Spreading the News

With the realization that I am no longer the person I was when I got engaged, I realized that the time to figure out who I am is now or never. I don't know what I want in life, or who I want to be. I don't think any of us truly ever know, but most people have a better sense of it than I do, that's for sure. One thing I do know is that I don't want to be the damaged girl who never amounted to anything because of a broken heart. I don't want to be the girl who let a man hold her back, who let a failed relationship keep her from loving again. I don't want to be the girl who forces herself to stay in one place because she's afraid to see greener grass.

And so, I decided since I don't want to be that girl, I'm not going to be. Remember how I wanted to run away from this place and all the harsh memories it holds and move somewhere different? Well, I fucking did it! Kind of. In the past few days, I've made great use of my copious spare time by getting serious about moving and even researching my dwindling list of likely cities. Taking everything into account, I decided to cross Austin and Chicago off my list. I know absolutely no one in Austin and though I love the vibe, I fear the slow pace might cause me to feel unsettled. I need distractions, lots of them. When it came to Chicago I realized two things. One, I would never survive the brutal cold. I'm just not that tough. And two, I would never survive the torture of having to scan every restaurant and bar to make sure Twenty-Five wasn't around.

So it all boiled down to Los Angeles and New York City. Both were strong contenders. On the plus side, Los Angeles has the appealing weather, and despite being clueless as to my next career move, there are endless possibilities there. It's not called the City of Dreams for nothing. But I've been in L.A. for the better part of a year and I have bittersweet feelings toward it, considering it's where this shitshow started in the first place. And it's awfully far from home. It's one thing to want to get away, but to move cross-country, be in a different time zone and so far from the comforts of home had me worried. When it came to New York City, I realized that it too offers a bounty of opportunities, yet comes with a clean slate. Those same bittersweet memories won't haunt me there. But you know what will? The damn cold.

So I looked at places to live in both cities, put in various inquiries and talked to people I knew that lived on each coast. And after much debate, I finally decided on a winner. . . .

Start spreading the news: You are looking at a future New Yorker! Ahhhhh! I'm doing it! I've purchased a one-way ticket and it's non-refundable! Having practically no idea what areas are suitable to live in, I've booked a three-week rental in the West Village, where the one and only Sarah Jessica Parker lives. I figure I can't go wrong being neighbors with only the greatest New York woman ever! That will give me exactly twenty-one days to find a permanent home. I've even ordered a pair of those faux fur snow boots all the fashion bloggers are always raving about.

I broke the news to my parents, and despite my mother crying when I told her, she's happy for me and knows I need this change. My father is obviously worried about the logistics, as any protective dad would be, but I've done enough research and number crunching to know a) I will likely be living in a shoe box, b) open-toed sandals are going to have to be purged from my wardrobe, and c) I'll probably be broke after a year. But none of those factors dampens my overwhelming excitement in this very moment as I imagine life as a single girl in New York Fucking City! I've got to learn how to correctly say "aaaapple" and "coooiifee," because I am going to be a New York City girl! I could live in a brownstone, just like Carrie, sip cosmopolitans with girlfriends, hail cabs, go to the theater, visit museums, run in Central Park! I can be whoever and whatever I want!

Aside from a fresh start, I'm not going to lie, part of me relishes this move as the ultimate fuck-you to Number Twenty-Six, who has a pronounced disdain for big-city life.

Sure I may be a lost soul right now, but if that's how it's going to be, then at least I can be lost in New York City and not Atlanta. I'm ready for something different to begin for me.

With my one-way ticket purchased, I'm both excited and scared. Then again, what do I really have to lose? It's time for me to do this. I've always been envious of friends who studied abroad or moved to a big city and wished I could do the same, but I took the safe route instead; hell, I got engaged to someone who lived five miles away from me! But this catastrophic journey has changed me. It's opened my eyes to a whole new world. A world that is bigger than Atlanta, bigger than me, bigger than my past.

That's the thing about a breakup, it's the perfect opportunity to leave the past where it belongs, and instead roll the dice, take a chance you wouldn't normally take, and reinvent yourself. It's the ammo everyone needs to face what we all fear the most: change.

Oftentimes, it's not other people or even ourselves that stand in our way of greatness, but this fear of change. We fear the idea of it so much that we try to avoid it at all costs, not without reason. Change brings with it uncertainty. It makes you think of all the what if's, which leads you to realize that you don't know the answers. So, you decide to stick to what you do know and take the safe route. Change brings with it the fear of failure. You figure you've dealt with enough setbacks in your life, so why bother trying anything else? Which brings us to perhaps the biggest reason we shy away from change. Because we fear it might lead to success. Funny how you can fear both failure and success, huh? It's as if we feel unworthy of happiness because we've become stuck in a world of sadness for so long. You get to a point where you become comfortable in this world, and accept your life as all you deserve, misery and all.

But what if instead of fearing and defying change, you just embraced it? Change is inevitable for every person and everything after all. It's what turns winter into spring, a seed into a tree, a teenager into an adult, a fashion fad into a faux pas, and a lover into an ex. You can hide from it, but it'll still happen.

But then you go through something horrific like a breakup and you stop fearing change—you actually crave it. Because just like the seasons, these shitty feelings you have will also have to evolve. Think about where you were a year ago, maybe even two. Now think about where you are right in this moment and all the events that have happened between now and then. Those are all changes in your life that you've managed to endure. I mean hell, I went from being in a courtroom to being on a reality television show, to being engaged and now being single. If so much change can happen then, why can't it happen now? That's the beauty of change, is that it works for us and against us. It's terrifying, yet hopeful. It can turn the best of times into the worst, but it can also turn the worst into an even better best. And when it does, you can look back at where you've been, what you've gone through, and smile because of where you'll be.

Your breakup has severed the ties that once held you back from redefining your life. Now there's no boyfriend saying he doesn't want to move to a new city, there's no difficult choice of trying to make a long-distance relationship work, there is nothing that ties you to where you are. You have nothing and no one stopping you from taking a great leap of faith toward something that has the ability to mold you into the person you've always dreamt of being.

It's time for you to realize that there is a great big world out there that exists, and it's waiting to be discovered by you. Sure, you've been holed up, consumed with this breakup, thinking that life consists of only yourself and this damn breakup. And while you may have hit the Pause button, the world has continued to play. It's a daunting realization that the world will go on with or without you, but that's just how life works. So, you have a choice, now. You can either choose to sit out and watch, or you can decide to get your ass up and get back in the game. And in order to do that, you have to be willing to accept the scary idea of change. You have to go out on a limb and say screw it, "I have nothing to lose, therefore anything is a gain."

Lesson learned: *There aren't a lot of silver linings to heartbreak . . . But this? This is a big one.*

DAY 55. 5:25 P.M.

The Relapse

I relapsed. And when I say relapsed, I mean R-E-L-A-P-S-E-D. Let's just say, I have officially broken my dry spell. Shit, shit, shit!

So here's the thing (you know it's going to be bad when the story starts with "here's the thing"). Despite engaging in a multitude of back and forth texting wars, unfollowings, and photo deletions, it's been fifty-five days since I last saw Number Twenty-Six. So there I am, going about my business at the gym, getting back to my pre-breakup fighting shape, which will be useful for my new life as a single girl in New York City, when out of the blue, I get a text message from none other than Mr. "REGRET" himself. Figuring a snarky or accusatory text is awaiting me, I decide to first check my social media, only to discover that I've neither said nor posted anything offensive enough to get me in hot water. Curious, I can't help but wonder what he could possibly want and read the text.

26: How r u?

ME: Ummm . . . Fine, how are you?

26: Good, whatchu up to?
ME: I'm at the gym. What's up?
26: Cool. I was wondering if u wanna grab lunch?

My shock turns to nausea. Something isn't right.

ME: Haha. Who has your phone?
26: Huh?
ME: Who is this?
26: It's me lolz.
ME: What's your favorite flavor protein bar?

Several security questions later, he'd successfully proven his identity enough for me to inconceivably believe that the person asking me to lunch is, in fact, my ex-fiancé. Why is he being so nice? Did he, like most men, possess the superpower of knowing just when we women have turned a corner, only to swoop in and fuck shit up for us all over again? As I lie on a dingy rubber gym mat I pretend to stretch, all the while really going back and forth in my mind on what all of this means and whether or not I should meet him for lunch. Could it be that his intentions are pure and this is his version of a peace offering? Is he just being an asshole, hoping I will say yes, only to tell me he was just joking? Or, is this lunch invitation really just a sex invitation? I mean, come on, no man wants to have a meal with his ex without indulging in a little dessert at the end, right?

Whatever his intentions are, they're affecting me enough to make me consider meeting up with him. *Don't lose control*, I think to myself. I'm stuck in that delicate post-breakup phase where I have successfully cried out all of my tears, some of the hatred toward my ex has subsided, and I'm moving on under *my* terms. I guess you could say I've begun to regain both power and control over my life. But with my move to New York just days away, I can't help but feel as though I'm leaving Atlanta with some unfinished business and it all centers around my ex.

Ultimately, I want things to be amicable between us, considering I was once engaged to this man, but so much damage has been done that I doubt peace is even a possibility. So why do I still find myself tempted to see him? Is it because my toxic relationship has become an addiction of sorts? Is his love my drug? The love I felt was the highest of highs, but the fights and the anger felt like the most painful of lows, yet I kept going back for more. Now, I find myself craving one last high, one final hit, and then maybe I can put it down forever. I need to finally find the power to stop letting this drug tempt me, and instead be able to live my life how I want to, soberly. And then it dawns on me. Somewhere between thinking he's being an asshole and me needing to kick the habit for good, I realize exactly what I need to do . . . F-U-C-K him! Figuratively, literally, symbolically, raunchily, all of it.

OK, don't get your panties in a twist and act surprised! There are very few things, if any, in this world that carry more power than sex. It is one of the greatest sources of temptation, the easiest way to mind-screw a man, and if you do it right, the most rewarding revenge imaginable. And in my case, it's just what I need to free myself. Plus, what do you do to a man that has broken your heart in every way imaginable; a man who has cursed at you, fought with you, fucked with your every emotion, and left you feeling completely powerless over your feelings, self-esteem, and life in general? You become the feisty fighter you are and you take back the power. You prove to yourself and to him that not only have you moved on but that you control your own life rather than your addicting relationship and breakup controlling you. How do you do that? S-E-X. After all, what says "fuck you," to a man louder than literally fucking him?

It's a risky move that could lead to my final descent, but I know I'm strong enough to face it. I can do this. I need to do this! If only to prove to myself that I am in the driver's seat of my own life; that I can have one last high and quit my ex addiction once and for all. Plus, it's been fifty-five days of hellish withdrawals, and maybe I want some damn dessert too!

And so, I agree to lunch the following day in hopes of emerging victorious! Plus, I'm secretly hoping that he's packed on the pounds and looking miserable, while I, on the other hand, will be looking my best, naturally of course. I spend the morning prepping for our . . . what do you even call it? We're not together so it's not a date, we have no business so it's not a meeting, I plan on sleeping with him so does that make it a booty call? Whatever it is, all I know is I'm determined to look hot and decide to make a pre-lunch to-do list:

- Workout in the morning. Extra crunches . . . check
- Shave legs . . . check
- Make sure I don't need a wax . . . check (thank God!)

Next up, I need to nail my makeup. I go for the "natural" look by applying some concealer and foundation complete with blush and, of course, a little contouring. I go light on the mascara but heavy on the clear lip plumping gloss. I give myself a simple blowout with the help of some volumizing mousse. My outfit, equally strategic, consists of black yoga pants to make sure he knows I haven't tried very hard, a white V-neck casual enough to reaffirm that I haven't tried very hard but is also low enough to show my cleavage and soft enough to feel like a bed sheet. Top it off with a leather jacket for a splash of badass and the look is complete.

As I glance in the mirror, I realize that despite being a few pounds thicker than I was before this breakup, I don't look so bad. Sure, it's largely thanks to the spandex yoga pants and an hour and a half of hair and makeup, but he doesn't have to know that. As far as I can tell, the only thing he'll be thinking when I walk in is, "damn, she looks good natural." Oh, if only he knew. . . .

Despite looking slightly sexy on the outside, as I drive to the restaurant, I'm losing my shit on the inside. So many different scenarios run through my mind.

Scenario 1: *I get to the restaurant, only to be stood up. (Lord, please no!)*

Scenario 2: *I don't get stood up but he looks so horrible that I can't imagine hooking up with him, which makes this entire lunch (and the hour plus of preparation) a complete waste of time.*

Scenario 3: *We meet for lunch, he looks hot, doesn't invite me back to his place, and I start to question whether* he *was the one who got away.*

Scenario 4: *We meet for lunch, we go back to his place and have sex, I leave with sex hair, more smitten than ever, which sends me straight back to rock bottom. (Also, Lord, please no!)*

Scenario 5: *We meet for lunch, have shitty dead-fish jackhammer sex back at his place, and I leave with zero* *feelings and zero satisfaction. (Not the worst option, but certainly not the most satisfying.)*

Scenario 6: *We meet for lunch, have decent sex, and I leave with nothing but a feeling of contentment at being the chick who hit it and quit it. (Secretly praying for this in the worst of ways, but sounds too good to be true.)*

With my scenarios in check, I pull into the restaurant's parking lot. I'm a few minutes late, on purpose. I want to not only guarantee that I'm not getting stood up but also make it evident that this lunch on a random weekday is in no way my priority. Finally, I exit my car and nervously walk into the restaurant to see him with his back turned toward the door. I know it's him because he's wearing the same damn pants and red V-neck he always wears. We greet each other with a hug and a kiss on the cheek before we take our seats next to each other in a semicircular booth in the corner. As we awkwardly sit side by side, I notice the grin on his face. It's the same one he had the first night I met him, and it once again triggers the same cheek-hurting grin I had all those months ago.

The conversation starts out shallow as we catch up, avoiding any heavy-hitting topics. It's awkward on so many levels. How could it not be? We are two ex-fiancés eating sushi together and the sexual tension between us is so immense, it's sake-bomb-worthy. He knows it, I know it . . . we both want to have sex, and the fact that I can see underneath the table that he is literally bursting at his pant seams for me makes me ecstatic. He's attempting to appease his appetite one spicy tuna roll after another, but all the sushi in the world isn't going to get him what he really needs and wants . . . me.

The waiter brings the check, and in textbook fashion, he asks if I want to come back to his place to see his dog. I oblige, obviously. And when he goes to use the restroom before we leave, I can't help but mentally pat myself on the back in delight. Ohhhh, men . . . so predictable.

We arrive at his apartment and his dog immediately jumps on me and starts licking my face. I've missed her. We move to the couch where we sit side by side. As I look around my old home, which looks the same minus some cute candles, clean toilet bowls, and of course the pile of my shit he dumped in the corner, I wonder how I ever lived here. It's not so much the masculine leather couches or his framed jersey still hanging above them that makes me realize how much this place wasn't my style, but more just the feeling in the air.

Nevertheless, we continue chatting as a basketball game plays on the large flat-screen television that sits atop a black metal entertainment stand. With each passing moment, we find ourselves closer and closer until finally we are cuddled up in each other's arms. He rests his head on my cheek and whispers, "This is nice." I press my cheek next to his and it only takes seconds before his lips find their way to mine. They feel foreign, yet familiar. My mind is racing, but I go with it and kiss him back and our lips begin moving faster as the kissing gets deeper. He moves his hand down to my shoulders and underneath my shirt as he claws at my waistline. Before I know it, our shirts are off and he's carrying me up the stairs that lead to our old bedroom. We continue kissing as he climbs each step, and I can't help but wonder if this is the first time he's ever carried me this way. We get to the bedroom where he gently tosses me on the bed and begins to unzip his pants. It's on!

Twenty-five minutes later . . .

I'm picking my clothes up from various parts of the bedroom—

my pants are on the dresser, my underwear has somehow gotten caught on the corner of the television, and my bra is nowhere to be found. As I get dressed and see him lying on his back, naked with a look of satisfaction on his face, I laugh silently at just how easy it was to get into his pants. I tell him I have to get going and though I don't say it, I know deep down that this is the last time I will ever see Number Twenty-Six and his naked body again. He puts on his pants and walks me down the stairs and to the front door. We kiss goodbye and I exit the apartment for the last time.

I walk through the parking lot, unlock my car door, and sit in the driver's seat for a moment. In the rearview mirror, I catch a glimpse of my reflection. All I can see is the bitchiest, most satisfied, fuck-you grin I've ever seen before. I put the car in reverse, slump back in my seat, and leave one hand on the gearshift (despite it being an automatic). It takes about a mile or so for the satisfaction to subside and the realization of what I just did to creep in. I can't decide how I really feel about all of it. My emotions are like a big crockpot combined with so many ingredients: a cup of power, a teaspoon of embarrassment, a heaping tablespoon of satisfaction, a few ounces of clarity, and a pinch of confusion. I try to remember the scenarios I made up along this very road just hours ago in an effort to decide which one prevailed. I think it's Scenario 6, but with everything that just happened, I really don't know. The only thing I know is that this rendezvous is coming with me to my grave! I repeat to myself the entire way home, "I will not tell a soul about this, I will NOT tell a soul about this, I will NOOOOOT tell a soul about this." (Until now. Oops!)

My desire for secrecy isn't derived from being some uber-private person, or even a feeling of remorse, but rather the powerful knowledge of what I just did, knowing that he knows what I just did to him, and most of all *secretly* knowing I have successfully taken back the power (plus, let's be honest, nobody wants to have to utter the words, "I just relapsed"). It's the first risky move I've made that's paid off in quite a while, and while I know I'm supposed to feel some kind of "moral hangover" about this, I feel empowered instead. And the feisty smirk that has finally returned to my face brings with it zero regret, zero remorse, and most of all, the power to move on.

The truth is, I got lucky (in more ways than one). I'm well aware, both now and then, that this spontaneous romp could have sent me right back to the hellhole it's taken me almost two months to crawl out of. And though my risk paid off, the question is still worth asking: Is it smart to hook up with your ex one last time, and if so how/when/why/wtf?!

Objectively, I realize there are myriad reasons *not* to have a last fling with your ex. It's a dangerous move, one that could toss you back into the trenches of heartbreak you've finally dug your way out of. There's also the moral hangover that a quick bang carries, and let's not forget that by hooking up one last time, you are effectively bypassing the bridge you've burned and taking a swim in murky waters, right into his arms (and pants). Basically, every rule in the (nonexistent) "breakup book" and basic common sense says not to do it. But every womanly bone in your body is craving one last hurrah. So what do you do? Well, you know what I did, but each scenario is different.

You can start by answering the following questions, yes or no:

1. Are you and your ex past the point of no return?
2. Do you need one last hit before you can kick the habit of thinking about your ex for good?

3. Are you ready to take back the power and stop letting this breakup and your ex define you?
4. Do you want to be the one who got away or what?

If you answered yes to all of the above questions, then congratulations, you're ready to embark on Operation Last Hurrah. If you answered no, have no fear, your time will come soon, dear. Now, it's time to plan. This risky mission has to be well thought-out.

STEP 1: *Get in the right mindset:*

First and foremost, under absolutely no circumstances are you to have even the slightest hope of repairing this broken relationship. You can't think maybe this hurrah will somehow bring you back together. You can't think this will be the ticket to pressing the Reset button and starting anew. If you do, then this is nothing more than a suicide mission and you should abort immediately!

Say it again: "My relationship is OVER!" This last hurrah is not about rekindling, reliving, or reviving. It's not even about sex. No, this is about giving yourself one last little hit before you are ready to quit your addiction and take back the power over your life.

STEP 2: *Do it for yourself:*

This is for you, and you alone. It's not to jilt him or exert payback for what you've been going through. This isn't about inflicting pain onto him. Now, with that being said, does a little satisfaction come from knowing you're using that asshole? Absolutely. But, this must be for YOU. This is the rare time where selfishness is not only acceptable, it's mandatory.

STEP 3: *Protect your future:*

If you've got the right mindset and are doing this for you, then your heart and integrity are protected, but that doesn't mean your future is. The only thing worse than being sent back into an emotional tailspin out of this one-time romp is for a baby to pop out of your belly ten months later and you've now signed up for eighteen years of joint parenting. (Or even worse, an incurable disease.) This means after you get done shaving your legs and looking hot, go to the drugstore and buy some condoms. Yes, it may feel taboo, but you as a woman are allowed to buy condoms just like a man does. Sure, it might feel skanky and embarrassing as the cashier rings you up, but let me just say, the power of not only buying condoms but whipping one out when the time is right trumps any mortification. Plus, not only does it make your intentions crystal clear to him, but you look like a motherfucking boss doing it.

STEP 4: *Get it done and get the hell out:*

What do you do after you get off work? You go home! Make no mistake, this is work—therefore, there is absolutely no reason to stick around after the job is done. No sleeping over, no cuddling in bed next to him with your head pressed against his bare chest. No having a chat afterward talking about how great that just was. None of it! The moment the deed is done, come hell or high water, you are to immediately put your clothes back on and get the hell out of there. Then, you are to walk directly to your car, smile in the rearview mirror, and drive off, never to return to the scene of the crime again. The only place you're off to is toward a man who will deserve you in all your powerful bad-assery.

So there you have it. It's in your hands now. If you're ready to kick the habit for good and need just one last hurrah, then have at it! Don't forget to hit the gym an extra time this week, get a wax, and enjoy taking back the power!

Lesson learned: *S-E-X . . . more like S-E- YESSSSSSSSS!*

DAY 57. 10:10 A.M.

You Can't Change History

The grin on my face has yet to subside. I can't believe how good I feel. I got laid and didn't attach any debilitating emotions to my sexcapade. Who am I? I mean, seriously, how reckless was I to have done such a fun and tantalizing thing? I'm feeling damn lucky that it panned out the way it did considering I could very well be back at rock bottom right now. Luckily, I'm not and with that have gained a little perspective on this breakup. It's as if knowing that I can have sex with him and feel nothing but self-satisfaction brings with it the realization that maybe this wasn't the end of the world after all. Maybe this breakup, though a little harder, isn't all that different from the twenty-five that came before it. It leaves me feeling as though I'm traveling down a road away from my past; the farther I drive, the smaller my relationship gets in the rearview mirror.

Yes, I am leaving behind my relationship, and my breakup. Which over the past fifty-seven days has brought about some rather not-so-becoming moments. Let's see, over the course of the past eight weeks . . .

- I've gained a few pounds.
- I've cried more tears than a river (sorry, Justin Timberlake, I win).
- My hair has grown at a Guinness-world-record rate.
- I've moved out.
- I eradicated him from my social media.
- I burned his shit.
- I purged my feelings in an interview.
- I had one last hurrah!

And that's not even including the $33 I spent on lipstick. Despite how much time has gone by, I still think about Twenty-Six and us every single day. Things constantly remind me of him. People remind me of him. When I see a couple holding hands, I am reminded of the days when we did the same. When I pass by a restaurant we used to frequent, I can remember all of our Friday night dates once filled with kisses and laughter. When I walk by the park we used to visit on sunny days, I can still picture us lying on a blanket in the grass while we played with our dog. Though I've seen the same couples and places for months, my feelings toward them have changed. The bitterness I thought would never go away has turned into nostalgia. Sure, it makes me a little sad to remember the good times, but the lack of animosity when I remember also brings me peace.

Because I know, no matter what, that once upon a time I was engaged to a man whom I loved very much. He was a man

I thought I'd spend the rest of my life with, the man my children would make Father's Day cards for, the man who would be by my side for eternity. Until, he wasn't.

Do I think I made a mistake in getting engaged? Yes. Obviously, considering it didn't last. Do I regret it? Yes. I regret the fact that I will never get that first proposal back; that moment won't go to my husband, but rather will always belong to my ex. But, I've never believed in living life free of regrets, it's too much pressure. In fact, I regret plenty of things: the terrible bangs I had in third grade, the hideous sequined corset I wore to the prom—hell, I regret what I wore last weekend. Regrets are mistakes that we learn from. They don't dictate the rest of our lives, they're just little glitches, and impulsive choices we made in the moment. But it's just that, a moment and the moment eventually passes.

It reminds me of the winter after I landed my first job. As a reward, I decided to save a few hundred dollars each pay period until I had enough to buy my dream purse: a Louis Vuitton Speedy. It took months, but finally I had saved enough to buy it. I loved that purse, from the smell of new leather to the tan trim, all the way down to the damn box it came in. I was in love with my bag and wouldn't go a day without it. But guess where that bag is now? . . . your guess is as good as mine. Odds are it's somewhere in my parents' attic or buried in a box deep in my dusty storage unit. Turns out, the bag wasn't that cute to begin with. And while I still have fond memories of saving up for it and the pride I felt handing over a wad of hundreds to the saleswoman and toting it around everywhere I went, the love for the actual purse has worn off.

And my relationship is no different. Yes, I'm comparing it to a

Louis Vuitton purse, which I think is actually quite generous. But like the purse, I can still remember the pride and love I felt whenever I talked about my future with Number Twenty-Six. But just as the purse went out of style, so did my relationship. And now they both belong in the past.

I won't deny that I loved that purse once upon a time, just like I won't deny I loved Number Twenty-Six once upon a time. Doing so would just be a slap in the face of love. The truth is, the moment Number Twenty-Six asked me to marry him was, to this day, the single most glorious moment of my life. I can't deny that the kisses I shared with him were the best I've ever had; that the laughs made my abs sore for days, but I didn't mind; that the gaze in his eyes made me feel happier than I ever had; and that the feelings I felt were deep and beautiful. And I don't want to deny it. I fell in love, and it didn't work out. And now, it's just part of my history.

Isn't that what all our relationships that end are, anyway? Little chapters in the pages of a book known as the story that is your life. Sure, you could tear out the pages because you don't like them, skip them, pretend they don't exist. But they do, and they always will. So why not just accept your story, as it is, for better or worse? Why not accept responsibility for the feelings that swept you off your feet, the emotions that made you giddy and the kisses that made you grin. Why not step away and see your relationship from the outside as just another chapter in an epic story? A chapter with two main characters who fell in and out of love in a story full of riveting plot twists, swoon-worthy characters, blow-up fights, and passionate makeups. A story that isn't over yet. Not even close. Because you're still in the thick of it. You have no idea what awaits you in the next chapter, nobody does. All you really know is that there *is* a next chapter. And now it's time to see how it begins . . .

Lesson learned: *Bad relationships go out of style, happiness never does.*

DAY 59. 9:44 P.M.

The End

It's my last night here in Kelly's house, and the word "bittersweet" doesn't do this feeling I have justice. Tomorrow, I officially embark on the next chapter of my life starting with my big move to New York City. I am excited, nervous, and downright terrified all at the same time. Though I'm not sure I'm making the right decision, I know moving away is a hell of a lot better option than being where I am now. I've come a long way, sure, considering fifty-nine days ago I thought my life was officially over. I have to chuckle knowing that my engagement ending was really my life beginning.

With my flight now less than twenty-four hours away, I look around the room that has served as not just my living quarters, but my sanctuary. So many tears have been shed in this room. So much pain exists in it. But, so much progress does too. And of all the memories that could come to mind in this moment, the one that, surprisingly, I haven't thought of in all of this time, is the one moment I can't ignore any longer. It's the moment that brought me to this room in the first place: the moment it all ended. In truth, the moment my relationship ended wasn't sudden. In fact, it had been looming for months. But one trip to Los Angeles would be the final straw that broke the back of a very weak, very exhausted and very unhappy me.

Number Twenty-Six and I had been invited to Los Angeles by the producers of our show to attend the live premiere of the latest season. It was to be an unprecedented shindig complete with a red carpet and a bevy of past contestants. The night before we were scheduled to fly out, another heated argument ensued, over something I can't for the life of me remember. That's the thing with volatile relationships, you start to forget what the fights are even about. Odds are it had something to do with how unhappy we were. That's another thing with volatile relationships; you actually find yourself having to discuss your happiness or lack thereof.

During the fight, as usual, we said our "it's over"s and "I'm done"s and went to bed in silence, unsure if we would even be getting on the plane the next day. And just like clockwork, the next morning was filled with "I'm sorry"s and "I love you"s. Hours later I would find myself feeling the high as I sat next to him on the plane, laughing and kissing as if everything was fine. But no high could change the fact that our relationship was in a very bad state, and we both knew it. To make matters worse, we were a day away from walking a red carpet where everyone was expecting us to gush about how insanely in love we were. There was no winning when it came to this trip; not going would set off alarms and spark rumors, but going could result in a disaster on live television. And though we chose to stick it out on this trip and hope for the best, I knew in my heart we were close to the end of the road. I just didn't know how close.

A few cocktails and four hours later, we arrived in L.A. all smiles. Maybe it was something about the California air that made us forget the previous night's fight—and the past three months of fights, for that matter—or maybe it was the buzz from all the screwdrivers we had sucked down. Either way, we had arrived in the city where we'd created so many beautiful memories together. If any place could magically press the Restart button on our relationship, it was this place.

Not so fast. On the ride from the airport, the buzz must have worn off because before we even made it to our hotel, another fight erupted.

"I wonder if [insert random chick's name] is here, she lives here now," Twenty-Six mumbled as he scrolled through Instagram on his phone.

Now, ordinarily, this wouldn't mean anything to me, but for some reason this name was suspiciously familiar. Certainly, he couldn't be talking about the girl he told me he had hooked up with days before coming on the show, right? No way. I knew about his past, so it wasn't news to me that he had hooked up with chicks before me, and this one in particular. There were no boundaries between us, and that included his dating history, which in all honesty I found funny. Plus, it wasn't as if I didn't have a past of my own. But there was no possible way he was actually referring to a prior hookup by name, let alone "wondering" if she was in town. No way.

Curious, I asked, "Wait, [random chick's name]? That's not the same chick you hooked up with days before you met me, is it?"

He stuttered nervously, "Umm yeah . . . it is, but it's not what you think. You see, umm . . . She just started working for me, selling vitamins on my team and I don't even really . . . I don't even have a lot of contact with her, someone else umm handles that."

I stared at him, bewildered, as I waited for his nervous rant to continue. "I mean, I would have told you, but I figured you'd probably get upset. It's not even a big deal, she works for me now," he said with more guilt in his voice than Lindsay Lohan at her trial.

What the fuck?

He continued babbling bullshit about how he didn't tell me because he knew I would get upset and he didn't want that. Effing right I would get upset. Let's think about this—rationally, of course. Our relationship is basically in the toilet, and the only reason it's not down the pipe is that neither of us has the guts to flush it like we should. We are in Los Angeles and will have to talk publicly about how happy we are, even though "happy" has become an extremely relative term in our relationship vocabulary. And before we even get to the hotel you're talking about a chick you used to hook up with? Oh, and let's just stab the stiletto in my eye and tell me that she now works for you and that you've kept this a secret. I can't possibly imagine why I wouldn't be over the goddamn moon hearing that a former booty call of yours has reentered your life. Hang on, let me open up the toolbox and get an effing screwdriver out so I can bolt this smile to my face, because that's the only way I am going to look happy about this.

Who the hell was this man sitting next to me? Who had he become? Had I turned him into this monster, or was the monster always lurking inside the dark-haired, athletic man with the megawatt smile I had once loved so much? I don't know, but I knew this wasn't the man I had agreed to marry. Tossing this woman in my face so casually (and yet awkwardly and guiltily) went against everything he supposedly stood for, and I was certain that had this conversation been the other way around, he would have lost his shit right there in the middle of Sunset Avenue.

Even thinking about that moment right now as I'm preparing

to make my move to the Big Apple pains me, because it makes me realize how far gone our relationship was. Why did I not just get out of the car and walk away? Forget my asking who *he* really was. The real question is: Who was *I* to be letting this nonsense happen?

Later that evening, we decided to go our separate ways for a few hours so I could enjoy dinner with the girls and he could hang out with the guys from our season. It was a much-needed break for both of us. As I sat at dinner with my girlfriends and reminisced about the good ol' days over cocktails, I was relieved to be away from Number Twenty-Six and feel happiness. But that feeling came to a screeching halt when mid-entrée my phone, which was rudely sitting out on the table, chimed, notifying me of a text from my "lovely" fiancé. *Oh boy*, I thought as I read it.

26: So, I hear u r at dinner with some dudes. Cool, Andi.

This allegation was followed by a thumbs-up emoji, which had become one of his trademark ways of expressing anger. *Gag me!* He was an artist when it came to accusing, blaming, and belittling all in one low-blow text. I looked around the table of eight women, and knowing a simple denial wouldn't be enough for him, I snapped a photo of the table clearly filled with girls and only girls. This wasn't the first time I'd felt the need to defend my innocence with the physical proof of a photo. I'm ashamed to say that this had become my usual response to his allegations of the sort. He didn't respond, but in my mind, it was strike two, and we'd been in California only a few hours.

After dinner with just the girls, we met my fiancé along with his friends at a bar across the street. After several awkward conversations, plenty of glares from him when I casually chatted with his guy friends, and a few too many drinks, I decided to call it a night. Tomorrow was the big day, and though inside I was struggling, as a firm believer that the only bags you should wear are on your arm and not under your eyes, I was determined to look damn good on the outside, which meant I needed my beauty rest. He, on the other hand, didn't have to worry about bags under his eyes and thus wasn't done for the night. So, as I meandered my way back to our hotel alone, he headed off to more bars with the guys.

I have no idea what time he came home that night—or should I say morning?—but it couldn't have been before three. I was awakened at nine by a text from a girlfriend alerting me to the fact that my fiancé had not only been out with the guys last night, he'd also been with a bevy of single chicks from the current season. Ironic, considering the text he sent me at dinner. While part of me didn't care and part of me felt disrespected, I desperately wanted to avoid another fight, so I said nothing. Well, almost nothing. I was starving so I asked if he wanted to go to breakfast. When he agreed, I was shocked considering he'd probably barely slept and was obviously hungover. I wondered if it was the guilt from the night before or if he was offering an olive branch—or maybe he was just hungry. We left the I-stayed-out-all-night-partying-with-single-girls elephant in the hotel room and strolled to a nearby café.

Over eggs Benedict and coffee, the two of us spoke of only one thing: how to get through the day's big red-carpet event, namely the ungodly number of questions pertaining to our happiness and the status of our upcoming wedding (which wasn't planned whatsoever), which were sure to be asked. We had to figure out an appropriate answer, and sadly it couldn't be a truthful one. I mean, what could I say? "Oh, well, our relationship blows, my fiancé came home at three in the morning after partying all night with a bunch of single hussies, we are not planning the wedding, we barely made it to this premiere without breaking up yet again, but other than that, yeah, everything is absolutely amazing"?

It's not exactly the easiest thing to tell people your relationship is shitty when you're wearing a giant diamond ring, cameras are capturing your every move, and you're surrounded by a bevy of supporters who truly want to believe in your "love." Though I wanted to keep it real and admit the struggles in our relationship, I think part of me wasn't willing to admit it to myself. I had fallen in love with this man, professed it to the world and even used the words "soul mate," and now I was eating those words faster than I was eating my eggs. We agreed that we'd attempt to dodge the questions like the plague, and if need be, simply say, "We are happy and ready to figure things out now that the show is all over." Not complete bullshit, but it sure smelled like it.

The awkward breakfast ended, thank goodness, and we walked back to our hotel so I could begin the arduous task of getting red-carpet ready and he could sleep off his hangover. As we exited the elevator, before entering our room, I thanked him for breakfast.

"It's about time you thanked me. I've been waiting for that the entire walk back."

Here we go again. I knew he was big on thank-yous and never missed an opportunity to lay into me if God forbid I forgot to say it, but this seemed a little extreme. See, this is exactly why there are knockouts in boxing. Instead of having to watch twelve agonizing rounds of little jabs here and there, one guy just cold-cocks the other and gets the shit over and done with. We, on the other hand, had moved on to what felt like round four with little jabs still coming and no sign of anyone hitting the mat soon.

"Ummm . . . okay." I scowled.

"You are seriously the most unappreciative person I have ever met in my life."

I paused as I silently thought in my mind how fucking ridiculous it was that my own fiancé was bitching about me not saying thank you for buying me a $12 plate of eggs and a coffee using the per diem we were given. I thought about staying silent and avoiding yet another fight. I tried to, but I just couldn't. He'd already gotten a pass on returning home in the wee hours of the morning stinking of cheap booze and even cheaper skanks. These personal attacks weren't going to fly. He was never short on dramatics and always big on extremes, so I shouldn't have been surprised or even bothered by this statement, but given all the tension of the trip and the day, I was. And as a result I completely lost it. In what could only be described as an out-of-body experience, I began sobbing hysterically and screaming at him that I couldn't handle this anymore; I couldn't handle the ridicule, the pressure, or the constant criticism, not from the world and especially not from my fiancé. He was supposed to be the one supporting me and protecting me, like he had promised, and instead he was the one hurting me the most. It wasn't just the words he used; it was a culmination of everything. From bringing up his ex-hookup in the car, to accusing me of being at dinner with guys only to come home at three in the morning, to now scolding me over something as stupid as thanking him for breakfast. Everything that had been happening between us for months boiled over inside of me in that moment, and I exploded. This, at last, was the knockout punch.

With tears streaming down my face and my heart pulsing through my chest, I did the only thing I could think of: I picked up the phone and called the airline. I was done. This was how it was ending, with me skipping out on the live premiere and instead bolting to the airport before hopping on the next flight back to Atlanta.

As the airline operator checked for available seats, Twenty-Six pleaded with me to hang up the phone and stay. I don't know why he even wanted me to, considering he had made his disdain for me pretty damn clear. I assume it was to avoid the humiliation that would undoubtedly result from my disappearance. He continued to plead as I continued to check for available seats. One final frantic plea and I did what I absolutely should not have done: I hung up the phone.

To this day, I'm disgusted at myself for staying. I'm not sure I'll ever know why I did. In hindsight, I think part of me knew the embarrassment that would prevail if I were a no-show, while part of me was still clinging to the hope that if we were around the people who had brought us together in the first place, somehow we could get back on track. It was the same excuse I had used for months, and yet no matter what he did, no matter how hurt I felt, no matter how bad things got, I continued chasing after this unrealistic dream. I continued craving the high I once had from the love we once shared. And I think most of me probably just wasn't ready to admit to myself that I was an addict staying in an unhealthy relationship that had become irreparable. Whatever it was, I stayed, and I regret it to this day.

The premiere, as it turned out, was fine—not great, but not the disaster it could have been. The people who knew us best could sense that something was off as we walked on the red carpet and posed for pictures together. I felt like a fraud for acting happy when inside I was filled with anger. At an event surrounded by adoring fans and people who were a part of our love story, I should have felt the happiness and love I once had for him, but I didn't. No event, no person, no reminders could bring us back to that blissful time. It was gone. I wasn't ready to admit to millions of viewers, or to myself, that beneath the cherry lip-gloss and contour makeup, I was in excruciating emotional pain. I wasn't ready to face the fact that we had failed everyone who believed in us and, worst of all, we had failed each other.

After the premiere, he went off with his guy friends and once again came back to the hotel in the wee hours of the morning. And once again I didn't care. All I cared about was getting out of Los Angeles, and this relationship. Before our flight departed, I went to Nikki's room to say goodbye. I crawled into her bed and immediately began to cry. I didn't have to say what was wrong. She knew; she had known for a while. "This is supposed to be me, ya know, the one crying and you comforting me," she joked. She was right. It wasn't long ago that I was the one listening to the drama about her failed relationship, and now the tables had turned. Before I left, she told me what I already knew: that I was miserable, that I was trapped, and that I needed to break free . . . immediately.

The flight back to Atlanta from the premiere in L.A. was spent in deafening silence. The car ride back to our apartment from the airport was equally noiseless, and we both knew something very bad was about to happen. In the back of my mind I knew that in all likelihood, this was the last flight we would ever take together, but still I didn't know if it was the last night we'd have together.

When we arrived home, I beelined it up the stairs as I lugged my suitcase behind me. When I got to the top, I walked straight into the closet where I laid my bag on the floor. I closed the door behind me and sat on the carpeted floor with my back resting on my still-zipped suitcase. And there, alone in a closet, I cradled my head in my hands and unleashed the tears that had built up inside of me for three thousand miles. As I sobbed like a grieving child, I buried my face between my legs in an attempt to muffle the sound of my weeping. Moments went by until I heard footsteps coming up the stairs. The door to the closet creaked open and Number Twenty-Six asked me if I was okay. I didn't respond, I didn't so much as turn to look at him. I just buried my head deeper. Without saying another word, he moved the suitcase over and sat on the floor behind me and wrapped his arms around my trembling body. We sat in silence for what felt like eternity until I finally was able to speak. I didn't raise my head, I didn't move my hands, I didn't even think about what I was going to say. Instead, five life-changing words uncontrollably left my mouth, "This is over, isn't it?"

I could feel him inhale deeply as he grasped me tighter. His voice cracked. "Yes, I think so."

I didn't respond. I didn't need to. In a relationship that had been filled with so many insulting words, so many painful arguments, nine words had finally shut both of us up for good. There we were, a couple once so madly in love, now sitting on the floor of a closet, both weeping. There would be no going to sleep that night in the same bed. There would be no waking up the next morning beside each other saying our typical "I'm sorry"s and "I love you"s. Not this time. Of all the conversations and fights, those nine words were the most brutal things we had ever said to each other. But they were also the most honest, mature, and impactful words as well. It was the calmest conversation we'd ever had. The tranquil vibe of the conversation was eerily different from the anger and animosity that had built over the past few months. The peaceful tone made me realize this was it. This was the end. What had begun as a burning love affair that blossomed thousands of miles on trips to France, Italy, and Belgium, followed by a romantic proposal in the Dominican Republic and my own happily ever after was over. All that was left was the non-returnable gift of a broken heart.

And though I didn't know it then, that peaceful conversation wouldn't set the tone for the aftermath. I guess just like our relationship, the recovery phase wasn't going to be easy. The highs weren't going to come without the lows, and the pain wasn't going to subside quickly.

But eventually, I would come out of it alive and would kick the habit, emerging stronger, happier, and free. I would see that this ending was really just the beginning for me.

That's the thing with a breakup, it is the end of something. But life is filled with endings. The good ones like a thrilling movie, a vacation, the glory days of college or an epic party, are all hard to say goodbye to. But all good things must come to an end. And all bad things must too. That's not to say that you should look at your relationship in its entirety as bad. In fact, I hope you can look at it and see both the good and the bad. The good parts are what made you fall in love and live in your own fairytale while the bad parts broke you down and made you feel like you were living a nightmare. But it's all over now. That chapter is done, but the story is just starting again.

Lesson learned? *Your story is far from over. Enjoy writing it.*

DAY 60. 2:05 P.M.

The Beginning

The day has finally arrived. The start to my new beginning is here! I woke up this morning with the surreal realization that within a few short hours, I'd be on a plane bound for my new home in New York City. I'd successfully gotten all my belongings into my suitcases and am attempting to zip them when there's a knock at the door. It's Kelly. She's coming to say goodbye. Through tearful eyes, she watches for a moment as I struggle to get the zipper around my overflowing suitcase, before deciding to sit on top of it in an effort to smush the already crammed clothes even more. After we finally get it zipped, she moves from on top of my suitcase to on top of my bed where we both lie back and try to hold it together. Within seconds, it becomes clear neither of us stands a chance, and we begin weeping. I grab her hand and interlock it into mine as I tell her how grateful I am for her. Not just for the generosity of opening her home to me but also—actually, more so—for her undying love and support. I mean here is a friend who without hesitation put me up in her home, cooked for me, drank wine for me, talked me off many ledges, and did it all, not for anything in return, but out of pure kindness. I tell her that I'll never be able to repay her.

"You can thank me by going out there and killing it in New York City," she responds.

"Deal."

We both begin to laugh. We joke about how pathetic I once was in this very room along with some of the hilarious moments we've shared in this house over the course of the past two months. And then, in true Kelly fashion, she goes to the kitchen and returns with a bottle of champagne and two flutes. She pops the cork and pours the bubbles into the glasses.

"Cheers to your new adventure," she toasts.

"Cheers to our friendship!"

We clink the glasses and sip on the bubbly as we continue to reminisce and talk about the Big Apple.

It dawns on me that this new venture is my first step in my own adaptation phase. I've cleansed out the toxins, I've replaced them with healthy nutrients. And now here I am choosing to live a life free from the toxins that once paralyzed me. Could it be that I have finally, successfully finished my first detox? (Other than the fact that Kelly and I are sipping champagne, I think so!)

An hour later, my parents arrive to take me to the airport. I schlep the suitcases through the living room and out to the driveway, where my dad hoists them into the back of his SUV. I say my final goodbye to Kelly, though we both know it's hardly the last she'll see of me. It's only a twenty-minute drive to the airport, but it feels so much longer as my dad drives and my mom and I sit together in the backseat holding hands. I'm desperately trying to avoid bursting out in a sob. The truth is, I'm terrified about this new chapter of my life, but I don't want my parents to know that. I don't want them to have to worry about me. I want them to feel like I'm going to be okay, that I am strong enough to make it in the big city, that I can do this! But, deep down, I know it isn't my parents that need convincing of all of this, it's me. *I* don't know if I will be okay and make it in the big city. I don't know if I can really do this. There's probably about a fifty-fifty chance that within a month I'll get eaten alive, or freeze to death. Hell, I fear that I might not even last a month. But I can't let them see my fear. It's important for me to keep a brave face. It's important, because it's time.

The ride is filled with small talk and my mother making plans to visit within a matter of weeks. Though she says it with excitement, I see a sadness in her teary eyes and hear the worry in her cracking voice. She's trying to hold it together, we both are. I catch a glance of my father in the rearview mirror and can see what he's thinking in his eyes. He's scared too. His youngest daughter has been through the ringer, she's still delicate and now she's moving a thousand miles away where he can't protect her. But he knows he has to let me go.

We arrive at the airport, and my father begins to unload my bags and hand them to the curbside check-in attendant.

"Where to?" he asks.

"New York City," I respond and hand him my Georgia driver's license.

He slaps orange tags that read HEAVY on my suitcases and hands me my boarding pass. I'm all set. I've made it to the airport and my bags have made it out of the car. Now all that's left is for me to get on the plane. But first, I have to say goodbye to my parents. Just like with Kelly, I know this isn't my final goodbye to them. Heck, my mom will probably come visit me before I've unpacked all my stuff. But I can't help but think that this is the last time I'll ever seem them again, as this person. For better or worse, New York will change me.

I hug my mother first, and as I let go, I see the tears she's been holding back streaming down her face. I wipe them away before drying my own. I lean in for another hug. I don't want to let go. I turn to my father, who isn't one to cry, but with tears welled up in his eyes, he's pretty close to losing it. Finally, the three of us embrace in one big final hug.

With my bags checked and my ticket in hand, I say goodbye and head toward the sliding double doors of Hartsfield-Jackson International Airport. The scene is all too familiar. Just a year and a half ago, I was walking through these same doors, looking back at my parents and joking that the next time they see me I could be engaged. And now here I am, having done that, and off to my next adventure. As I enter through the doors, I look back one last time, to see my dad with his arm draped around my mom's shoulder as they stand by the car. I take a deep breath and wave goodbye. The doors close.

After I make my way through security and to my gate, I find an empty corner chair looking out at the runway and take a seat. I put on my sunglasses and begin to cry. I don't know exactly why I'm crying. I feel an overwhelming sense of fear, but also an odd sense of freedom and relief and most of all excitement. But all of it seems to be overcome by anxiety. I tell myself what I'm feeling is natural considering I am literally a two-hour plane ride away from starting a new chapter of my life, without a clue as to what it holds.

The gate attendant comes over the loudspeaker and informs us that the plane will begin boarding shortly. There's no turning back now. This is happening. This is the next step on a journey that I've taken in the past year and a half, a journey that has shown me not only a whole new world but also a whole new me. A weaker one at times, but a stronger one at others. I never expected my world to come crashing down the way it did, but then again, I never expected my world to take off the way it did either. Sure, there will be moments when I will reminisce about the past, and I'll feel everything from anger, to sadness, to forgiveness and strength. There will be times where I'll still feel damaged, but isn't that just how it goes? Life isn't just sunshine and roses, we can't truly have the sweet without the bitter.

At the end of the day, my engagement is over. My reality television days are behind me and so is the city I've called home for almost all my life. I am emotionally and physically moving on from a life, from a relationship, and from a version of myself that I didn't like. But the point is, I'm moving on from it. Maybe that's the gift that comes with hitting rock bottom; you get a chance to be a phoenix and rise from the ashes. Sure, the way down sucks, it's sad and comes with unremitting pain, until suddenly you can't get any lower, you can't hurt any more, and you can't go anywhere but up.

I walk down the Jetway and board the plane. I take my window seat, lifting up the shade, and watch as the luggage gets loaded into the plane. Finally, we push back. The plane begins to accelerate and we are wheels up. I continue staring out the window, this time glancing at the city below me. It's the city I once called home, where so many memories were made. The city where that one casting call changed my life forever. It's the city where I thought I would spend the rest of my life with the man I had fallen so deeply in love with. The city that I am now leaving behind. As the plane climbs higher and higher, the buildings of downtown Atlanta get smaller and smaller until finally, all I can see is a sheet of clouds. My old home has vanished from sight.

A tear falls from my eye and I pull down the shade. I recline in my seat and close my eyes. I smile as I envision the new city that awaits me. It's the city that will be the setting for yet another chapter in my story. A story that has so many pages written, yet so many still waiting to be written. And though there are plenty of mysteries and possibilities that come with each new chapter, I plan to greet each of them with an open heart, a healed heart, and most of all, a heart that will forever believe in love.

Because no matter how bad it gets, no matter how tumultuous and painful the end of a relationship can be, no matter how much you think your life is over and you are forever damaged, there comes a moment when you find that the storm has finally passed. The sunshine has dried up all the rain, and you, my friend, have survived. It's the moment where you look at the scar that came from heartbreak, and see it not as a scar of weakness but as a scar of resiliency and strength. It's the moment when you finally realize that maybe, just maybe, it *is* okay.

This is that moment.

—The Beginning—

ACKNOWLEDGMENTS

There are so many people I'd like to thank for not only helping me with this book but helping me through the many discombobulated chapters of my life.

First off, to everyone who makes up "Bachelor Nation," thank you, thank you, thank you. I can say with 100 percent certainty that this book would have never happened without you! To the fans, thank you for your incredible show of love and loyalty, not only to me, but to every person who has graced your television screen on Monday nights. Though I will never feel worthy of your immeasurable support, I will forever be grateful for it. To everyone who worked on the show—from producers, to casting directors, to the entire crew—I thank you for taking a chance on a gal from Atlanta, Georgia, and giving her such an unbelievable and life-changing adventure.

To my family, you are my rock, my world, my happiness. Mama, thank you for being the coolest grandmother and allowing me to share my dirty secrets with you. Rachel and Elie, thank you for keeping my secrets and also keeping Mom and Dad from going insane throughout this entire experience. Dad, thank you for not disowning me as your daughter after what I've put you through these past few years. I swear to you, I will never make out on national television again. Lastly, Mom, there are no words capable of justly describing the insurmountable love and appreciation I have for you, so I will just say this . . . thank you for having been and always being "my person."

Thank you to all of my girlfriends who got me through one of the darkest times in my life. Though my misery may have been an excuse to drink copious amounts of wine, it's a misery I overcame thanks to you. Kelly, I will never be able to express my gratitude for you. Without hesitation, you took me into your home, and more importantly, your heart, never asking anything in return. You are the epitome of generous, the definition of selfless, and a friend I am beyond grateful to have.

To "Team It's Not Okay," especially Kirsten Neuhaus and Sulay Hernandez, thank you for making this crazy idea for a book a reality. A special thank you to everyone at Simon & Schuster and Gallery Books, including Jen Bergstrom, Kristin Dwyer, Meagan Harris, Liz Psaltis, Diana Velasquez, and Lisa Litwack—thank you for having my back through this entire process and being the baddest group of women in the entire publishing world. Abby Zidle, you are the most trusting, enthusiastic, and brilliant editor in the world, and I am the luckiest woman to be able to call you my boss. Thank you for taking such good care of my firstborn child.

And last but not least, thank you to every ex-boyfriend of mine. For better or worse, each of you taught me some of life's most valuable lessons, which have inspired me to change for the better and come to the realization that sometimes it's the broken roads that lead to the most beautiful destinations.